You and Your Living-Educational Theory

Through the narratives of practitioner-researchers, this practical guide shares the proven processes, phases and supports that are most effective for generating living-educational-theories with values of human flourishing. Filled with case studies and continuing professional development activities, this book supports readers to conduct a values-based inquiry to improve their lives, describing and explaining how they influence themselves, others and the places where they live and work.

There are four parts to the book, guiding readers through the process of creating and sharing their own living-educational-theory:

- Part One is designed to meet the needs of the beginning researcher as they start a project to improve their practice.
- Part Two builds on Part One to address the deeper, more complex requirements of those interested in more academic projects potentially for accreditation at the Master's level.
- Part Three focuses on PhD/doctoral studies.
- Part Four focuses on applying this knowledge more widely to living our educational responsibilities as global citizens.

This book will serve as a useful guide, as opposed to a fixed template, to support readers in living their values more fully. It is an essential resource for all practitioners interested in establishing a Culture of Inquiry to create their own living-educational-theories. These are explanations of values-based professional development within their school community and can be submitted for academic accreditation.

Jacqueline Delong is a retired Superintendent of Education and Adjunct Professor, currently an International Mentor for Master's and doctoral students who need support for their Living Educational Theory research. You can access many of her writings from 1995 to 2023 at: http://www.actionresearch.net, http://www.spanglefish.com/ActionResearchCanada/ and https://ejolts.net/.

Jack Whitehead is a Visiting Professor at the University of Cumbria, UK, and an Extraordinary Professor of Community-Based Educational Research at North-West University, SA. He is a former President of the British Educational Research Association. You can access many of his writings from 1967 to 2023 at: https://www.actionresearch.net/writings/writing.shtml.

You and Your Living-Educational Theory

How to Conduct a Values-Based Inquiry for Human Flourishing

Jacqueline Delong and
Jack Whitehead

LONDON AND NEW YORK

Designed cover image: © Getty Images

First published 2024
by Routledge
4 Park Square, Milton Park, Abingdon, Oxon OX14 4RN

and by Routledge
605 Third Avenue, New York, NY 10158

Routledge is an imprint of the Taylor & Francis Group, an informa business

© 2024 Jacqueline Delong and Jack Whitehead

The right of Jacqueline Delong and Jack Whitehead to be identified as authors of this work has been asserted in accordance with sections 77 and 78 of the Copyright, Designs and Patents Act 1988.

All rights reserved. The purchase of this copyright material confers the right on the purchasing institution to photocopy pages which bear the photocopy icon and copyright line at the bottom of the page. No other parts of this book may be reprinted or reproduced or utilised in any form or by any electronic, mechanical, or other means, now known or hereafter invented, including photocopying and recording, or in any information storage or retrieval system, without permission in writing from the publishers.

Trademark notice: Product or corporate names may be trademarks or registered trademarks, and are used only for identification and explanation without intent to infringe.

British Library Cataloguing-in-Publication Data
A catalogue record for this book is available from the British Library

Library of Congress Cataloging-in-Publication Data
Names: Delong, Jacqueline, 1945– author. | Whitehead, Jack, author.
Title: You and your living-educational theory: how to conduct a values-based inquiry for human flourishing / Jacqueline Delong, Jack Whitehead.
Description: Abingdon, Oxon; New York, NY: Routledge, 2023. | Includes bibliographical references and index.
Identifiers: LCCN 2023005245 (print) | LCCN 2023005246 (ebook) | ISBN 9781032438672 (hardback) | ISBN 9781032438726 (paperback) | ISBN 9781003369158 (ebook)
Subjects: LCSH: Education—Research—Methodology. | Teachers—Self-rating of. | Reflective teaching.
Classification: LCC LB1028 .D426 2023 (print) | LCC LB1028 (ebook) | DDC 370.72—dc23/eng/20230503
LC record available at https://lccn.loc.gov/2023005245
LC ebook record available at https://lccn.loc.gov/2023005246

ISBN: 978-1-032-43867-2 (hbk)
ISBN: 978-1-032-43872-6 (pbk)
ISBN: 978-1-003-36915-8 (ebk)

DOI: 10.4324/9781003369158

Typeset in Bembo
by codeMantra

Contents

Foreword   *ix*

PART ONE
Beginning   **1**

  1.1 Intent and Purpose   1
  1.2 Why Should You Create Your Own-Living-Educational Theory?   2
  1.3 What Is a Living-Educational-Theory?   5
  1.4 What Do We Mean by Values and Living Contradiction?   8
  1.5 What Really Matters to You in Improving Your Practice?   10
  1.6 Support: Critical Friend, Cultures of Inquiry and Ways of Knowing and Being   10
  1.7 Choosing a 'Doable' Concern for Investigation   14
  1.8 Asking an Educational Question – How Do I Improve What I Am Doing?   15
  1.9 Using the Living Educational Theory Planner   16
  1.10 Workshop for Creating Your Own Living-Educational-Theory   18
  1.11 Ethical Issues   18
  1.12 Data Collection: Text, Digital and Visual Data   19
  1.13 Data Analysis   23

1.14	Organising the Data	25
1.15	First Draft of Research	26
1.16	Literature	29
1.17	Second Draft of Research	30
1.18	Methods and Methodologies	31
1.19	Validation Group	33
1.20	Creating a Culture of Inquiry for the Creation of Living-Educational-Theories	34
1.21	Final Draft of Your First Report	35
1.22	Publication	41
1.23	Conclusion to Part One	41

PART TWO
Master's Level Inquiries — 45

2.1	Development in Philosophical Base from Parts One to Two	45
2.2	A Curriculum for a Living Theory Approach to an Educational Inquiry	51
2.3	Stage 1. What Constitutes an Educational Inquiry?	53
2.4	Your Living-Educational-Theory Methodology	60
2.5	Strengthening Data Collection and Analysis from Part One	63
2.7	Including Ideas from the Literature in Your Living-Educational-Theory	71
2.8	Stage 2. Formulating and Carrying Out a Living Educational Theory Research Inquiry	72
2.9	Stage 3. A Final Draft of Your Action Inquiry Report	78
2.10	Validation, Rigour and Using the Ideas of Others	80
2.11	The Validation Group as a Conversational Research Community	83

2.12 Rigour and Using the Ideas of Others — 84

2.13 Creating a Living Educational Theory Community — 85

2.14 Creating Your Own Living Theory Community — 87

2.15 Educational Conversations/Dialogue as Research — 87

2.16 Dialogical Relationships in Cultures of Inquiry for the Creation of Living-Theories — 88

APPENDIX ONE
Martin Forrest's Use of Validation Groups — 90

APPENDIX TWO
Peggy Kok's Use of Richard Winter's Six Principles of Rigour — 99

PART THREE
Doctoral Level Inquiries — 111

3.1 Setting the Stage for the Study — 112

3.2 Developments in the Philosophical Base from Part Two to Part Three — 121

3.3 Master's to PhD: What's Changed? — 133

3.4 Approximate Timelines and Schedule of Research — 151

3.5 Available Resources — 152

PART FOUR
Living Our Educational Responsibilites As Global Citizens — 155

4.1 Developments in the Philosophical Base — 155

4.2 What Is Our Meaning of Educational Responsibility as Global Citizens? — 157

4.3 EJOLTs as a Vehicle for Extending the Living Educational Theory Social Movement — 164

4.4 Our Contributions to Previous Educational, Action Learning and Action Research Conferences and Their Publication — 165

4.5 The Contributions of Other International Living Educational Theory Researchers	168
4.6 Living Educational Theory in Cultures of Inquiry as Global Professional Development	171
4.7 International Educational Mentoring by Creating Cultures of Inquiry Around the Globe	172
4.8 Digital Visual Data and Dialogue as Methods	179
4.9 Researching Supportive Supervisors, Communities and Universities Through Expanding Boundaries in the Living Educational Theory Social Movement	183
4.10 Addressing and Avoiding Colonisation	184
4.11 The Role of Social Media	188
4.12 Implications of Our 'Educational Responsibility' as Citizen Scholars for the Living Educational Theory Movement	192
References	*197*
Index	*211*

Foreword

How this book can guide you

We are hoping that this book will serve as a guide as opposed to a template to help you in creating your own living-educational-theory. Through the narratives of practitioner-researchers, including ourselves, we share the processes, phases and supports that have worked for us and others. In addition, we have provided visual supports through YouTube and other platforms. The addresses for the video recordings (urls) are included in the text version as well as in the electronic one.

The process of living-educational-theory (Whitehead, 1989) creation is rarely sequential (some would say, never). You may find that following the way that we have conceived this creative process fits your learning style, but you may prefer to skim the whole and come back to various points in the book. It is only limited by your own inventiveness.

While it is certainly feasible to work through the inquiry on your own, you may find it eminently more enjoyable and easier to reach completion with the help of others. This help may include a Culture of Inquiry (Delong, 2002) where a group of like-minded individuals come together in a safe, caring, democratic space to support each other as they create their living-educational-theories.

There are four parts to the book: Part One is designed to meet the needs of the beginning practitioner-researcher; Part Two builds on Part One to address the deeper, more complex requirements of those interested in more academic projects potentially for accreditation. Part Three focuses on PhD/doctoral studies. Part Four focuses on living educational responsibilities as global citizens. You may go back and forth between the four parts to meet your needs.

To get started, all you need is an inquiring mind and a commitment to improvement.

PART

Beginning

1.1 Intent and Purpose

Part One of this book is dedicated to those practitioners who are new to Living Educational Theory research, who want to improve their practice and who want to know for sure that they are improving with evidence-based explanations of educational influences in learning. It bears noting that this process is for everyone, in every age group, in any line of work and in any position: it is transformative for teachers, students and administrators, for nurses, nursing instructors and administrators, for global community developers, for parents of small children and for retired military personnel. The Living Theory space of practice has no limitation but there must be a practice, some aspect of your life, to study and improve.

We invite you to create your own-living-educational theory and take this opportunity to personalise your own learning as continuous professional development, not through someone else's agenda. This model of professional growth links research and practice and leads to substantive change. Bev McDonald, one of the early adopters in the Brant Country Board of Education, wrote that she had "grown as a professional" and

> I have had the opportunity to reflect and review Literacy in the Primary Grades and to implement a very exciting literacy program in my classroom. Throughout the whole process, I have felt in complete control of all aspects, along with my two colleagues.
> (Halsall & Hossack, 1996, p. 24)

The book outlines the investigative process for the beginner with specific activities and examples from our experience. Support is a critical component in the learning and growth and includes

DOI: 10.4324/9781003369158-1

opportunities to dialogue, cultures of inquiry, critical friends, and guidance from mentors. When supports are in place, creating your own living-educational-theory:

- Focuses activities on learning and improvement
- Facilitates self and peer assessment
- Increases the sense of self-awareness, control and confidence
- Provides a different and wider lens for the practitioner and her students/colleagues
- Fosters continuous cycles of action, reflection and review
- Recognises and confirms individual ways of knowing
- Strengthens the voice of the practitioner and the student
- Creates and shares new knowledge
- Recognises different cultural experiences
- Contributes to professional dialogue and professional development
- Transforms lives and contributes to human flourishing
- Enhances sociohistorical and sociocultural understandings and their influence in the researcher's practice.

The most significant experience for the novice learning to create their own living-educational-theory is finding confidence in their own 'I', recognising their embodied knowledge and exploring the implications of asking, researching and answering their question, "How do I improve what I am doing?".

In Part One, we introduce you to the process of creating your own living-educational-theory as a novice, giving you all that you need to create your first research project using the Living Theory approach to research. We take you through the steps so that you get the support you need and have confidence in your knowledge and your capacity to share it as you focus on a small and manageable part of your practice and try to improve it.

1.2 Why Should You Create Your Own-Living-Educational Theory?

We feel that it is important to differentiate between self-study and Living Theory: all Living Theories are self-studies but not all self-studies are living-educational-theories. Living Theories are, by the nature of the question with 'I' at the centre, a study of self. However, self-studies may not involve using your values as explanatory principles in explaining your educational influences in your own learning and in the learning of your students as a contribution to the evolution of an educational knowledge base. We have been active in the field of self-study and our work has been inspired by self-study research. In fact, Jack was one of the founding members of the Self-study in Teacher Education Practices (S-STEP) Special Interest Group (SIG) in the American Educational Research Association (AERA) in 1993. We have presented papers in S-STEP over many years, and we have written chapters in several self-study texts (Kitchen et al., 2020; Whitehead, 2009; Whitehead et al., 2020).

We recognise that there are a variety of ways in which teachers can study themselves and their practices. In Narrative Inquiry, for example, researchers use narrative to help them create meaning in what they are doing; in Autoethnography, researchers focus on the implications of cultural influences in their practice and understandings. Researchers can also focus on Action Research which can include different schools of thought such as the Critical Theory school of Action Research. This gives priority to understanding the political, economic and living cultural influences in their practice and understandings. Living Theory researchers include insights from these different approaches to improve what they are doing and in generating valid, values and evidence-based explanations of their educational influences in learning.

We believe that teachers are the decisive element in the classroom and, therefore, it is a professional responsibility of teachers to engage in this form of self-study research. They can then ensure that they are creating an energising, life-affirming educational climate where learning and learners can thrive rather than simply survive. The purpose of self-study research is not to pump up the ego of a self-serving self but to research and generate knowledge of the educational influences in learning that contribute to the knowledge base of teaching and learning.

The theories of psychologists, sociologists and others concerned with education can be useful for teachers to draw on when they try to improve their practice. However, how these theories are expressed in practice can be very different, as Ginott (1972) eloquently pointed to when he wrote:

> I have come to the frightening conclusion: I am the decisive element in the classroom. It is my personal approach that creates the climate. It is my daily mood that makes the weather. As a teacher

I possess tremendous power to make a child's life miserable or joyous. I can be a tool of torture or an instrument of inspiration. I can humiliate or humour, hurt or heal. In all situations it is my response that decides whether a crisis will be escalated or de-escalated, a child humanised or dehumanised.

(p. 15 and 16)

Why should we use Living Theory research to improve our lives? We believe that what distinguishes a teacher as a professional educator is that they continuously research their practice to improve their educational influences in their own learning and in the learning of their students and to contribute to the evolution of an educational knowledge base. We know that the idea of contributing to the educational knowledge base as a distinguishing characteristic of a professional in education may be contentious, but it is an assumption we make in our work in enhancing professionalism in education. We believe teachers can do this by researching their practice, integrating insights drawn from the knowledge of others, and holding themselves accountable by contributing the validated knowledge they generate to the growth of an educational knowledge base.

Michelle Vaughan (2019) describes the impact of this work in an excerpt from her June 2019 article in *EJOLTs*:

I embarked on this journey to have a better understanding of what lies at my core, yet what I have come to realize is that this journey was indeed about bringing my core to the surface and creating the space to let it flow outward with confidence and purpose. When we talk about cores, they are often hidden, as in the middle of the earth or even the center of an apple, but this work is about exposing them and bringing them to the light for examination and discussion. Once my inside was revealed, I felt the sense of wholeness described by Moira Laidlaw (1996), the fragmented pieces of things that were important to me suddenly aligning themselves to create a scene that made sense for this first time. I found I could not do this work alone, and through the mentorship I received from those within this field, I was encouraged to talk about my work, share my thinking and expose my core. While initially uncomfortable, once I started, I found that I could not stop. Like a good book, I would share my story with anyone who would listen, making new pathways for this energy to travel.

(Vaughan, 2019, p. 76)

What particularly distinguishes Living Theory research from other forms of self-study is the generation of an evidence-based explanation of educational influence in learning. The explanations include the clarification of their life-enhancing values. These are the values that give meaning and purpose to our lives, form our explanatory principles of our educational influences in learning and the standards by which we hold ourselves accountable as professional educators. We will further discuss our meaning of values later in Parts One and Two.

1.3 What Is a Living-Educational-Theory?

In this book, we will show the implications for you of adopting a research methodology that focuses you, the researcher, on creating and making public your valid values-based explanations of your educational influence in your own learning, the learning of others and the learning of social formations within which you live and work. Generating such explanations of educational influences in learning is what distinguishes Living Educational Theory research. This is a form of self-study, practitioner-research whereby you clarify your embodied life-affirming values as they emerge in the course of researching aspects of your practice to understand, improve and explain it. These values form the principles and standards by which you explain and evaluate your educational influences in learning. You do this while contributing to your 'field'-related practice such as health and social care, community, education and management.

In his seminal paper on Living Theory, Jack proposed that the aim of a living-educational-theory account is for the writer to make a valid claim that they understand their own educational development:

> I'm assuming that all readers of this Journal will at some time have asked themselves questions of the kind, 'How do I improve my practice?', and will have endeavoured to improve some aspect of their practice. I believe that a systematic reflection on such a process provides insights into the nature of the descriptions and explanations which we would accept as valid accounts of our educational development. I claim that a living educational theory will be produced from such accounts.
>
> (Whitehead, 1989a, p. 41)

Whitehead (2008) asserts that: "A living-educational-theory is an explanation produced by an individual for their educational influence in their own learning, in the learning of others and in the learning of the social formation in which they live and work" (p. 104). A living-educational-theory emerges as an individual explores the implications of asking, researching and answering a question of the kind, 'How do I improve what I am doing?' The 'I' in such a question often experiences themselves as a 'living contradiction' in the sense that they recognise that while holding certain values, they are either negating these values in their practice or not living them as fully as they can. This tension or concern of being a living contradiction stimulates the imagination to think of possible ways of improving practice.

To begin, you will consider ways in which you might improve your practice. After you imagine new possibilities, one possibility is selected and forms the over-arching research question. The next step is to create an action plan to explore the question. You act on this plan and gather data that will enable a judgement to be made on the effectiveness of the action in living your values more fully. You then evaluate the effectiveness of the actions and modify your concerns, plans and actions in the light of the evaluations. A living-educational-theory is produced as an explanation of your educational influences in your own learning, in the learning of others and in the learning of the social formations that influence your practice and understandings. Your living-educational-theory is shared with a validation group of some 3–8 peers that you select. They suggest ways of improving the explanation in terms of its comprehensibility, the evidence used to justify assertions made, the extent and depth of the sociocultural and sociohistorical understandings that influence the explanation and the authenticity of the explanation in terms of you living your values as fully as possible.

In generating your own living-educational-theory, it is important that you are not constrained by the imposition of any methodology such as action research, autoethnography, case study or narrative inquiry. Each individual generates their own living-educational-theory methodology in the course of generating their own living-educational-theory. This capacity of each individual researcher is known as their 'methodology inventiveness' (Dadds & Hart, 2001).

> We have understood for years that substantive choice was fundamental to the motivation and effectiveness of practitioner research (Dadds, 1995); that what practitioners chose to research was

important to their sense of engagement and purpose. But we had understood far less well how practitioners chose to research, and their sense of control over this, could be equally important to their motivation, their sense of identity within the research and their research outcomes.

We now realise that, for some practitioners, methodological choice could be a fundamentally important aspect of the quality of their research and, by implication, the quality of the outcomes. Without the freedom to innovate beyond the range of models provided by traditional social science research or action research, the practitioners in our group may have been less effective than they ultimately were in serving the growth of professional thought, subsequent professional actions or the resolution of professional conflicts through their research. In this, we find ourselves sympathetic to Elliott's claim (1990:5) that 'One of the biggest constraints on one's development as a researcher, is the presumption that there is a right method or set of techniques for doing educational research.'

(Dadds & Hart, 2001, p. 166)

In generating your own living-educational-theory methodology, you can draw insights from any other methodology where those insights are appropriate, for example, in the use of an action-reflection cycle as described above and in the use of narrative as used below. In generating a living-educational-theory, it is usual to use any methods that are appropriate to researching and answering the question, 'How do I improve what I am doing?' Sometimes a Living Theory researcher must develop their own methods for their inquiry:

> The originality of the paper lies in the use of a method for using empathetic resonance with video-data to clarify the meanings of energy-flowing values as explanatory principles in explanations of educational influence in learning.
>
> (Whitehead, 2010, p. 89)

Whitehead also focuses on the importance of the flows of life-affirming energy with values that carry hope for human flourishing in explanations of educational influence in learning. There will be further explanation of these concepts.

1.4 What Do We Mean by Values and Living Contradiction?

1.4.1 Values

You will note that 'values' are mentioned many times in the course of discussion of Living Theory and, indeed, in this book. There may not be a common understanding of the nature of values. Values are defined as, 'principles or standards of behaviour' (Concise Oxford English Dictionary, 2004). We are of the opinion that we understand them when we see them and as Feyerabend (1990) stated that "… values can only be clarified and understood in the course of their emergence in practice" (p. 17).

While some differentiate between intrinsic and extrinsic values (Common Cause Handbook, p. 20), we do not. We intend to adhere to our values consistently whether in our personal or work lives and when we do not, we find ourselves to be 'living contradictions'. This does not preclude values from changing over time and, in fact, they often do. The Common Cause Handbook points out:

> Values, then, are one important influence on our actions and the way we see the world. Understanding them reveals a major underlying connection between a vast array of major issues—racism, human rights, community welfare, women's empowerment, youth exclusion, biodiversity loss, sustainability. Concern and behaviours related to these problems are all associated with a set of related values. [71] Such an understanding also reveals an important way in which progress on these issues is influenced by education, the media, and other social institutions. Values are engaged and strengthened by our experiences—and we are all a part of each other's experience, whether we like it or not.
>
> (p. 42)

In his writing on "conversations on educational values", Andy Larter shared the following:

> A few years ago, if you had asked me what my values as a teacher were, I would probably have replied that I valued student autonomy, the teacher in the role of facilitator, learning being fun yet worthwhile, talk as an important learning process and the emphasis placed on the process rather than purely the outcome. If this strikes you as

vague it is because my thinking at that time reflected my somewhat glib utterances about what I valued as a teacher. I feel that there is nothing unusual in this. During a DES course at Bath University (12/6/85) it appeared that many colleagues on the course were finding it hard to express what they felt to be their values. I feel that this is not because teachers are an unprincipled lot, but rather because much of what we do is taken for granted or implicit in our work.
(https://www.actionresearch.net/writings/jack/cycle1.pdf, p. 8)

Your values are evident in your actions and provide a screen or decision-making tool to judge whether you have improved. Because the expression of energy in the meanings of values such as justice, democracy or "loved into learning" (Campbell, 2011) cannot be communicated using only words on pages of text, we use video-data in a visual narrative to help with the public communication, the ostensive expression, of these meanings.

1.4.2 Living Contradiction

It is usually worthwhile video recording a lesson before you design your action plan. The video recording is a most powerful reflector of what you are doing and can often reveal contradictions between what you believe yourself to be doing and what you can see yourself doing. We refer to this experience in terms of being a living contradiction. All the teachers we have worked with have reported the experience of seeing themselves as living contradictions as they recognise, often in a surprising context, that they are not living their educational values as fully as they believed.

For example, Margaret Jensen of Hardenhuish School wanted to encourage her students to read what are considered to be the best parts of Shakespeare's writings. However, with the help of video, Margaret reported the experience of seeing herself as a living contradiction as she was taking the best parts in the reading of Shakespeare. This was also confirmed in pupils' written reports. Andy Larter examined his feelings on viewing a video recording of his response on being given a racist poem. Andy wanted to encourage his students to talk about their racist poem. Videos showed that Andy's responses got in the way of this encouragement. They actually prevented the kind of exploration he wanted to have with his pupils. Erica Holley of Greendown School reported her surprise on seeing transcript evidence which showed that she, rather than her pupils, were asking the questions which

Erica wanted the pupils to ask. This was a similar experience to Jack's experience of seeing himself as a living contradiction whilst watching a video of his classroom in which he believed that he had established inquiry-learning with pupils asking their own questions. Like Erica, Jack could see that he was giving his pupils the questions to ask.

It is often the experience of oneself as a living contradiction which stimulates the imagination to think of ways of overcoming this experience in a desired direction. While acting to improve your practice, it is often useful to gather data which will enable you to make a judgement on the effectiveness of your actions in terms of the pupils' learning.

We delve more deeply into 'Values' in Part Two.

1.5 What Really Matters to You in Improving Your Practice?

The Values Exercise that we use in workshops (see full workshop in Part Two) can be done alone or, even better, with a partner. Time for reflection will help with the process. We ask you to think about what really matters to you, both personally and professionally, in your practice and tell/write a story about an incident where you felt that passion and shows you working with someone that demonstrated that passion in action. It can be any length, but a page is plenty. The meanings of your values are usually clarified and communicated as they emerge through your actions as identified in your storytelling. They provide you with the evaluative criteria you use to judge improvements in what you are doing.

This is where another person is helpful (can be on videoconference, phone or present). When you read the story, write down all the values that you or your partner hear being expressed implicitly. Having someone listen to what really matters to you, we mean really listen, is amazingly energising and uplifting. If the list is long, over 20 values, some of them may be grouped together.

If you are working alone, you would share this story and list of values later with a partner who can be your critical friend.

1.6 Support: Critical Friend, Cultures of Inquiry and Ways of Knowing and Being

We think that it is worth emphasising that conducting Living Educational Theory research is challenging without suitable supports. We encourage you to find like-minded individuals to help you share your stories, challenge your assumptions and to comfort you when you run into obstacles or feel overwhelmed.

1.6.1 Critical Friend

The significance of the critical friend is three-fold: she or he can encourage and support your inquiry; your critical friend can provide data to support your claims to know your values; and they can challenge your claims. While we all espouse certain values and intend to live by adhering to those values, sometimes we violate our values and are 'living contradictions' (Whitehead, 1989a). A critical friend can be essential to this revelation and provide direction on overcoming this non-alignment with our values.

1.6.2 Culture of Inquiry

During the course of Jackie's thesis (Delong, 2002), she unveiled what she thought was a prerequisite space, a Culture of Inquiry, for educators to influence themselves, others and social formations. This Culture of Inquiry space is an environment for giving voice to teachers. She frequently exhorted them not to allow others to speak for them, to represent their embodied knowledge for and by themselves. She invited them into a Culture of Inquiry, a culture of love and support and encouragement, to unveil their embodied knowledge and create their own living-educational-theories.

If you are able to encourage a group of three to five to join you in a research journey, you can engage in "loving educational conversations" (Vaughan & Delong, 2019) and contribute to the creation of a Living Theory Culture of Inquiry where individuals are encouraged, supported and "loved into learning" (Campbell, 2011) as they create their own living-educational-theories.

> When we use the language of Living (Theory) culture of Inquiry, we are meaning the creation of a safe, supportive space where you are enabled to make explicit your values and make yourself accountable for living according to those values. Moreover, it is an environment where it is safe to be vulnerable. You learn to recognize when you are not living according to your espoused values and are what Jack Whitehead calls a living contradiction. Action-reflection cycles based on asking questions like "How can I improve my teaching of these children?" become as natural as breathing. Experiencing values

such as loving kindness and "loved into learning" in this democratic, non-hierarchical environment and recognition of your embodied knowledge, encourages you to take responsibility for your own learning. When we use the language of a Living culture of Inquiry we mean the unique living and embodied expressions of this living culture in the individual's practice.

(Delong, 2013, p. 26)

While groups of like-minded practitioner-researchers provide the ideal situation for encouraging and supporting you, an individual mentor can provide the same environment:

In an email (150619), Cathy Griffin, a former student, current school principal and long-term friend, described a Living Theory culture of inquiry in her response to our Skype conversation:
Cathy Griffin and Jackie Delong in a living culture of inquiry https://www.youtube.com/watch?v=vEoc-rNG4xE

A Skype session with you is a reflective, research space for me. I automatically prepare for a conversation by returning to my values and examining what I am doing in my work and my life. I enter the conversation knowing that you will be a loving listener with concern for my health and well-being above all. I also enter the conversation knowing that, as an astute LET (Living Educational Theory) researcher, you will help me identify and clarify important points in my journey to improving what I am doing and will validate or question the claims I make about my practice. That sounds so technical and 'researchy'. But the reality is much different than that because of the love that underpins the relationship and because of the loving actions you make in line with your values. For example, in the clip above, you honour my time more than once by checking if my household is getting up and needs my attention and by suggesting a next meeting time that suits my schedule which may be more complicated. You voice concern that I don't spend my weekend looking for a video clip for you but take time to relax. You voice your love at the end of each email and voice call. It may seem trite to an onlooker, but it is foundational to the work we do together. The unconditional love is an example of your values in action (ontology) and your intentional creation of a space in which it is safe to do Living Educational Theory action research.

(Delong, 2019)

In their December 2019 joint paper, Jackie and Michelle Vaughan described a Culture of Inquiry:

> Experiencing values such as loving kindness and being loved into learning within this democratic, non-hierarchical environment, and the recognition of their embodied knowledge, enables individuals to improve their lives and practice by creating their own living-educational-theories "…which includes 'I' as a living contradiction, the use of action reflection cycles, the use of procedures of personal and social validation and the inclusion of a life-affirming energy with values as explanatory principles of educational influence" (Whitehead, 2009, p. 182). It is a democratic space where individuals are "loved into learning" (Campbell, 2011), where they feel supported and encouraged to share their embodied knowledge and their vulnerabilities, where 'loving educational conversations' contribute to each one creating their own living-educational-theory using their own methods and methodologies with what Dadds and Hart (2001) call 'methodological inventiveness'.
>
> Removing hierarchies is challenging and simply saying there are none is not acceptable. I have found that creating a non-hierarchical space develops when the individuals come to recognize their own embodied knowledge, a knowledge that only they have and others do not. They may know less than the teacher/mentor about a discipline or a process but much more about their knowing and ways of knowing.
>
> It is the experience of both of us that, to make learners feel safe and trusted, the facilitators need to be vulnerable themselves and establish that they love the individuals in the group. Essential to the building of a Living Theory culture of inquiry is 'loving them into learning'.
>
> (Vaughan & Delong, 2019, p. 71–72, https://ejolts.net/files/349.pdf)

Ideally, for your Culture of Inquiry group you would have a facilitator who has created their own living-educational-theory with you on site or virtually via videoconference.

1.6.3 Ways of Knowing and Being

As global citizens working with practitioner-researchers around the world, we have become increasingly aware that our Western ways of knowing and being are often at odds with other cultures, behaviours and expectations. In 2010, in a Skype educational conversation Jack said to the Bluewater Master's class that he found that the Canadian humility, he saw and heard, got in the way of sharing and critiquing the researcher's embodied knowledge. One of his students, Peggy Kok (Leung), was very clear that she felt Jack's suggestions for opening up and emancipating space for his students were instructions and directives. Because of her background as a Chinese woman from Singapore, she took a long time to realise that she was being encouraged to be creative in her own terms. When Moira Laidlaw worked in China from 2000 to 2006, she found the students so accustomed to the transmission mode that they struggled to take responsibility for creating their own questions.

While teaching in the Master of Education program at the University of Prince Edward Island, Canada, Liz Campbell experienced a tension with many of her international students from China not only in their adherence to compliant behaviours but also in the validity and rigour processes. They were living a cultural dissonance that Liz had to deal with directly so they could see themselves as knowledge producers.

Parbati Dhungana of Nepal designed a new model of professional development where the teachers examine their values and plan for their improvement based on their own concerns. This would be contrary to local policy which mandates the content and process of professional development programs from above. In her research, she found the tension of teachers expecting to be told what to do was challenging to overcome. We have encountered this tension many times. Teachers often need encouragement in believing and understanding that they already have embodied knowledge that can evolve as it is made public through the knowledge-creating activities of the teachers as they ask, research and answering their questions, 'How do I improve what I am doing?'. Sometimes the tensions are the result of limitations in their contexts and cultures that may create obstacles to their freedom and capacities to generate their own knowledge and contribute this knowledge to their professional knowledge base.

1.7 Choosing a 'Doable' Concern for Investigation

Before we start the next section using the Living Theory Action Planner, we need to make the link between the unveiling of your values and starting on the journey of an investigation of a concern or problem in your practice. With your values in mind, you might consider how you could live your values of hope or joy or authenticity more fully and then how that way of living might assist you in improving your actions in your context. When it comes to choosing an area of focus for improvement, it is important to keep it within your capacity and the resources available to you. It is an admirable goal to want to improve the lives of children in poverty; however, unless that is within your realm of influence, it might be better to confine it to wanting to improve the life of one child, one group of children or one family. Your projects need to be 'doable'. Moreover, time is a limited resource.

1.8 Asking an Educational Question – How Do I Improve What I Am Doing?

Your fundamental commitment as a Living Theory researcher is to ask yourself a practical question concerning improvements in your practice. Your own 'I' in a question of the kind, 'How do I improve what I am doing?', is both a subject and an object in your inquiry. There is also an assumption in Living Theory research that you will have already had the experience of resolving practical problems by defining action plans, acting, evaluating and modifying actions in the light of evaluations. You should check the questions and form of the action planner below to see if it corresponds to your approach to problem solving. It is being used in our research network as a useful introduction to Living Theory research but is by no means a prescriptive template.

There are a number of ways for you to formalise your inquiry. You may already be engaged in the process of improving your practice and wish to move directly to the action planner. If you do this then the part of the process which we would like to stress concerns question 4 in the action planner below. This question is designed to help you gather the kind of evidence which will enable you to justify or contradict your belief that your living and learning is improving.

A characteristic of many of the first Living Theory research reports we have seen is the omission of evidence related to the quality of students' learning or of your learning. We stress that the central purpose of teaching, which is to arrange conditions to enable pupils to learn, does not usually provide a focus for the evidence produced in first Living Theory reports. We mention this in the hope that we can encourage you to include evidence in your first report which enables you to justify a claim to have understood something about your pupils' learning and your influence in this learning. We will share specific examples later.

For those who would prefer a period of reflection before engaging with the action planner, we suggest you move ahead to the sections, on 'conversations with colleagues', 'on your concerns and values', 'on contradictions in practice' and 'on gathering evidence', before returning to the action planner (p. 14).

1.9 Using the Living Educational Theory Planner

LIVING EDUCATIONAL THEORY PLANNER FOR IMPROVING LEARNING

NAME and WORKPLACE

The Living Educational Theory Planner and Action Planner are used interchangeably in this book. Living Theory researchers usually ask questions which are directed at improving the quality of their own practice, their understanding of their practice and the social context in which their practice is located. The action planner is usually organised through discussions which help to clarify the nature of the inquiry, 'How do I improve..............?'. We have always found the following five questions useful and manageable:

1. What is your concern/What do you want to improve?
2. What are your reasons for your concern?
3. What might you do to improve your practice?
4. How will you know that your practice has improved? How are you going to find out? What kind of data will you need to collect to use as evidence to enable you to make a judgement on the outcomes of your practice in terms of the quality of your own or teachers' and/or pupils' learning?
5. What kind of resources will you need to enable you to implement your plan?

FRAMEWORK AND RATIONALE FOR LIVING THEORY RESEARCH

NAME and WORKPLACE

Issue/Question Response

The Living Educational Theory planner/action planner is usually organised through discussions which help to clarify the nature of the inquiry, 'How do I improve…?'

1. What do I want to improve in my practice?

2. What will I do about it?

3. How will I know that my practice has improved? What kind of data will I collect to enable me to make a judgement on the outcomes of my practice in terms of the quality of my own or teachers' and/or pupils' learning?

4. How will I evaluate the educational influences of my actions?

5. How will I demonstrate the validity of the account of my educational influence in learning?

6. What kind of resources will you need to enable you to implement your plan?

Copyright material from Jacqueline Delong and Jack Whitehead, 2024, *You and Your Living-Educational Theory*, Routledge

1.10 Workshop for Creating Your Own Living-Educational-Theory

We have presented a 'how to' workshop many times in many countries and conferences. An example workshop in Norfolk, Vermont, USA, at the ALARA Conference 19 June 2018, conducted by ourselves and Marie Huxtable is described in full in Chapter Two of Part One.

1.11 Ethical Issues

First, you do not need anyone's permission to write your thoughts in your journals or to video record your own practice for informal, not-for-credit research. The issue becomes essential when you decide to make public your writing/video clips that involve other people. You do need the written permission of those in your context that you may be quoting or videotaping when you are about to make your writing public. You want to continue to live in your community and maintain your positive relations with those people. As Linda Tuhiwai Smith points out,

> Insiders have to live with the consequences of their processes on a day-to-day basis for ever more, and so do their families and communities. For this reason, insider researchers need to build particular sorts of research-based support systems and relationships with their communities. They have to be skilled at defining clear research goals and 'lines of relating' which are specific to the project and somewhat different from their own family networks. Insider researchers also need to define closure and have skills to say 'no' and the skills to say 'continue'.
>
> (Smith, 1999, p. 137)

Second, if you are conducting this research as part of an accredited degree, you will need to follow the University's ethical review process (REB). You cannot begin your research without REB approval and that approval would require written consent at the onset. We address this process in Part Two.

There are two benefits of publicly asking for help and for permission to share: one is that you check that those affected are comfortable with their role in the process, and you are engaging them to support you in finding evidence for your claims to know. There should be no surprises; that is, no one mentioned in the research for publication should be surprised to see themselves in the writing and/or video data.

1.12 Data Collection: Text, Digital and Visual Data

It is important to make a clear distinction between data and evidence. Data is information that is collected that might be useful in making sense of one's research. Evidence is data that is used to justify or refute a claim to knowledge in an analysis of the data. In this process, a variety of data collection methods, primarily qualitative, are used.

For the first-time inquirer, the process is focused on the practical areas of your life that you are trying to improve. The data that you collect should focus on one or two of these that will help you to make a judgement about any kind of improvement in learning that you are seeking. We focus on the most common, most accessible data in Part One of the book and deepen the sophistication of data collection and analysis in Parts Two and Three.

1.12.1 Your Values and Intentions

Gathering this data is perhaps best done through audio/video recordings of conversations with colleagues who question you about your purposes and the intentions in, for example, a future set of lesson plans. While these conversations can be time-consuming to transcribe, they can be most rewarding because of the data they contain. For videos uploaded to YouTube on 'private', there is a 'transcribe' function (three dots) at the right-hand corner under the visual.

1.12.2 Lesson Plans and Student Work

You might need to answer questions such as,

- What do you mean by an improvement in learning? or
- What are you trying to do about learning that would be sufficient in getting this process going? or
- What can you use as evidence to show learning is taking place?

Some examples of work from your students can serve to show improvement over time. As another possibility, if you can get the students asking their own improvement questions and their plans for improvement, they can provide evidence of improvement over time.

To keep the project doable within the time and resources available to you, you might consider focusing your improvement question on trying to improve the learning of one student or a small group of students in one area such as a mathematics or language skill or a learning strategy such as group work or using assessment feedback for improving writing. Photocopied or camera copied examples of pupils' work over time can give some evidence of the way in which the pupils are relating to what you are doing. In art and technology, you can photograph the pupils' work as it is developing. When you collect the student work, make a photocopy and file it by name and date either in a folder in a bankers' box or on your computer. A copy with a picture from your phone of either your lesson plan or the student work can be printed or filed electronically. You might also make an audio or video record on your phone or in a Zoom conversation of any comments that you want to make about what learning you see taking place.

Audio-recorded conversations with your camera with pupils as you move round the class are also a good source of evidence on the way you are relating to the pupils. An audio or video recorder (swivel cameras are ideal) set up in the room can record what is occurring for analysis later.

1.12.3 Journals

Journals are commonly used because they help you to keep regular notes on what is happening in your life as a researcher. They can be in text form or a video journal. The important part of journal writing is making regular contributions to it. Since our memories are usually very good but not sufficiently accurate for research purposes, notes in a daily planner can be useful in recording thinking, actions and conversations. Keep in mind that the journal is your journal and how much of it you share is entirely up to you.

It can take many forms including a pen and paper diary with a line drawn down the last third of the right side for reflections on the journal entries, an on-line journal on your desktop or phone or a video journal in which you orally make notes of your day. Constructing a website can provide a location for noting your thinking, photos, videos, so you can see the progress over time. We have found sites like Wordpress and Spanglefish very easy to use. We will discuss analysis of the data in the journal later but suffice to say, the video journal is perfect for individuals who dislike writing but the drawback is that it must be transcribed and that is time-consuming. There is a transcription of YouTube videos available-three dots on the bottom right of the visual.

Keeping a journal can be an opportunity to be creative by including drawings and sketches and/or poetry, to abandon sequence and expiate emotion such as anger or joy. It is important to include everything as leaving out something might mean an important piece of evidence is lost. Worrying about writing something of significance can prevent you from getting started or viewing what you have written as mundane may stop you from continuing. We often view our lives as boring when they are very interesting to others and provide a knowledge base of the real lives of practitioners.

Post-it notes are very handy to carry in your pocket to make quick notes of what was said or done. What to write is up to you but can include words, drawings/paintings, photos, videos, collages, artefacts and quotations.

The amount of time spent on it is a personal decision but we encourage a regular, daily time. For Jackie during workdays, it was at the end of the day with a favourite libation, usually around 10–11 at night, as it provided a means to reflect on the day, unload the tension and unwind.

1.12.4 Emails

Another way of documenting your actions and reflections is through emails. They can be self-addressed but if another person, a critical friend, reads, questions and responds, the interaction provides a documentation of the learning and improvement journey. The emails provide date and time, the correspondents and the subject of the dialogue. The emails must be saved, however, in a specific email or computer folder or be printed for a paper-based folder. Keep in mind that once sent, emails can become public information even if they were intended to be private.

1.12.5 Photographs

Included in visual data is the photograph. What is captured in that instant in a photo may not be seen until the photo is viewed and can provide data to support your claim or, alternatively, show you acting contrary to your values. A 'loving gaze' (Buber, 1970) can be so much more alive and evident in a photo of a teacher and her pupil than through words alone. It is relatively easy to insert a photo using INSERT mode as opposed to drag and drop so that the photo is stable. For visual learners, the photo can inspire a flood of ideas to stimulate the writing.

1.12.6 Video-Recordings

Visual data is also available to you through video recording your lesson, your meeting, your interactions with students or colleagues or recording your reflections. You may set the camera on a tripod and sit it in the corner of the classroom and let it run. You will need to stay within the scope of the camera range to be recorded unless you have the swivel camera that will follow your movements. You may also have an opportunity in the curriculum to engage students in the operation of a camera for their understanding of technology or using video for research. You have the right to video record your own actions without permission but including others, students, educational assistants, colleagues does require permission in the event of publication.

After some experience with the video recording process, Jackie's Master's students found the value in it for data collection and data generation as Liz Campbell explains:

> Using a living educational theory methodology enables me to make use of methodological inventiveness to capture, investigate and articulate my values and experiences and to develop my own living educational theory. This methodology embraces the use of alternative research and video is one way to capture, explain and represent my lived experiences that represent this valid yet alternative way of knowing. I agree that it is difficult to measure if we resort to the traditional measuring tools of empirical, scientific ways of knowing. In order to measure a living educational theory, it is essential to consider alternative ways of measuring these alternative ways of knowing. Video has the potential to capture what I can't relay with words (at this particular junction in my writing career) and, in some cases, it can portray knowledge I am not even aware of yet. In addition, video provides another voice for layered reflection and evidence that is measureable; you can see and hear energy flowing values which enhance the ability to feel life affirming energy.
>
> (Campbell, 2011, p. 111)

1.12.7 Interview and Questionnaire

The traditional methods of interview and questionnaire can be used. Interviewing your pupils, provides a means to obtain their opinions on some aspect of their learning or your teaching.

1.12.8 Policy Documents

An individual's practice takes place within a social context that is likely to be influenced by local, regional, national and global policies. Such policy documents can be used as data that can be used in an analysis to provide a context for understanding their influences in practice and understandings.

1.12.8 Previous Reports, Meeting Agendas and Minutes

You can use previous reports, meeting agendas and minutes as data that can be used as evidence in an analysis of a present explanation of educational influences in learning.

1.13 Data Analysis

The aim of analysis in Living Theory research is to generate a valid and evidence-based explanation of your educational influence in your own learning and in the learning of others (an explanation of your educational influence in the learning of social formations usually comes later, after the initial data analysis). There is a clear distinction between data and evidence. Data is the information you gather. You use data as evidence to justify your explanation of influence.

It is advisable to set regular times for analysing the data that you have collected so that you can continue to modify your teaching strategies so that you are teaching the way the student can learn as a responsive teacher. Waiting until the end of the project can be overwhelming with the volume of data to analyse and may mean missed opportunities to address the needs of the student.

The most common data collected for a first project is close at hand and easily manageable and thus we focus on Student Work, Journals and Emails. More extensive data analysis is outlined in Part Two.

1.13.1 Student Work

When spread out on a table or computer screen the work of your students, along with your lesson plans with your intentions for the learning, you will see patterns or themes in them. They may include obvious improvement in learning of the student or, alternatively, a blatant lack of learning or regression; may include disconnect from your intentions in the lesson plans and the learning of the student; may include connection between the lack of the students' comprehension of the skill and their behaviour.

By looking at the first samples of student work as a baseline, a pattern will emerge that shows the progress or lack thereof and the specific areas of progress or difficulty. From this data analysis, you will be able to reflect on your teaching and their learning to enable you to change or modify your plan for addressing the needs of the student. Writing out that plan and sharing it with a critical friend and with the students will demonstrate your learning and direction for improvement. It is important to engage the students in taking responsibility for their own learning.

1.13.2 Journals

Keeping a journal whether electronic or paper-based provides regular data not only on your intentions and responses to people and events but also the emotions and balance in your life. By analysing your reflections on the right third of the page or screen, themes and patterns will emerge that will provide data of how you are responding both intellectually and emotionally to challenges in your life and work. This data can provide evidence of your improvement and/or continuing challenges to living according to your values and to living a good and productive life.

Over a two-month period, you might notice that you wrote that you were upset about the distracting behaviour of a particular student over five times. That might not have come to your attention had you not written it down. Seeing this issue would prompt you to look further into the reason for her misbehaviour to uncover the source of the student's distress as well as a means to relieving your own discomfort.

It is important not to leave too much time before you produce an evidence-based explanation of your educational influences to share with others in a validation exercise. If you leave it too long you are likely to suffer from data overload.

To begin, we suggest that you use the action-reflection cycle to generate your evidence-based explanation as outlined in LIVING EDUCATIONAL THEORY PLANNER FOR IMPROVING LEARNING above.

1.13.3 Emails

Reviewing the data set of your email communications can provide a wealth of information about your actions with regard to your area of proposed improvement. With the lens of that area of focus in mind, you will see the changes over time, whether they are positive or negative and the responses of your critical friend or colleague to your claims to have improved. Themes or patterns may emerge of which you were completely unaware and which may be useful in determining the focus of your actions for the next cycle of action and reflection.

1.14 Organising the Data

A location for the data collected from journals to reports to video recordings is a personal matter. Some of the examples that we have seen and experienced includes bankers' boxes with labelled files, computer folders and sub-folders, artwork drawings and canvases and surfaces with materials under themes. This holistic display that Jackie used makes the data visible and accessible. Jackie spread out her data on a table in her recreation room. This allowed her to see in visual form the processes and patterns of her learning. Jackie had to add new surfaces as the data trail grew.

Another data display method is a data wall. Liz Campbell (2011) used chart paper on the wall of her office in order to see the patterns in it. She writes,

> The *living wall* is my attempt to combine practice and principle in a creative way that will provide a template or strategy that may help or inspire other reflective practitioners to generate their own living educational theories.
>
> (Whitehead, 1989)

The *Living Wall* is a physical representation of the internal (my thoughts) and external (my actions) me —the inner and outer "I" unfolding in time—my living educational theory (Whitehead,

1989). It serves many purposes from the very practical to the abstract. I started the wall because I felt an urgent need to organize my thoughts and the traditional structure offered by a Major Research Project outline was not working for me; in fact, the situation was actually worse than that because the suggested (and I am very fortunate that this was not required) structure actually hindered my thinking process and stifled my creativity. I could not work within this framework and I certainly felt a conflict with the suggested outline and the living educational theory methodology (Whitehead, 1989) I was using. I am certainly not suggesting that everyone would or should sense the conflict; simply that one existed for me. The nature of the living educational theory methodology is such that a traditional five-chapter outline might be the perfect structure for an individual if that is how their research unfolds. The structured outline was far too restrictive and prescriptive for me. It made me feel like I was being intentionally self-destructive as I forced myself into the corsetry of the system. I found myself looking for material to fit within the parameters and when I made my research fit, it seemed to lose something—I felt disfigured. My voice disappeared from the page and my ideas, which seemed to flow previously, now seemed stagnant and dull—the internal rhythm was hijacked.

(Campbell, 2011, pp. 100–102)

1.15 First Draft of Research

It is wise to produce your first embryonic explanation some six weeks into your inquiry. There are at least three good reasons for taking this action. One is that description of your journey to date helps to prevent what can become data overload, where you have so much data that you can lose any sense of purpose and comprehensibility. Two is that it can be helpful in that you can check that the data that you are collecting and analysing is directly related to your question. An interesting aspect of data collection and analysis is the issue of collecting the wrong data for the question you have posed on "How can I improve?" When two of the Brant Country teacher researchers, Tom Wilson and Jeff Churchward, discovered that the data that they had collected did not answer their question, "What strategies can be used to facilitate a three-way partnership between parent-child-teacher in a child's learning?", they were dismayed to find that they needed to start over.

A third reason is that you may find that based on your data analysis, your question has changed. Joanna Finch, a Grade 6 teacher, started with an initial question, "How am I going to help my students better communicate their problem-solving ideas?" and changed it to "How am I going to assist my students to improve their reasoning skills?" She wrote,

> I believed that I needed to shift my research/teaching focus from that of communication to reasoning so the students would have a secure framework of thought processes in place before communicating about them. If they couldn't reason through a problem, recognizing their own difficulties, how could they communicate about it?
>
> (Delong, 2001, p. 102)

This is where your validation group can be most helpful in keeping a focus on both your practice of improvement and your practice as a researcher in generating valid explanations of educational influences in learning.

Here is an example of a first draft report showing Tina Jacklin's evaluation criteria and what she has produced early in the process. We share it in typed text but the original was marked up with handwritten notes:

How I want to be evaluated

1. Is there evidence of growth as I proceed through the Action-Reflection cycle?
2. Is there evidence that I have become aware of my values and beliefs?
3. Is there evidence that I have lived my educational values in my practice?
4. Is there evidence that my learning has influenced the learning of my students?

Draft #1 Getting ideas down

Changing Attitudes: Gaining Skills

Inexperienced, nervous, unprepared, excited, I faced my class of 13 students who were squished together in a corner of the library. This was definitely not the ideal learning environment. How was I to create a sense of community, a safe place to learn and take risks when I only saw the students an hour a day? By the end of the first week of school I realized that the students I was working with had a strong dislike for school. They would say things like may-day, may-day, I can't read/write, and I hate reading/writing. I needed to find a way to change their attitudes and subsequently improve their skills since 11 out of the 21 students were non-readers and all but two of the others were reading below level. I Have strong belief that children must feel safe before any real learning takes place. Is this a claim?

Soon my class grew to 22 students and I was given more time to work with them. It was at this time that I began collaborating with Brenda on a Books and Buddies program. I thought that this program accompanied with a great deal of encouragement and praise, fun activities in the classroom, and little homework would help to improve the students' view of school. (Why I assigned little homework is linked to one of the reasons the children had learned to dislike school.)

A few months into the school year I was discouraged. I was still hearing from that children that they hated virtually everything at school including physical education and art. I discussed this with Brenda and she thought that there was a discrepancy between what the children were saying and what we were seeing in the classroom. They said they hated things but once they had begun the task they seemed to enjoy themselves. (Old habits die hard). This is when I began having the students write in a buddy journal, as Brenda had suggested. In this journal, they were allowed to express things they disliked, enjoyed or thought needed to be improved in the buddy program. I gave them a place to have a voice. It was in this journal that I began seeing that many of the students actually enjoyed taking part in reading buddies. They were having trouble difficulty, at times, getting their buddy to listen and work. So we began sharing some of the difficulties and the successes we were having and how to solve some of the problems. The students shared a great deal and began helping each other to solve problems. I also shared. Many of the problems they were having honestly were problems I also had in the classroom. I think this helped them see themselves as "teachers". A sense of community had developed in the classroom.

I really saw the improvement in my students' attitudes in March when a new student arrived in my classroom. She was having difficulty reading. When she came to read to me she said, I can't read. It's too hard." It was at this time that I sat back and realized that I hadn't heard those words in such a long time. The students had come so far. They were saying things like "Don't tell me that word. I can figure it out myself." One girl's public speech was titled,

'I Love Books." The students had really begun to understand what reading was about and had developed confidence as readers. (See reading strategies and what is reading.) This confidence was apparent after we tested their reading ability again in June. All of the kids were readers. (Support for my claim.)

I knew I had done my job in May when one of the students who had held firmly all year that he hated all aspects of school, came up to me and said, I'm a good writer!" I knew then that he had opened himself up to learning.

You can access all of Tina's six drafts and more information on getting started at: http://www.actionresearch.net/writings/jack/cycle1.pdf

1.16 Literature

When you are just starting on the Living Theory journey, the emphasis is on your embodied knowledge so that you are keeping the writing about you and your 'I'. It can be distracting if you look to others who claim to know more than you do and, in fact, do not and could not know more about your life and work than you do. We find that everyone has some literature that has influenced them whether poetry or fiction or philosophy. It's a matter of reflecting back on how that influence has emerged. For example, Jackie found the writings of Stephen Covey (1989, 1990) very influential in her thinking early in her research. She found his language of 'True North principles' and an 'Inside-Out' approach to professional development and self-improvement, provided insights and helped her to articulate her value of care and support for others.

In addition, most of us have integrated literature from our various disciplines, such as curriculum, pedagogy, history, psychology, into our practice. Research in these fields has influenced our lives in both positive and negative ways, either confronting or confirming our knowledge and experience. We are not always aware of that influence and may need to reflect on the influence in order to be explicit. In Living Educational Theory research, we recognise that we are being influenced all the time and need to acknowledge that influence.

Having said that, you will find references within this book to certain authors, whom we have found helpful in providing insights into expressing our values and framing our questions, especially practitioner-researchers who have shared their Living Educational Theory research in *The Educational Journal of Living Theories (EJOLTs)* available at https://ejolts.net, in *The Canadian Journal of Action Research* at https://journals.nipissingu.ca/index.php/cjar and in the Grand Erie District School Board repository of classroom research at https://www.actionresearch.net/writings/ActionResearch/purpose/index.html

Summary:
   Living Educational Theory Research
   in a Culture of Inquiry by

- Values-based inquiry
- Action-reflection cycles
- Multimedia to collect or analyse data
- Personal and social validation
- Share findings on a comfortable stage
- Changing teaching practice
- Improving student learning

1.17 Second Draft of Research

For a second draft, some additional expectations might include:

1. A refined question
2. Your context
3. A bit about your methodology and methods
4. The analysis of more extensive data
5. Your findings to date
6. A few references

For a second draft, you may have changed or refined your question. You will have more data that you will have analysed to deepen your explanation of your influence and improvement. There will be an expectation that you will show the influence of the literature on your learning although still at a minimal level as the emphasis is on your embodied knowledge of teaching and learning in your classroom and/or school. The emphasis is still on sharing data that provides evidence of improvement: as a teacher in the classroom, it could include data showing improvement in student achievement as a result of a change in pedagogy; as an administrator in a school, it might include an improvement in teacher voice in professional development activities; as a nurse in a hospital, it might include an improvement in patient well-being.

There would be an expectation that you share your context so that the reader can more fully understand your claims to have improved.

1.18 Methods and Methodologies

We know that there can be some confusion about the different meanings of a method and methodology and we try to be clear about the distinction:

- A Method is a way of collecting data or a technique of analysis.
- A Methodology provides the rationale for how the research is carried out.

A methodology provides the theoretical analysis of the methods and principles associated with the contribution to knowledge being made in the research.

A Living Theory researcher uses whatever methods are useful in the inquiry, 'How do I improve what I am doing?' In our early research, both of us used action reflection cycles as **a method** in our inquiries. We mean this in the sense that:

1. we expressed a concern grounded in our experience of believing that we could live our values more fully in our practice;
2. we imagined ways forward and chose an action plan to act on;
3. we acted and gathered data on which to make a judgement on the influence of our actions;
4. we evaluated our actions in terms of our values; and
5. we modified our concerns, ideas and actions in the light of our evaluations.

Living Theory researchers generate their unique living-theory-methodology as they create an explanation of their educational influences in their own learning, in the learning of others and in the learning of the social formations that impact on their practice and understandings. A living-theory-methodology can use insights from different methodologies such as Narrative Inquiry, Action Research, Phenomenology, Ethnography, Autoethnography, Case Study and Living Theory research.

We have found Creswell's (2007, pp. 53–58) descriptions of five qualitative research approaches to narrative research, phenomenology, grounded theory, ethnography and case studies to be one of the best introductory texts on these methodologies. For each of the five approaches, Creswell poses a definition, briefly traces the history of each approach, explores types of studies, introduces procedures involved in conducting a study and indicates potential challenges in using each approach. He also reviews some of the similarities and differences among the five approaches 'so that qualitative researchers can decide which approach is best to use for their particular study'. We emphasise that a researcher need not choose one of these methodologies. As a researcher, you can draw insights from any of these approaches together with insights from action research and narrative research without choosing between them in the development of their own living-theory-methodology as you create your living-educational-theory. For more information, see https://www.actionresearch.net//writings/arsup/livingtheorymethodologies.pdf

The most common research approach used for creating living-educational-theories is that of an autobiographical or a self-study form of action research. In 1953, Stephen Corey produced the first textbook on action research in education on 'Action Research to Improve School Practices'. On 24 May 2020, a search in Google on Action Research generated over 3,730,000,000 references. There are now many different schools of action research. Most include some form of action-reflection cycles of planning, acting, evaluating and modifying. This method of inquiry, using an action planner, involves the action researcher studying their own practice in order to improve it.

An important text in the history of action research is Wilf Carr's and Stephen Kemmis' (1983), 'Becoming Critical; Knowing Through Action Research' with many of these ideas included in their 1986 publication on 'Becoming Critical'. Carr and Kemmis applied Habermas' (1976) critical theory to distinguish their critical approach to action research from other approaches. They retained the action-reflection cycles in their action planner while emphasising the priority of sociopolitical, historical and cultural influences in the knowledge generated through action research.

In several other publications, Jack Whitehead and Jean McNiff stressed the importance of the knowledge created by action researchers as they researched the processes of improving their practice. This knowledge included insights from explanatory principles derived from social science theories and methods (McNiff & Whitehead, 2009a, 2009b, 2011; Whitehead, & McNiff, 2006).

It is important to avoid confusing methods with methodology. In Living Educational Theory research, a methodology explains the process through which a living-educational-theory has been generated.

1.19 Validation Group

All researchers are concerned about their work being valid and not merely anecdotal. To address this concern, the explanations are strengthened by subjecting them to the responses of a validation group. One of the distinguishing characteristics of Living Theory is that the researcher must make public the story of their research in a way that is open to others to evaluate its validity. A Living Theory methodology includes the processes of validation.

Validation groups are guided by the idea of testing theories or ideas, critically discussing the investigation or study and providing suggestions for improvement. The group size is not absolute but usually consist of three to five peers. A validation group can help to enhance validity by focusing on responding to a practitioner-researcher's explanation of educational influence, in relation to four questions posed by the researcher based on Habermas' (1976, pp. 2–3) criteria for social validity:

1. How could I strengthen the comprehensibility of my writings?
2. How could I improve the evidence I present to justify or challenge my assertions – that is what I claim to be true?
3. How could I enhance my awareness of the cultural and sociohistorical influences that affect my writings in terms of what I believe to be right?
4. How could I demonstrate more convincingly my authenticity in the sense that I am living my values as fully as I can (Whitehead, 2010, p. 101)?

The TRAC acronym created by Liz Campbell (2013) generates the questions. Liz writes:

Shared struggles and common values are revealed and made explicit through the use of reflective writing, videotaping, and individual and collaborative review and analysis of the writing and video footage. We refer to Habermas' concept of social validity to test knowledge claims as we ask and seek feedback for the question 'Am I on TRAC?' i.e. truthful, right, authentic and comprehensible (Habermas, 1976, pp. 2–3). This is not to suggest that there is an imposed moral agenda; however, there is the intention of enhancing our individual understanding of our values and influences and hoping to improve our lives and the lives of others. (p. 51)

Does it sound:

> **T**rue?
> **R**ight?
> **A**uthentic?
> **C**omprehensible? (TRAC)

1.20 Creating a Culture of Inquiry for the Creation of Living-Educational-Theories

We mentioned earlier the importance of a critical friend and a supportive community in a safe, supportive space where you are enabled to make explicit your values and make yourself accountable for living according to those values. Moreover, it is an environment where it is safe to be vulnerable. Creating a Culture of Inquiry requires the facilitator to gradually build a non-hierarchical environment of democracy and mutual respect in order to establish 'power with' and eliminate 'power over' relationships. It's important to overtly check for the comfort of each individual, see where attention needs to be paid and gently solicit involvement from the quiet voices.

When the facilitator demonstrates her vulnerability (Delong, 2009), others in the community are released to more fully share their own discomfort and vulnerabilities. You learn to recognise when you are not living according to your espoused values and are what a 'living contradiction' (Whitehead, 1989). Some groups 'gel' almost immediately while others seem to take more time. "Educational conversations and dialogue as research" (Delong, 2019; 2020) are significant features of a Culture of Inquiry.

How would you go about creating that community? First, you might see if there is a group that has already formed that you could join. Second, you could create one either in person or virtually through videoconferencing programs such as SKYPE, Teams and ZOOM. At least to start, there needs to be an organiser who invites people virtually or welcomes them to the session and asks each person to share a catch-up or what's going on in their life and research.

Sometimes the topic has been pre-set or emerges from the sharing. Then the group can decide the logistics such as time, dates, locations or sites, size of group.

The effectiveness of mentoring of practitioner-researchers in Cultures of Inquiry to create their own living-theories has a significant history in a variety of contexts (Delong, 2001, 2019; Vaughan, 2019; Vaughan & Delong, 2019). After the introduction to exploring your values, the steps to the process can be taken in a gradual sequence as per the Living Theory Planner. Some participants get anxious about seeing the end product and our advice is to 'trust the process'. The 'perfect' question is not always discernible at the beginning and more often emerges in the process of writing and sharing your stories and keeping journal notes. After several months of collecting data and sharing in the Culture of Inquiry, patterns and themes emerge, evidence of having lived according to your values and/or not adhering to your values. Through analysis of the data, these themes can confirm the direction of your research to improve or take you in a different direction.

1.21 Final Draft of Your First Report

For a final draft, once you have generated an evidence-based explanation of educational influence in learning, some additional expectations might include:

1. A cover page with your question and a short biography
2. An abstract that summarised the research
3. Your socio-historical context
4. Your methodology and methods
5. Your findings
6. Your next steps
7. References

For the Final Draft of your First Report of creating your own-living-educational-theory, the length is not important, unless it is being submitted for academic accreditation in an Institution that specifies the length. If you have answered your "How can I improve" question with adequate evidence to support your claims to know, a few pages will suffice. As an example,

An Action Research Project on Improving Students' Written Communication in Mathematics

George Neeb, Grand Erie District School Board, May 2000

My research question was, "What can I do to improve students' written communication in Mathematics?"

Introduction

I was concerned when the students at my school obtained the lowest results in the Mathematics section on 1998–1999s Grade 6 Provincial Assessment. Upon analysis of the sub tasks, I found that one of the poorest results was the students' ability to communicate understanding in Mathematics.

1998–1999 Mathematics Results

PERCENTAGE OF STUDENTS ACHIEVING A LEVEL 3 OR 4

Problem Solving	13%
Understanding Concepts	13%
Application of Mathematical Procedures	26%
Communication of Required Knowledge	13%

Although problem-solving and understanding of concepts were also weak, I concentrated on communication because it is embedded in all the scores. I was also concerned that, because the provincial assessment is written, students who have trouble with writing are not being assessed accurately on their mathematical ability. Most of my students are stronger orally and the test demands high levels of writing to explain reasoning.

"It is easier to say it verbally. In math I can never think of what to write." Student

In the past, I had never thought of written math responses as needing the time and dedication of language skills. I felt students should just write a response and move on, without really thinking of ways to teach them to do so. I do believe that students need to improve their understanding of math concepts, but I also believe students have much knowledge that is already there but not showing up in the test results. Students need practice and encouragement in sharing in the written form. I decided I would try to teach students to write math responses the way I teach them in Language using a writing process. In essence I borrowed a "Language" technique to apply to mathematics. This strategy is a form of integration on my part.

Methodology

Under the guidance of Diane Morgan, Educational Consultant and James Ellsworth, Curriculum Coordinator, and as part of an action research group, I studied my classroom practice during 1999–2000. Data collection included student work samples, EQAO test scores and sub tasks, regular journal keeping, and videotaping class lessons. We were trained by Educational Consultant Ruth Sutton to use corrective feedback. With the support of Diane, James and critical friends in the group, I analyzed and shared my learning.

Procedure

I planned to develop ways to improve writing by coaching students to build on knowledge that was already there and use their oral ability as a starting point to written responses. I planned to motivate students and encourage them to help each other to feel more confident about writing the provincial assessment. This would be accomplished through the following strategies:

1. *Use a process writing approach to solving math problems*
2. *Use corrective feedback (Sutton, 1997) with students*
3. *Explicitly teach problem-solving steps and strategies*
4. *Clearly outline evaluation expectations*
5. *Teach the required math terminology*
6. *Replicate testing circumstances in the classroom*

Process Writing to Solve Math Problems

Commonly in my practice, I encourage them to talk over ideas with others (like prewriting), then write a response using a problem-solving model (drafting), then re-read their response (proofing), share their response with others (conferencing and corrective feedback), and finally, make any changes in ideas and edit for clarity (final draft). I encourage students to do more than one draft of their responses, just like authors do several drafts of stories.

"Conferencing with others about my math answers helped me to notice my mistakes and help others."

Student Corrective Feedback

Although students were using corrective feedback (Sutton, 1997) in their conferences, I think it is still important to discuss it directly here. Students need to be taught how to help others improve their work and teachers need to understand the importance of this skill and how to use it effectively. I taught students to focus on making two statements to the writer: "You did well...." and "You could improve your answer by...." I reinforced repeatedly that telling someone their work was "good" or "excellent" really does not help them. Everyone can improve in some way. I would always have my students use a conferencing sheet to evaluate how well the stories they were sharing met certain requirements. Students had to staple this formative evaluation onto their stories when they handed in drafts for me to read and I encouraged them to use this feedback to revise their stories before handing them in. I thought this sheet would work for math responses so I had the class help me decide what we should look for in a question. They came up with suggestions and, over time, we realized that there was a standard practice to writing a complete math response.

Problem-Solving

Then I found an actual "Steps for Math Problem Solving", GEDSB document which we used as a basis for our model, conferencing and feedback form. These were the steps:

Explicit Evaluation and Practice Tests

Students need to know how their responses are being evaluated. In class, I always have rubrics ready before the students start on an assignment so they know what I am looking for in a Level 3 or 4 answer. Using the overhead, I showed students the actual rubrics for the provincial tests. Although the rubrics are very general, we had a lengthy discussion on what each section meant. When we took up the practice tests together, I modelled responses based on the rubrics sent by EQAO and clearly identified why I was doing what I was doing in the response.

Findings and Conclusions

Students need to buy into the importance of written communication in the test setting (and the importance of the skill in everyday life). One way was to leave Mathematics and discuss the Reading section of the provincial test.

I asked students to explain how they thought they would receive a reading score. Most assumed they would be reading to someone. I explained that their reading score was based on the writing they did about the story they read, the reasons why we have been doing response journals all year! This helped them see that writing was clearly important.

Students need to be prepared to answer questions independently. It is important for them to realize that they will not have the corrective feedback they had in the classroom on the provincial test. In the third term, I gradually removed the conferencing option so students would solve the problems more independently.

Students greeted the writing process approach to math with enthusiasm. The class was unanimous in agreeing this not only made math journalling more fun, but it actually did help their mathematical understanding. A few said it helped them to clarify their ideas and make their responses better.

"I liked conferencing with others about my math answers because I got to see what other people thought of my work before I handed it in." Student

Summative Evaluation

Even if the conferencing and sharing only made math more enjoyable, it was still a help because I believe the more enjoyable the experience, the more effort will be put into it. My own practice of corrective feedback to students has improved this year. I feel more confident giving students' strengths, weaknesses, and next steps comments with marks being optional. This formative approach helps students see how they can improve as opposed to just receiving a mark and ignoring the comments. I still use summative evaluation but with corrective feedback in mind, and I give students opportunities to improve their work after they have received the feedback.

In working independently in third term, I found many students still did as well in their responses because they could conference alone, using the corrective feedback ideas discussed in class. Students were re-reading their responses, going through the "Steps for Math Problem-solving" independently and also revising and editing. Some were even doing second drafts.

I videotaped students hard at work and conferencing, using the camera as my eyes. Usually I was quiet, just observing, sometimes asking questions. This gave me a wealth of information about my students. When I viewed the tapes later, I found I was seeing things I had not noticed (who was working with whom, who was more on task, who was giving helpful advice). I could also listen to my own questioning and see how students were responding to me. I then showed the video to them. This offered us a process for formative student self-evaluation, teacher–student evaluation, and teacher self-evaluation.

I have seen incredible growth in my students' mathematical communication. We still have a way to go, but I believe I have implemented some techniques to help students that will become part of our everyday classroom programming.

I had students give feedback on math this year. They made some powerful statements about their own learning:

"Problem-solving is my favourite part of math because it is both fun and challenging."

"I find it easier if I have discussed the problem rather than having to do everything in my head."

"I have improved in problem-solving. When I first started I was bad at it. Now it's my favourite part of math. I don't know how I improved, I just did."

Our school results are in from last year's Provincial Assessment. I have only analyzed the data from the Grade 6 students that I taught last year. I have compared the data to the previous year's scores (mentioned above – none of these students I taught). I am happy to report an increase in communication (and all mathematical scores).

Comparison of Mathematics Results

PERCENTAGE OF STUDENTS ACHIEVING A LEVEL 3 OR 4

	1998–1999	1999–2000
Problem Solving	13%	34%
Understanding Concepts	13%	26%
Application of Mathematical Procedures	26%	46%
Communication of Required Knowledge	13%	25%

Concluding Comments

Again, with the support of James Ellsworth, I am continuing my research during 2000–2001 to see if I can sustain my learning and continue to improve student learning and achievement. I am presenting my research at the Ontario Educational Research Conference in December 2001.

I continue to work towards improving student communication in mathematics, and strive to include corrective feedback strategies in all areas of my program.

Reference

Sutton, R. (1997). *The Learning School*. Salford: RS Publications.

Bibiographical Note

Name: George Neeb
Current Position: teaches Grade 6 at North Ward Public School, Paris, ON.
Academic Background: BA Psychology McMaster, Hamilton, ON, BEd, Western, London, ON, Masters of Arts in Teaching, McMaster
Areas of Interest: member of ETFO, member of Community Builders focusing on building an inclusive community in schools, enjoys Visual and Dramatic Arts
Mailing Address: 33 Lincoln Ave, Brantford, Ontario N3T 4S6
© Nipissing University 1998–2011
http://oar.nipissingu.ca/archive-Vol4No2-V424E.htm (Neeb, 2020)

1.22 Publication

You can access details of eight volumes of Passion in Professional Practice that show how initial living-theory explanations can be published at:
   https://www.actionresearch.net/writings/ActionResearch/index.html

You can access details of ten years of issues of the Educational Journal of Living Theories (EJOLTs) to see how you improve your publications to the professional level of a refereed international journey at: https://ejolts.net/

1.23 Conclusion to Part One

As a living-educational-theory is emerging with data to provide evidence to support your claims to know and your validation group confirms the validity of your argument, a report ensues that meets the tenets of a Living Theory:

What is Living Educational Theory (Living Theory) research and what are living-educational-theories (living-theories)? A brief resume:

'Living Educational Theory' (Living Theory) (with upper case) research refers to a lexical definition of meaning which distinguishes Living Theory research, whereas 'living-educational-theory' (living-theory) (with lower case) refers to the unique embodied and ostensive expressions of meaning in explanations of an individual's educational influence in learning.

Whitehead's 1985 paper presents his notion of a living form of educational theory and in his 1989 paper he coined the term 'Living Theory' to denote a distinct form of theorising and research whereby an individual produces an 'explanation of their educational influence in their own learning, the learning of others and the learning of social formations'.

An individual's living-educational-theories (living-theories) are living, that is they are evolving and they are lived as they are embodied and expressed by the researcher through their practice. Researchers' living-theory accounts provide explanations and standards of judgement of 'improving practice' in terms of their relational and ontological values that are clarified as they emerge and evolve through their research. A 'living-educational-theory' is the particular/unique living-educational-theory generated by individuals to explain their educational influences in learning in enquiries of the kind, 'How do I improve what I am doing?'. An individual's living-educational-theory account includes evaluations of past learning and an intention to improve practice in the future in ways that are not yet realised in practice. Improvement in practice is understood as practice that contributes to a world in which humanity can flourish and is expressed in the values-based living standards of judgement (Laidlaw, 1996) of the Living Theory researcher.

Living Theory research is a form of self-study research in which practitioners research questions that are important to them to generate their values-based 'explanations of their educational influence in their own learning, the learning of others, and the learning of social formations' (Whitehead, 1989). They use various research methods such as Action Research, Narrative Enquiry and Autoethnography. Living Theory research is distinguishable by the form of logic, epistemology, explanations, standards of judgement and units of appraisal.

The evolving history of Living Educational Theory research can be seen in publications dating from 1967, many of which can be freely accessed from http://www.actionresearch.net.

To learn more about Living Theory research and the connections to the rest of the book, watch this video:

Jack Whitehead outlines the Living Theory process for novices https://youtu.be/9VTciLigPGI (Delong, 2020b)

You may also want to visit and join the conversations in the EJOLTS community space (http://www.ejolts.net), and on EJOLTs Facebook and Living Theory Facebook group and EJOLTs on LinkedIn.

In addition to being free of grammatical and structural errors, the following checklist may be helpful to see if all elements of a valid project have been included:

1. An 'I' question
2. Your social, historical and political context
3. Your Living-Educational-Theory methodology and methods used
4. Evidence of reflection
5. Data to support your claims to know
6. Data Analysis process
7. Validation process
8. Findings
9. Next steps
10. References

You can access more information on IMPROVING YOUR ACCOUNT AND DEVELOPING ACTION ENQUIRY from: http://www.actionresearch.net/writings/jack/cycle2.pdf

PART

2 Master's Level Inquiries

Part Two builds on Part One to address the deeper, more complex requirements of those interested in academic projects, potentially for accreditation at the Master's level. It focuses on our suggestions for both tutors and students. The increased academic requirements at the doctorate level are developed in Part Three. You may wish to go back and forth between the three parts to meet your needs.

2.1 Development in Philosophical Base from Parts One to Two

In building on the philosophical base of Part One, we continue to focus on making public and evolving the practical knowledge that is being expressed in inquiries of the kind, 'How do I improve what I am doing?'. In our support for tutors and students in such continuing inquiries, we deepen and extend the philosophical understanding we bring into our pedagogy for Living Educational Theory research.

In Part Two, we are continuing to focus on making public, practical educational knowledge, the knowledge being expressing in everyday practice, together with **its evolution** in explanations of educational influences in one's own learning, in the learning of others and in the learning of the social formations that influence practice and understandings. In Part Two, we are focusing on a curriculum for a Living Educational Theory research approach to an educational inquiry that develops the beginning inquiries in Part One into work of Master's quality.

In Part One, we focused on starting an educational inquiry into the question, 'How do I improve what I am doing?'. We advocated the use of action-reflection cycles to engage in a systematic inquiry into improving your practice and into making public an explanation of your educational influences in your own learning and in the learning of others. In Part Two, we continue to explore the implications of asking, researching and answering such questions whilst emphasising the deepening and extending of explanations of educational influence in one's own learning and in the learning of others. This involves a growing understanding of the nature of the educational knowledge that is created in justify claims to know one's own educational influences in one's own learning and in the learning of others.

What we also want to do in Part Two is to emphasise the processes for strengthening the data that is collected and used to generate a valid, evidence-based explanation of educational influences in learning. We will explain how to integrate insights from the ideas or theories of others, in the generation of a living-educational-theory. Finally, we emphasise the importance of working within a Culture of Inquiry, in communities of other practitioner-researchers, that supports Living Educational Theory research.

By focusing on the evolving living-educational-theories that are emerging from your question, 'How do I improve what I am doing?', we avoid what became known as the 'intellectualist legend'. This is the belief that intelligent actions presuppose a recognition of propositions that are governing the actions. We are assuming that practitioner-researchers are already engaged in educational practices without such a recognition of those propositions. Gilbert Ryle explained the problem of the intellectualist legend in relation to his meaning of efficient practice.

The methods used for gathering and analysing data can be drawn from a range of methodological sources bearing in mind Gilbert Ryle's point, as explanations of educational influences in learning are produced:

> Efficient practice precedes the theory of it; methodologies presuppose the application of the methods, of the critical investigation of which they are the products. It was because Aristotle found himself and others now intelligently and now stupidly and it was because Izaak Walton found himself and others angling sometimes effectively and sometimes ineffectively that both were able to give to their pupils the maxims and prescriptions of their arts. It is therefore possible for people intelligently to perform some sorts of operations when they are not yet able to consider any propositions enjoining how they should be performed. Some intelligent performances are not controlled by an interior acknowledgement of the principles applied in them.

> The belief that it is not possible for people intelligently to perform some sorts of operations when they are not yet able to consider any propositions enjoining how they should be performed, was known as the intellectualist legend. The crucial objection to the intellectualist legend is this. The consideration of propositions is itself an operation the execution of which can be more or less intelligent. But if, for any operation to be intelligently executed, a prior theoretical operation had first to be performed and performed intelligently, it would a logical impossibility for anyone ever to break into the circle.
>
> (Ryle, 1973, p. 31)

'Efficient practice' is vitally important in Living Educational Theory research. What we mean by 'efficient practice' is that practitioner-researchers already have embodied knowledge that is expressed in practice. The task of Living Educational Theory research is to help to make public, this embodied knowledge, to evolve this knowledge in the process of making it public and to share this knowledge in a way that is relatable and useful to others. We are stressing the importance of not imposing theoretical abstractions on explanations of educational influences in learning, as if these abstractions can explain an individual's educational influence. However, we are also emphasising that insights from these abstractions can be drawn into a living-educational-theory, as we show below in the sections on validation, rigour and using the ideas of others.

The importance of including the practical principles used by a practitioner-researcher to explain educational influences in learning as a living-educational-theory and a contribution to Living Educational Theory research can be appreciated when you consider the following mistake in the disciplines approach to Educational Theory. The mistake was that the approach explicitly **replaced** such explanations in Educational Theory, by abstract principles from the disciplines of Education. Jack experienced this 'replacement' in his studies of Educational Theory at the London Institute of Education in 1968–1970. The explanations Jack was creating, as a science teacher, were focused on his educational influences in the learning of his pupils. In the Disciplines Approach to Educational Theory, these explanations were not only ignored but attempts were made by his tutors to replace his practical principles with principles from the theories of the disciplines of education. This mistake was recognised by

Paul Hirst (1983), one of the principal proponents of the disciplines approach to Educational Theory:

> ...Principles justified in this way have until recently been regarded as at best pragmatic maxims having a first crude and superficial justification in practice that in any rationally developed theory **would be replaced by principles with more fundamental, theoretical justification. That now seems to me to be a mistake**. (our emphasis). Rationally defensible practical principles, I suggest, must of their nature stand up to such practical tests and without that are necessarily inadequate.
>
> (p. 18)

As a tutor you might, because of a particular commitment to a discipline of education, act in a way that seeks to replace the practical principles used by your student to explain their educational influences in learning, by principles from a discipline of education. This could be because, as a tutor, you may believe that your primary responsibility is to initiate your student into a discipline of education rather than in supporting them in the generation of their own contribution to Living Educational Theory research through the generation and sharing of their own living-educational-theory.

To help tutors and students retain a focus on the values-laden practical principles that can explain educational influences in learning, while at the same time valuing contributions from the disciplines of education, we make a clear distinction between 'education research' and 'educational research'.

In our experience, there has been a tendency to lose sight of the importance of 'educational' influences in learning within the language of research in education. With the following two examples, one from UK and one from USA, we want tutors and students to be aware that academics from the disciplines such as philosophy, history, sociology, psychology and leadership in education continue to impose their own conceptual frameworks and methods of validation on educational research. First, in his Presidential Address to the British Educational Research, Geoff Whitty writes about changing the name of an Educational Research Association to an Education Research Association:

> I have so far used the broad term education research to characterise the whole field, but it may be that within that field we should

reserve the term educational research for work that is consciously geared towards improving policy and practice.

(Whitty, 2005, pp. 172–173)

Whitty does acknowledge that one problem with this distinction between 'education research' as the broad term and 'educational research' as the narrower field of work specifically geared to the improvement of policy and practice is that it would mean that BERA, as the British Educational Research Association would have to change its name or be seen as only involved with the latter (p. 173).

A similar move has been made by a senior administrator in the American Educational Research Association, to replace educational by education. On complaining to the editors of AERA publications about this replacement Jack received a note that included a recommendation from a senior administrator of AERA that the term education research rather than educational research should be used.

We include these references and correspondence to emphasise the importance of seeing a responsibility of educational researchers and education researchers to distinguish these different forms of research. There is no necessity in education research for researchers to explain their educational influences in their own learning, in the learning of others and in the learning of the social formations that influence practice and understandings. However, this is a necessary condition of educational research. At the heart of these explanations of educational influences in learning are values-laden practical principles. This is because education is a values-laden practical activity.

As we encourage students to include ideas from others in their Living Educational Theory research we also encourage the formulation of a professional inquiry, as we did in Part One using the action-reflection planner (this may be an individual or group inquiry). This includes the production of short pieces of autobiographical writing to help to locate inquiries in their particular contexts and to outline the unique constellation of values which provide the motivations to improve practice. To start this process we often advocate the creation and sharing of a living-poster that can be added to the 2021 homepage of living-posters at https://www.actionresearch.net/writings/posters/homepage2021.pdf.

The reason we focus on the importance of these values is that they form the explanatory principles that are the heart of explanations of educational influences in learning. We stress the difference between descriptions and explanation in educational research. Descriptions enable us to be clear about what is going on. Explanations enable us to be clear about why it is going on. Explanations provide the reasons why something is happening in the way that it does. Hence the importance of values as explanatory principles. When a person asks, 'How do I improve what I am doing?' the implication is that the person could be doing something better. In other words, it implies that the person is not yet living his or her values as fully as they could be. When we experience this feeling, that we are not living our values as fully as we could do, this is a sufficient reason for explaining why we are doing something. If we feel that our values of freedom, justice or care are not being lived as fully as possible, we give the reasons for acting in terms of seeking to live these values (or others) as fully as possible.

In accepting an educational responsibility, to extend one's cognitive range and concern in learning for oneself with values of human flourishing, we can also accept an educational responsibility for supporting this learning with others. While we can write and talk about these values in meanings that include the words social justice, freedom, compassion, care, democracy, love, equality, respect and educational responsibility, the meanings we focus on are clarified as the embodied values we express in our practice. This is how Joy Mounter (2008b) explains her value of educational responsibility as she moves from a language of learning to the language of educational responsibility:

How do I recognise the move from the language of learning to the language of educational responsibility?

> …Each practitioner researcher clarifies, in the course of their emergence, in the practice of educational inquiry, the embodied ontological values to which they hold themselves accountable in their professional practice. (Whitehead, 2005) I have spent the last two years exploring my values and beliefs in the classroom and working with the children in my class to develop our skills and reflections as learners. As educational researchers we need to go beyond the language of learning into a language of educational responsibility; a responsibility to ourselves and the children, looking at educational explanations and evaluations of our living values in our class. This essay will move from the language of learning to clarifying the meaning of the educational responsibility I feel towards the children in my care. My intention in this paper is to contribute to the knowledgebase of education with my own

living educational theory, exploring my values and the influences in my learning and of the children in my care, while looking at the insights I have gained from other education theories. Hirst (1983) explores this issue, helping us to clarify our desire to create and not replace our own 'living educational theories'.

(See https://www.actionresearch.net/writings/tuesdayma/joymounteree207.pdf)

In clarifying the meanings of values, it is not sufficient to use words alone. We make a clear distinction between lexical definitions of the meanings of the words we use and our ostensive expression of meaning. In lexical definitions, words are defined in terms of other words. For example, we can define punishment as the intentional inflicting of pain, by somebody in authority on somebody who has broken a rule. The ostensive expression of the meaning of punishment would include the embodied meanings experienced in the process. The introduction of Foucault's (1977a) Discipline and Punish contains such an expression of meaning in the experience of the punishment of a regicide.

The meanings of our embodied expressions of values are expressed in what we do and are clarified, in the course of their emergence in our practice. We explain below how digital visual data from practice can be useful in clarifying the meanings of embodied expressions of values.

We now turn to the importance of a curriculum for a Living Educational Theory approach to an educational inquiry before focusing on the nature of a living-educational-theory methodology.

2.2 A Curriculum for a Living Theory Approach to an Educational Inquiry

Accredited programmes of professional development usually involve a curriculum that is accredited by a University, or other accrediting body. The following outline of a curriculum is an example of the kind of pedagogical support we, as tutors, have given to practitioner-researchers in the development of their accredited programmes together with the criteria for assessment. The outline for tutors is designed to personally communicate with students. It is organized in terms of purpose; organization; content (i) what constitutes an educational inquiry (ii) formulating and carrying out a Living Educational Theory inquiry (iii) final draft of a living-educational-theory (iv) assessment.

2.2.1 Purpose

We see the purpose of our tutoring is to support explorations of the implications of asking, researching and answering an educational inquiry of the kind, 'How can I improve what I am doing?' in whatever context a student is seeking to improve. Our tutoring is focused on how to carry out an educational inquiry into improving practice, within the fundamental principles of Living Theory research which we explain below. We locate the significance of the approach in institutional, local, provincial and national governmental policies as well as the literature that is relevant to your inquiry. We use 'I' and 'you' below to communicate to students.

2.2.2 Organisation

We usually start our sessions by focusing on participant's understanding of what constitutes an educational inquiry. This includes a focus on the values you use to explain what you are doing and that you use to judge improvements. This leads into the design of short action inquiries into areas of the participant's choosing. We are thinking of inquiries which will use the group as a peer learning set in which issues and problems related to an individual's inquiry will be addressed and discussed in detail. A final draft of the action inquiry report will then form the basis for self and peer assessments.

We have organised the sessions to progress in three stages:

Stage 1. What Constitutes an Educational Inquiry?
Stage 1 focuses on the wide range of individual educational inquiries. It includes: the generation of your living-educational theory methodology; strengthening your data collection and analysis from Part One; including ideas from the literature in your living-educational-theory.

Stage 2. Formulating and Carrying Out a Living Educational Theory Research Inquiry

Stage 3. A Final Draft of Your Educational Inquiry Report.
Stage 3 focuses on strengthening validation, rigour and using the ideas of others in your final draft of your educational inquiry report before submission for accreditation.

2.3 Stage 1. What Constitutes an Educational Inquiry?

This section includes some details of the following inquiries:

- How can I enable the gifts and talents of my students to be in the driving seat of their own learning?
- How can I enhance the educational influence of my pupils in their own learning, that of other pupils, myself, and the school?
- How can I conduct a worthwhile inquiry into effective homework in my primary school?
- How can I improve my practice by communicating more effectively with others in my role as a professional educator?
- How can I change the culture of a school?
- A Living Educational Theory of Knowledge Translation: Improving Practice, Influencing Learners, and Contributing to the Professional Knowledge Base

It also includes:

- Your living-educational-theory methodology
- Strengthening your Data Collection and Analysis from Part One. This includes an introduction to the use of visual data as evidence in constructing an explanation of educational influences in learning.
- Including ideas from the literature in your living-educational-theory

In Stage 1, we usually extend understandings of the history of action research with the following information:

Stephen Corey (1953) produced the first text book on action research in education on 'Action Research to Improve School Practices'. On 7 January 2022, a search in Google on Action Research generated over 4,200,000,000 references. There are now many different schools of action research. Most include some forms of action-reflection cycles of planning, acting, evaluating and modifying. This method of inquiry, using an action planner, involves the action researcher studying their own practice in order to improve it.

An important text in the history of action research is Wilf Carr's and Stephen Kemmis' (1983), "Becoming Critical; Knowing Through Action Research", with many of these ideas included in their 1986 publication on Becoming Critical, Education, Knowledge and Action Research. Carr and Kemmis applied Habermas' critical theory to distinguish their critical approach to action research from other approaches. They retained the action-reflection cycles in their action planner while emphasizing the priority of sociopolitical, historical and cultural influences in the knowledge generated through action research.

In several other publications, Jean McNiff and Jack Whitehead (McNiff & Whitehead, 2009a, 2009b, 2011) stressed the importance of the knowledge created by action researchers as they researched the processes of improving their practice, without giving a priority to explanatory principles derived from social science theories and methods.

McNiff and Whitehead also stressed the importance of individuals generated their living-educational-theories in their action research in their 2006 publication Living Theory Action Research (Whitehead, & McNiff, 2006).

As Living Educational Theory researchers, we identify more closely with autoethnography than the other methodologies while continuing to draw insights from the other methodologies, such as narrative inquiry and self-study. We particularly like the following about autoethnographic texts:

> In these texts concrete action, dialogue, emotion, embodiment, spirituality, and self-consciousness are featured, appearing as relational and institutional stories affected by history, social structure, and culture, which themselves are dialectically revealed through action, feeling, thought, and language.
> (Miller, 2009, p. 739)

Our doctoral theses, (Delong, 2002; Whitehead, 1999) can be seen, in the above sense, as autoethnographic texts. They are also living-educational-theory autoethnographies in the sense that the relational and institutional stories are presented within our explanations of our educational influence in my own learning, in the learning of others and in the learning of the social formations that influence my practice and understandings. In relation to phenomenography, Tight (2016) states:

> All of the data collected is then treated collectively for the purposes of analysis, such that the focus is on the variations in understanding

across the whole sample, rather than on the characteristics of individuals' responses.

(p. 320)

As Living Educational Theory researchers, we might draw on such variations in understanding across a 'sample', in the generation of a living-educational-theory, but the individual's explanation of educational influence in learning cannot be subsumed within an analysis from a phenomenographic analysis of a 'sample'.

We explain that our meaning of 'what is educational?' goes beyond learning. While learning is necessary for something to be seen as educational, it is not sufficient. Not all learning is educational in the sense that the learning includes values of human flourishing. We are sure that you will recognize that some of your own learning has had to be unlearnt as you work out for yourselves what it means for you to live a good and productive life. We are also sure that you will recognize that history is full of examples of the learning in cultures and social formations that has negated these values. We were both born at the end of the Second World War where over 51 million lives were lost in fighting to impose or to resist the imposition of control by particular societies, on others. History has also many examples of individuals and groups learning to treat other individuals as less than human. The 2020 global phenomena of 'Black Lives Matter' is focused on ensuring that the values of equality and social justice are at the heart of educational learning within our cultural learning and influences.

It is important to note that we encourage the use of the Living Theory/Action-Reflection Planner described in Part One as a framework for your inquiry at the Master's level.

Here, we provide examples of educational inquiries drawn from professional practice. These examples are deeper and more extensive than the beginning inquiries in Part One and have been accredited on Masters' programmes. Access to many of these inquiries is provided at: https://www.actionresearch.net/writings/mastermod.shtml

The examples include:

How can I enable the gifts and talents of my students to be in the driving seat of their own learning? Sally Cartwright.

Into this narrative I wish to pull together strands that have been woven together, to form an exciting tapestry for both the student and teacher to develop their gifts and talents. For the student there is a new qualification from the English Examination Board AQA called the Extended Project Qualification, which appears to meet a need to develop the skills of independent and interdependent learning. For the teacher there is the opportunity afforded by the concept of an Educational Living Theory (Whitehead, 2008). (See https://www.actionresearch.net/writings/tuesdayma/scgandtnov08.pdf)

How can I enhance the educational influence of my pupils in their own learning, that of other pupils, myself and the school? Joy Mounter.

This assignment will build on my previous work (Mounter, 2008a), enabling the reader to share the journey we have undertaken and feel the change in language, beliefs and living values. Whitehead (2005) summarises this journey of exploration and development of one's own embodied ontological values which we hold ourselves accountable to. We move through our journey from teacher and pupil, filling the vessel with knowledge, through the self-awareness and awakening as a learner, understanding the roles and changeability of teacher/ learner/ coach/ mentor/ c-creator. Our journey is shared through not only the words of this assignment, but through the design of the flow and choice of vocabulary. My journeying involves doubt and uncertainty, the end is hidden until that point is reached, and I want you to share those qualities of my authentic journey through this account. The point and my writing will only become clear when you reach the end. The style and 'flow' are reflective of this, almost tangible but just the certainty out of grasp. Through this assignment you will share the journey, the drawing together of the threads at the end of the journey through reflective thought, mirrored in the conclusion of my writing. Our journey is challenging perceptions of researchers and pushing beyond current research. Bruce-Ferguson (March 2008) explores the courage and open-mindedness it takes to move away from traditional research processes and representation. (See https://www.actionresearch.net/writings/tuesdayma/joymounteree3.pdf)

How can I conduct a worthwhile inquiry into effective homework in my primary school? Tim Heath.

I indicate how I will apply the practitioner-action-research methodology to an inquiry into effective homework.

My account may be of interest to others undertaking school-based inquiries, particularly those for whom the action research approach is unfamiliar. It may also be of interest to established action researchers as a reminder of how very unfamiliar their methods can appear to prospective researchers.

To call the product of my inquiry 'worthwhile research' I was hopeful that I would do more than merely plan, implement and evaluate a school-based initiative. I hoped to learn and apply trusted inquiry techniques to create a lucid, novel account that would be:

- Empirical
- General
- Authoritative.

These are the marks of a broadly scientific, or positivistic, methodology. I was not naive enough to suppose this process would be straightforward. I certainly anticipated difficulties in satisfying these criteria within a small-scale inquiry and, more fundamentally, was suspicious of their application to the complex social setting of a school.

My training allows me to claim an understanding of the powerful and convincing methods employed by natural scientists. Fully aware that these methods could not be applied directly to children's learning, I was keen to discover how social scientists generate knowledge. I expected to tread what I fondly imagined would be a well-worn path from the natural sciences to the social sciences. Little did I realise how quickly that path becomes indistinct… (See https://www.actionresearch.net/writings/module/thhome.htm)

How can I improve my practice by communicating more effectively with others in my role as a professional educator? Mark Potts.

In this dissertation I seek to show my learning as an educator as I try to improve my practice and gain an understanding of how it is that I influence others. Using my own values as an educator and drawing on ideas such as presencing (Scharmer, 2000) and mindfulness (Claxton, 1997), I seek to understand better how I communicate with others and connect with them at a deeper level, influencing their actions. Words are not enough to express my meaning and therefore I have presented this dissertation with video clips to try to demonstrate my meaning more completely. It is written as a narrative with events recounted mostly chronologically. There is a limited amount of re-ordering. This is the narrative of my life as a teacher researcher with many different demands on my time. I have taken time, usually during school holidays, to reflect on the problem of how to be a more effective communicator allowing slow, unforced development extending over a year. This approach has allowed my deeper thoughts to surface and to guide my writing. I have so many interactions each day with my colleagues and my students that I seek here to understand how I can ensure good intuitive responses, making a lot out of a little. (See https://www.actionresearch.net/writings/monday/mpmadis.pdf)

How Can I Change the Culture of a School? Ruth Mills.
My living theory action research project sought to explore and answer the question, "How can I change the culture of a school?" When a principal begins at a new school, the first thing he or she discovers about that school is the culture. This project examined the data connected to brain-based research and the connection between environmental stress and learning. It also looked at what research says about the role of the principal in creating and sustaining a peaceful school culture. The research focused on the Roots of Empathy program and shows how this program impacted the culture of a particular school over time. (See https://s3-eu-west-1.amazonaws.com/s3.spanglefish.com/s/11596/documents/ruth%20mills/rmillsmed21aug09opt.pdf)

A Living Educational Theory of Knowledge Translation: Improving Practice, Influencing Learners, and Contributing to the Professional Knowledge Base. Jen Vickers-Manzin and Jan Johnston

Abstract

This paper captured our joint journey to create a living educational theory of knowledge translation (KT). The failure to translate research knowledge to practice is identified as a significant issue in the nursing profession. Our research story takes a critical view of KT related to the philosophical inconsistency between what is espoused in the knowledge related to the discipline of nursing and what is done in practice. Our inquiry revealed "us" as "living contradictions" as our practice was not aligned with our values. In this study, we specifically explored our unique personal KT process in order to understand the many challenges and barriers to KT we encountered in our professional practice as nurse educators. Our unique collaborative action research approach involved cycles of action, reflection, and revision which used our values as standards of judgement in an effort to practice authentically. Our data analysis revealed key elements of collaborative reflective dialogue that evoke multiple ways of knowing, inspire authenticity, and improve learning as the basis of improving practice related to KT. We validated our findings through personal and social validation procedures. Our contribution to a Culture of Inquiry allowed for co-construction of knowledge to reframe our understanding of KT as a holistic, active process which reflects the essence of who we are and what we do. (See documents/brock_vickers-manzin_jen_-and-_johnston_jan_2013.pdf) (Vickers-Manzin, 2013)

Before we turn to the importance of strengthening your data collection methods and the analysis of your educational influences in learning that you used in Part One, we shall consider the generation of your living-educational-theory methodology. This is followed by a deeper and more extensive understanding of validation, rigour and using the ideas of others in such explanations of educational influences in learning.

2.4 Your Living-Educational-Theory Methodology

A distinguishing feature of Living Educational Theory research is that the researcher creates and publicly shares an explanation of their educational influence in their own learning, in the learning of others and in the learning of the social formations that influence the practice and understandings in enquiries of the kind, 'How do I improve what I am doing?' As Living Educational Theory researchers, we recognize that there is no existing methodology that is appropriate for exploring the implications of asking, researching and answering the question, 'How do I improve what I am doing?' The reason that no existing methodology can answer the question is because of the dynamic nature of the question. 'What I am doing' is continuously changing with the evolution of both 'I' and the context. Hence the necessity for the Living Theory Researcher to recognize the need to create an appropriate living-educational-theory-methodology in the course of its emergence in researching and answering the question. In this process, a unique living-educational-theory methodology is generated. While having to create their own living-educational-theory methodology, Living Theory researchers are fortunate in having access to a wide range of insights from other methodological approaches.

We will distinguish the five methodological approaches that Creswell (2007) claims a researcher must choose between, from Living Educational Theory research. This is followed by descriptions of action research, autoethnography and phenomenography. You could draw on insights from these in creating your own living-educational-theory methodology as you generate your explanations of educational influences in learning in inquiries of the kind, 'How do I improve what I am doing?'

Dadds and Hart (2001) describe clearly the need for "methodological inventiveness". We repeat from Part One that this is the inventiveness that we believe is needed to go beyond other methodological approaches while drawing insights from these approaches, where appropriate, in generating your own living-educational-theory research methodology:

> The importance of methodological inventiveness
>
> Perhaps the most important new insight for both of us has been awareness that, for some practitioner researchers, creating their own unique way through their research may be as important as their self-chosen research focus. We had understood for many years that substantive choice was fundamental to the motivation

and effectiveness of practitioner research (Dadds, 1995); that what practitioners chose to research was important to their sense of engagement and purpose. But we had understood far less well that how practitioners chose to research, and their sense of control over this, could be equally important to their motivation, their sense of identity within the research and their research outcomes.
(Dadds & Hart, 2001, p. 166)

If our aim is to create conditions that facilitate methodological inventiveness, we need to ensure as far as possible that our pedagogical approaches match the message that we seek to communicate. More important than adhering to any specific methodological approach, be it that of traditional social science or traditional action research, may be the willingness and courage of practitioners – and those who support them – to create inquiry approaches that enable new, valid understandings to develop; understandings that empower practitioners to improve their work for the beneficiaries in their care. Practitioner research methodologies are with us to serve professional practices. So what genuinely matters are the purposes of practice which the research seeks to serve, and the integrity with which the practitioner researcher makes methodological choices about ways of achieving those purposes. No methodology is, or should, cast in stone, if we accept that professional intention should be informing research processes, not pre-set ideas about methods of techniques…
(Dadds & Hart, 2001, p. 169)

We are justifying the creation of a living-educational-theory methodology in the creation of a living-educational-theory in relation to our responses to Creswell's (2007) ideas on: narrative research, phenomenology, grounded theory, ethnography and case studies; Ellis' and Bochner's (2000) ideas on autoethnography; Whitehead and McNiff's (2006) ideas on action research and Living Theory research; Tight's ideas (2016) on phenomenography.

A living-educational-theory, as an explanation by an individual, of their educational influences in their own learning and in the learning of others, can be understood as a form of narrative research in that it begins with the experiences as lived and told by the researcher. Within the narrative what distinguishes the story, as a living-educational-theory, is that it is an explanation of the educational influences of the individual in their own learning and in the learning of others. Not all narratives are living theories, but all living theories are narratives.

Living-educational-theories are phenomenological in that they begin from the experience of the phenomenon the researcher is seeking to understand. The purpose of a living-educational-theory differs from the basic purpose of phenomenology in that the purpose of phenomenology is to produce a description of a universal essence while the purpose of a living theory is to produce a unique explanation of the individual's educational influences in learning.

A living-educational-theory is similar to a grounded theory in that the intent of a living-educational-theory is to move beyond description and to generate a valid explanation for an individual's educational influence in his or her own learning and in the learning of others. Living Educational Theory research differs from Grounded Theory in that the theory is not an abstract analytic scheme of a process. A living-educational-theory is an explanation for an individual's educational influence in learning where the explanatory principles are not abstract generalizations. The explanatory principles are the energy-flowing values and understandings the individual uses to give meaning and purpose to their life and to explain their educational influences in learning.

A living-educational-theory is similar to ethnographic research in paying attention to the educational influences of the cultural norms within which the researcher is acting and researching. It differs from ethnographic research in that it does not focus on an entire culture group. A living-educational-theory is an explanation of an individual's educational influence in their own learning, in the learning of others and in the social formations in which the researcher is living and working. In engaging with the cultural influences in the individual's learning, especially in the learning of social formations, living theorists include an understanding of cultural influences in the explanations of their educational influences in learning. These influences can be emphasized in the application of Habermas' (1976) four criteria of social validity to strengthening the validity of explanations of educational influences in learning, especially with the criterion of demonstrating an awareness of the normative background from within which the researcher is speaking and writing.

A living-educational-theory may sometimes be mistaken as a case study. Stake (2005) refers to case study as a choice of what is to be studied within a bounded system. Living-educational-theories, generated from a perspective of inclusionality, as a relationally dynamic awareness of space and boundaries, are aware of the experience and expression of a life-affirming and unbounded energy flowing through the cosmos. The main difference between a case study and a living-educational-theory is that a case study is a study of a bounded system while the explanatory principles of living-educational-theories are not constrained by a bounded system. Living-educational-theories articulate explanatory principles in terms of flows of life-affirming energy, values and understandings that are transformatory and not contained within a bounded system, they contribute to the creation of their own boundaries.

If you are conducting an inquiry of the kind 'How do I improve what I am doing?', with the intention of improving your practice and generating knowledge in your living educational theory, we think that you will need to embrace Dadds' and Hart's (2001) idea of methodological inventiveness, in the creation of both your living-educational-theory and your living-theory-methodology (Whitehead, 2009).

2.5 Strengthening Data Collection and Analysis from Part One

We emphasise the importance of visual data in clarifying and communicating the meanings of the values we express in educational practices and that we use to give meaning and purpose to our lives in education.

2.5.1 Visual Data

The main difference between data collection and analysis from Part One is that we now focus on clarifying the meanings of your values as these emerge in your practice. These values are used as explanatory principles in your explanations of your educational influences in your own learning, in the learning of others and in the learning of the social formations, that influence your practice and understanding.

The reason that we stress below the importance of digital visual data is that they focus on showing what you are doing as you inquire into your contribution to your educational influences in the learning of others. The digital visual data allows you to move the cursor backwards and forwards along a video clip so that you can point to the places of greatest resonance as you experience and see yourself expressing your values in your practice. Here is an illustration of what we are meaning from the data collection and analysis of Cathy Griffin.

As a classroom teacher, Cathy Griffin (2011) wrote about her processes of data gathering and analysis in her presentation at the 2015 conference of the Action Research Network of the Americas, where she received the award of Young Researcher of the Year. Cathy used video with her students in order to record their action research questions and to get feedback about her teaching. She wrote that four of her students read their personal research questions. After creating their questions, she sorted students into research groups based on the themes of their inquiries. The themes included focus, group work, independence in learning, interacting with others and conflict management and fear of talking in front of the class. Rather than getting ideas from books, the students worked individually and in groups to develop action plans based on what they already knew and what they wanted to improve.

In her role as principal of an elementary school, Cathy worked with a struggling teacher who had not been doing well on her appraisal. Cathy gave her a camera to tape her instruction with prompts of what to look for, i.e. body language. This helped a lot: the teacher came back to say that she had started practising the lessons with her husband who doesn't know the math program. She says that she can focus on the kids now that she knows the material which resolved the earlier problem of focusing on the material and not the students. While this was Cathy's first foray into video use for teacher performance, she is a veteran at using video data as evidence to support claims to know:

> Cathy Griffin's expertise in creating short video clips from long tapings to demonstrate evidence of life-affirming energy and empathetic resonance is described in the following excerpt from our AERA 2013 paper.
> (Campbell, Delong, Whitehead & Griffin, 2013)

To analyse video, Cathy scanned the video at high speed for:

a. Life Affirming Energy (Whitehead, 2002): increased movement, gestures or dialogue that indicate passion and values. Changes in body language or dynamics between group members: tension, conflict, support, celebration, etc.
b. Empathetic Resonance: "moments when we recognise the energy flowing values of the other, the activity of the participants is increased, or there is evidence of tension."

(p. 8)

Identified sections of video were transcribed, watched and analyzed by the group to determine what was important during the process and as evidence of our deepening culture-of-inquiry.

From CathyeditARNAjdd250415docx p. 30 http://www.actionresearch.net/writings/arna/ARNAjdd260415.pdf

In this paper, are several examples of the positive effect on practitioners researching their practice as a form of professional development:

Video 2.1. https://www.youtube.com/watch?v=A6mw9gbSwO0

Jackie uses a visual display to avoid data overload

One of the issues in data collections and analysis is organization and learning style. For some practitioner-researchers, data in files and boxes work fine. For other, more holistic thinkers, having the data spread out and visual is essential. Jackie found that she needed to see the data holistically:

> How can I transform the story of my learning through five years studying my practice that is visually and physically spread out in my recreation room on a huge table? What would it look like to show the meaning of the values I hold and transfer the documentation on the table to reveal my learning? How can I describe and explain my learning within my internal capacity and energy to sustain my own learning and to engage and support the learning of teachers and administrators for the purpose of enhancing student learning? Looking at the photos puts me in touch with my values: I
>
> I am different people in different contexts with the values I hold as the unifying force. The story appears like rivulets running across the plain to converge into a river of knowing and theorizing about my life as a superintendent.
>
> In terms of my own learning the spider plant metaphor that Gareth Morgan (1988) uses may help to explain how I learn a skill or aspect of knowledge and teach others what I have learned. Once the other person has learned the skill, he/she becomes independent of the direct support as an autonomous individual. The list of my learning and teaching is long: the action research process, the use of digital still and video cameras, staff development and leadership, curriculum, assessment, and special education and so on.
>
> Much of my data collection, analysis, synthesis, and writing concerns the role of the professional educator, my role as teacher and as learner. I am creating myself in a process of *improvisatory self-realization* (Winter, 1989) using the art of the dialectician, in which I hold together in a process of question and answer, [my] capacities for analysis with [my] capacities for synthesis:

What I think distinguishes my work as a professional educator from other professionals such as architects, lawyers or doctors is that I work with the intention of helping learners to create themselves in a process of improvisatory self-realisation (Winter, 1998). Stressing the improvisatory nature of education draws attention to the impossibility of pre-specifying all the rules which give an individual's life in education its unique form. As individuals give a form to their lives there is an art in synthesizing their unique constellations of values, skills and understandings into an explanation for their own learning. I am thinking of the art of the dialectician described by Socrates in which individuals hold together, in a process of question and answer, their capacities for analysis with their capacities for synthesis (Whitehead, 1999).

(Delong, 2002, p. 279)

Jack's use of visual data in communicating flows of life-affirming energy with values of human flourishing in a TEDx talk.

In an EJOLTS article Jack wrote:

Because of the importance of digital visual data in my research, for the communication of meanings of embodied expressions of life-affirming energy with values of human flourishing, I include here the recording of my 18-minute TEDx talk at the University of Bolton on the 24 October 2019 on Living Educational Theory research. I include this video as I have been told that it is a very clear expression of my meaning of Living Theory research. Educational Journal of Living Theories 12(2): 1–19, http://ejolts.net/files/346.pdf

Video 2.2. TEDx talk https://www.youtube.com/watch?v=Jf1kFHLdiPY

I chose the image above because, as I move the cursor along the clip, I see myself expressing and communicating a flow of life-affirming energy with values of human flourishing. I am also encouraging the participants to generate and share their own living-educational-theories as contributions to enhancing the educational influence of Living Theory research as a global social movement.

(Whitehead, 2019, pp. 2–3)

Here is a visual example of this process using the 3:10 minute video below of Jacqueline Delong at the International Conference of Teacher Research in 2007. Jackie is responding to a question about support for teacher researcher by describing the 'Grand Erie SWAT team' that responded to a teacher's request for help. As we move the cursor backwards and forwards around 2:49, we share an expression of the life-affirming energy that Jackie expresses in her educational relationship and that is included in the explanatory principles that explain Jackie's educational influences in her own learning, in the learning of others and in the learning of the social formations that influence practice and understanding.

Video 2.3. https://www.youtube.com/watch?v=qsECy86hzxA

Another way of organizing data visually can be seen in Liz Campbell's wall map

In the following excerpt from our EJOLTs article (Campbell et al., 2013), we share the use of video recordings as data, a visual way of storing and analyzing data and the concept of "Being Loved Into Learning".

To frame our research process for the reader, Liz videotaped the evolution of our understanding of the Living Theory Action Research Process. Liz Campbell can be seen to be engaging in the action research process, as we understand it from Whitehead and McNiff (2006), in the following clip and her explanation of methodology emerging from expressing her energy-flowing values such as "Being Loved into Learning:

See 54 seconds into the 18:44 minute video of Liz Campbell for an expression of being loved into learning (Video 2.4. http://youtu.be/zmBcrUsDG8s)"

In 2018, Liz was awarded her doctorate by Nipissing University in Canada, for her thesis:

Loved Into Learning: A Narrative Inquiry Exploring How Love Has Influenced Me As A Teacher. Retrieved 14 June 2020 from https://www.actionresearch.net/living/campbellphd/campbell-phd2018.pdf

2.5.2 Strengthening Your Alternative Forms of Data Representation

As well as emphasising the importance of visual data from your educational practice for clarifying and communicating the meanings of your expressions of your values that you use as explanatory principles in your explanations of educational influences in learning, we also highlight the importance of alternative forms of data representations (Campbell et al., 2019)

In her Abstract Liz writes:

My interpretive qualitative study explores the generation of my living educational theory as I introduce love into my practice and discover the obstacles and challenges to living more fully according to my values of love, hope, and joy. Using a narrative inquiry methodology and methodological inventiveness, I draw on 6 years of data collection from my personal journals and lived experiences to make the process of living narratively explicit.

We do urge you to read Chapters 5–7 to see how Liz has used different forms of representation in her explanations of educational influences in learning in the generation of her living-educational-theory.

Chapter 5:

- How Has Love Influenced Me as a Teacher? .63
- How Did I Get Here? 63
- Why Did I Stay? 67
- Where Did I Experience Unconditional Love? 69
- What Is My Inner Voice Telling Me? 71
- What Did I Do That Was Different? 73
- How Did I Begin? 73
- How Did I Tell My Students I Loved Them? .75
- What Did I Share? 76
- How Did I "Manage" the Classroom? 76
- What Resources Were Available? 77
- How Did I Set the Tone? 79
- How Did We Embrace Self-Directed Learning? 81
- How Did We Embrace Democracy? 83
- The Four Questions. 83
- On Being Present 84
- A Different Perspective 86
- Or So It Seemed: Interlude Two 88
- What is my truth? 92
- Truth: Accountability interferes with authenticity 93
- Truth: Choice is an illusion within public schools 95

Chapter 6:

- How Did Love Influence Me as a Researcher? 97
- Researching With My Values 98
- BARN Is Born 99
- Creating a Collaborative Community—BARN 100
- Sustainability of BARN 103
- Publicly Sharing Our Work 103
- Meaningful Research 103
- How BARN Gave Me Hope 108
- BARN Summary 110
- Or So It Seemed: Interlude Three 112
- Passing the Torch 113

Chapter 7:

- How Did Love Influence Me as a Learner? .117
- Background 117
- Or So It Seemed: Interlude Four 118
- To the brook and back 118
- My Spiritual Death 119
- Awakening Hope 122
- Learning to Love the Questions 124
- Being Love as I Retire 125
- Call of the Sea 127
- The Blessing 129
- What Is My New Path? 131
- Or So It Seemed: Interlude Five 132
- How Did I Reconnect With Nature? 134
- Where Do I Go From Here? 138
- Or So It Seemed: Interlude Six 139
- Is it time to rip the bandage off? 139
- How was I wounded and how did I wound others? 139
- Why did I allow wounding of self and others? 142
- How can I heal? 145

While Liz focused on a form of narrative for presenting her doctoral thesis, many Living Educational Theory researchers use action-reflections cycles to give a systematic and rigorous form to present their explanations of educational influences learning. For example, Máirín Glenn (2006), in her living-educational-theory thesis on, *Working with collaborative projects: my living theory of a holistic educational practice*, exemplifies how Living Educational Theory research can draw insights from Action Research in her use of a form of an action-reflection cycle to provide a disciplined form for her thesis. This use of action-reflection cycles can be clearly seen in the titles of Chapters 6–7.

Chapter One: What were my concerns? Examining the background and contexts of the research. (pp. 33–60)

Chapter Two: Why was I concerned? Examining my understanding of my practice as I clarified my ontological values. (pp. 61–94)

Chapter Three: What could I do about my concerns? Examining issues around methodology. (pp. 95–132)

Chapter Four: What did I do about my concerns? Developing key insights around my research in terms of an emergent understanding of my practice. (pp. 134–170)

Chapter Five: How do I use technology to enhance a dialogical and inclusional epistemology? Examining how technology and holistic approaches to education can merge. (pp. 171–207)

Chapter Six: How do I evaluate my work? Developing epistemological justification – demonstrating validity. (pp. 208–252)

Chapter Seven: How do I contribute to new practices and theory and to the education of social formations? Examining how I show the significance and potentials of my work. (pp. 253–285)

(7.1) Section 1: The significance of my research in relation to my own learning. (pp. 254–262)

(7.2) Section 2: The potential significance of my research in relation to the learning of others. (pp. 264–274)

(7.3) Section 3: My educational influence in the education of social formations. (pp. 274–283)

In Chapters 7.1–7.3, Máirín goes further than the use of an action-reflection cycle in generating her living-educational-theory. Máirín offers her living-educational-theory as an explanation of her educational influence in her own learning, in the learning of others and in the learning of the social formations that influence her practice and understandings. You can see how Máirín focuses on these explanations of educational influence in Sections 7.1–7.3 above. This explanation moves Máirín's research from an Action Research approach into Living Educational Theory research.

Máirín also shares her insights of seeing the interconnectedness of people and their environments as a locus of learning which may be embraced through technology. This insight is particularly relevant to today as Living Educational Theory researchers are exploring their formation of a global social movement to spread the influence of Living Educational Theory Research with values of human flourishing.

While the examples from Liz Campbell and Máirín Glenn are drawn from their doctoral inquiries, we do encourage Master's researchers to engage with this work as they can contain helpful ideas and sources of inspiration.

Glenn, M. (2006). *Working with Collaborative Projects: My Living Theory of a Holistic Educational Practice.* PhD Limerick University. Available from: https://www.jeanmcniff.com/glennabstract.html (Accessed 23 June 2020)

As we focus on the creation of your valid, evidence-based explanations of educational influences in learning, we want to emphasise the importance of integrating insights into your explanations from the ideas of others.

2.7 Including Ideas from the Literature in Your Living-Educational-Theory

Because of the importance of a research methodology in clarifying the principles used in explaining how the inquiry takes place, we have clearly distinguished (above) the methodologies of narrative inquiry, case study, phenomenology ethnography, autoethnography, grounded theory, action research and Living Educational Theory research. With our students, we share the following paper from Jack on 'Justifying your creation of a living theory methodology in the creation of your living educational theory' from https://www.actionresearch.net/writings/arsup/livingtheorymethodologies.pdf.

I have found Creswell's (2007, pp. 53–58) descriptions of five qualitative research approaches to narrative research, phenomenology, grounded theory, ethnography and case studies to be one of the best introductory texts on these methodologies. For each of the five approaches Creswell poses a definition, briefly traces the history of each approach, explores types of studies, introduces procedures involved in conducting a study and indicates potential challenges in using each approach. He also reviews some of the similarities and differences among the five approaches 'so that qualitative researchers can decide which approach is best to use for their particular study'. I shall emphasise the point below that a researcher need not choose one of these methodologies. As a researcher you can draw insights from any of these approaches together with insights action research and autoethnography without choosing between them in the development of their own living theory methodology as you create your living-educational-theory. You can access a 2008 paper of mine on Using a living theory methodology in improving practice and generating educational knowledge in living theories in the Educational Journal of Living Theories (EJOLTS) at http://ejolts.net/node/80.

As you formulate and carry out your living-educational-theory research inquiry, we stress the importance of sharing your draft explanations with a Validation Group and of strengthening your engagement with ideas of others in the literature we reference below in Stage 2.

2.8 Stage 2. Formulating and Carrying Out a Living Educational Theory Research Inquiry

A draft of your inquiry 'design' will be a focus for group discussion such as that described below as Martin Forrest subjected his draft explanation of educational influence to the critical discussion of a Validation Group. Questions can be raised about the feasibility of the inquiry. Is it doable? Do I have the resources to do it? What kinds of data will I need to enable me to make judgements on the quality and effectiveness of my inquiry as I create an explanation of my educational influences in learning? As you carry out your inquiry there will be opportunities for reporting back to the group on issues and problems arising. During this time, it is envisaged that you will consider the integration of the methods and conceptual frameworks from the disciplines of education into an educational inquiry e.g. conceptual analysis, theories of learning, the use of autobiography, autoethnography, action research and narrative in the presentation of qualitative research.

Texts that we recommend are intended to support your engagement with ideas that you can use to extend and deepen your cognitive range and concern as you recognise the potential colonisation of Western views of knowledge (Smith, 2012), in representing and communicating the meanings we are expressing in our educational practices. The texts are intended to strengthen the scholarship and rigour of your research. Here are some of the ideas that we have found helpful in deepening and extending the scholarly and rigour in the creation of our own living-educational-theories.

We accept Foucault's (1977b) distinction between the 'specific intellectual' as opposed to the 'universal intellectual'. Foucault says, that for a long period the 'left' intellectual was acknowledged as a champion of truth and justice. The intellectual was a spokesperson of the universal in the sense of moral, theoretical and political choices. In opposition to the universal intellectual, he describes the specific intellectual in terms of an engagement in a struggle at the precise points where their own conditions of life or work situate them. Foucault takes care to emphasise that by 'truth' he does not mean 'the ensemble of truths which are to be discovered and accepted'. By 'truth', he means the ensemble of rules according to which the true and the false are separated and specific effects of power attached to the true. The struggles 'around truth' are not 'on behalf' of the truth, but about the status of truth and the economic and political role it plays. While we identify with Foucault's idea of the 'specific intellectual' and understand his point about the status of truth, our own research is focused 'on behalf' of truth in seeking to spread the educational influences of living-educational-theories with values of human flourishing.

Foucault, M. (1977b) Intellectuals and power – A conversation between Michel Foucault and Giles Deleuze, in Bouchard, D. F. (Ed.) *Michel Foucault, Language, Counter-Memory, Practice*. Oxford: Basil Blackwell.

We also accept Lyotard's (1986) point about formulating rules for ourselves in generating the explanatory principles that we use in our explanations of educational influences in learning:

> A postmodern artist or writer is in the position of a philosopher: the text he writes, the work he produces are not in principle governed by pre-established rules, and they cannot be judged according to a determining judgement, by applying familiar categories to the text or to the work. Those rules and categories are what the work of art itself is looking for. The artist and the writer, then, are working without rules in order to formulate the rules of what will have been done.
> (Lyotard, 1986, p. 81)

Lyotard, F. (1986) *The Postmodern Condition: A Report on Knowledge*. Manchester: Manchester University Press.

All living-educational-theories are stories or narratives that communicate a valid, evidence-based explanation of educational influences in learning. We found Kathy Carter's (1993) paper on stories very helpful in reinforcing our use of narrative as a research method:

> ...Attraction to stories has evolved into an explicit attempt to use the literatures on 'story' or 'narrative' to define both the method and the object of inquiry in teaching and teacher education. Story has become, in other words, more than simply a rhetorical device for expressing sentiments about teachers or candidates for the teaching profession. It is now, rather a central focus for conducting research in the field.
>
> (Carter, 1993, p. 5)

Carter, K. (1993). The place of story in the study of teaching and teacher education. *Educational Researcher*, 22(1), 5–12, 18.

The texts also serve to highlight the importance of intercultural translation as our Living Educational Theory research communities include participants from different cultures. For example, when Moira Laidlaw started her six years of Voluntary Service Overseas in China, Moira already had a PhD in a Living Theory approach to educational inquiry where asking questions is of fundamental importance. Teaching in China helped her to understand that some cultures do not support such questionings, especially of authorities. This recognition helped Moira to develop her pedagogy in a way that acknowledged the difficulties of encouraging such questions while retaining her belief in the value of educational inquiry.

Whitehead, J. (2016). Review of de Sousa Santos, B. (2014). *Epistemologies of the South: Justice against Epistemicide*. London: Paradigm Publishers. Available from: https://ejolts.net/node/288 (Accessed 8 June 2020).

We recommend your engagement with the following texts, if you want to deepen your understanding of some of the issues of representation and politics surrounding the academic legitimisation of your living-educational-theory.

We found the writings of Elliot Eisner (1988, 1993, 1997) very helpful as we encountered scepticism in the Academy over our submission of our living-educational-theories for academic legitimation and his emphasis on alternative ways of representing data.

Eisner, E. (1988). The primacy of experience and the politics of method. *Educational Researcher*, 17(5), 15–20.

> Knowledge is rooted in experience and requires a form for its representation. Since all forms of representation constrain what can be represented, they can only partially represent what we know. Forms of representation not only constrain representation, they limit what we seek.

Eisner, E. (1993). Forms of understanding and the future of educational research. *Educational Researcher*, 22(7), 5–11.

> My address this afternoon is partly the story of a personal odyssey and partly a confessional…My hope is that at least some of what puzzles me will intrigue you. Indeed, I hope it intrigues you enough to want to join me.

Eisner, E. (1997). The promise and perils of alternative forms of data representation. *Educational Researcher*, 26(6), 4–10.

> This article addresses the potential strengths and weaknesses of alternative forms of data representation. As educational researchers become increasingly interested in the relationship between form of representation and form of understanding, new representational forms are being used to convey to "readers" what has been learned.

In this stage of the inquiry there will also be an emphasis on engaging with ideas that are at the forefront of the educational inquiries published in Journals such as the Educational Journal of Living Theories (EJOLTS), Educational Action Research (EAR), the Action Learning Action Research Journal (ALARj) and the Canadian Journal of Action Research (CJAR). To show that we are practicing what we are advocating, here are some of our recent publications in these Journals that we believe you will find useful in strengthening the scholarship and rigour in your living-educational-theory.

Delong, J., Whitehead, J. & Huxtable, M. (2019) Where do we go from here in contributing to 'The Action Learning and Action Research Legacy for Transforming Social Change?'. *Action Learning Action Research Journal*, 25(1), 65–73. Workshop presentation at the 2019 ALARA Conference in Norwich University, Vermont, USA. Retrieved 8 June 2020 from https://www.actionresearch.net/writings/jack/jddjwmhalarj19.pdf.

> The workshop brought together researchers who are engaged in action learning/action research inquiries of the kind, 'How do I improve what I am doing and live, as fully as possible, my values that carry hope for the flourishing of humanity?' Participants comprised researchers physically present in the room, those present through SKYPE and those who have a virtual presence in the form of their living-posters at http://www.actionresearch.net/writings/posters/homepage020617.pdf.
>
> This workshop focused on living-theory accounts created by educational practitioner researchers, including those engaging as AL/AR practitioners, which are contributing to a legacy for transforming social change. The living-theories used in the workshop included those accredited for doctoral degrees in different universities around the world. The workshop demonstrated the communicative power of multi-media narratives with digital visual data to clarify and communicate the meanings of embodied expressions of values that carry hope for the flourishing of humanity. Ideas, critically and creatively engaged with included current social theories such as de Sousa Santos' (2014) ideas on 'epistemicide'. These ideas were used to show how Western academic reasoning and epistemology can be understood and transcended in the generation of the living-educational-theories of individuals, grounded in their experiences and contexts.

Vaughan, M. & Delong, J. (2019) Cultures of inquiry: A transformative method of creating living-theories. *Educational Journal of Living Theories,* 12(2), 65–88.

> As we approach the question, "How do I improve my practice?" we are simultaneously working towards, "How do I make the world a better place and invite others to do the same?" This article documents the nature of our influence on ourselves, and those around us, using the methodology of Living Theory research and creating Cultures of Inquiry in a myriad of contexts that can serve as intentional spaces for personal exploration of values as living standards of judgment and explanatory principles. A culture of inquiry is a safe, supportive space wherein practitioner-researchers are enabled to share their vulnerabilities, to make explicit their values, and to hold themselves accountable for living according to those values. We argue that creating Cultures of Inquiry through our personal and professional interactions, and embodying key values that

are embedded within them, can contribute meaningfully to the growth of the field of Living Theory research. By inviting others into the world of Living Theory research, we are actively working towards creating and sustaining Living Theory research as a social movement with our current community and intentionally inviting others to join.

Whitehead, J., Delong, J., Huxtable, M., Campbell, L., Griffin, C. & Mounter, J. (2019) Self-Study in elementary and secondary teaching: A living theory approach. Second edition of the *International Handbook of Self-Study of Teaching and Teacher Education*. Dordrecht: Springer. Retrieved 8 June 2020 from https://www.actionresearch.net/writings/jack/jwjdmhlcccjmSSTEP2019.pdf.

In this chapter we present examples of Living Theory research, a form of Self-Study, which shows teachers, teacher educators and administrators researching to improve their teaching and the educational experience of students and contributing the knowledge they create in the process to a professional educational knowledge base. We clarify the relationship between education and educational research and show how Living Theory is distinguished within other forms of Self-Study research. Consideration is given to the opportunities and challenges of promoting this approach, and other forms of Self-Study research, as ways to improve practice in schools. We show the development of ideas since Whitehead's contribution 14 years ago, in 2004, to the first International Handbook of Self Study on, 'What counts as evidence in self-studies of teacher education practices?'. Our emphasis in this chapter is on practising educators, their professional development and gaining academic recognition for the embodied knowledges of master and doctor educators.

Whitehead, J. (2020) Moving from action research to activism with living theory research. *Canadian Journal of Action Research*, 20(3), 55–73. https://journals.nipissingu.ca/index.php/cjar/article/view/467).

This paper follows the organisation of the successful proposal: (1) The research and action aims: (2) methodology, theoretical tools and methods; (3) results, outputs, program changes and events... The results, outputs, program changes and events demonstrate the spreading global educational influences of Living Theory research.

Huxtable, M. & Whitehead, J. (2020) Enhancing educational influences in learning with a living theory approach to pedagogical action research in higher education. *Educational Action Research*, 29(2), 310–327. Final draft before publication https://www.actionresearch.net/writings/jack/mhjwEAR0620.pdf.

> The last 20 years have seen a growing interest in researching pedagogy in Higher Education with action researchers playing a part in this growth. However, there are few studies that analyse the educational influences in learning of the action researcher in their own pedagogy in Higher Education. Hence the focus of this paper on enhancing educational influences in learning with a Living Theory approach to pedagogical Action Research in Higher Education. This paper presents an analysis of such educational influences. The analysis explains our educational influences in the learning of students who have progressed from the springboard provided by Action Research to recognising and valuing themselves as knowledge creating researchers who are contributing to a global knowledgebase. The analysis draws on data from supervising and tutoring successfully completed masters and doctoral programmes of professional development with teachers and other professional educational-practitioners.
>
> The meanings of educational practice, educational influences in learning, educational pedagogy and educational research are clarified. In the discussion we show how a Living Theory approach to pedagogical Action Research in Higher Education enables students to engage in the highest levels of learning, creating and contributing knowledge with values that carry hope for human flourishing.

Now that you have completed the second stage focusing on formulating and carrying out a Living Educational Theory Research inquiry, we share some ways in which you can strengthen the validity and rigour of your explanation. We also emphasize the importance of extending and deepening your cognitive range and concern through your critical and creative engagements with the ideas of others.

2.9 Stage 3. A Final Draft of Your Action Inquiry Report

You will need to present a final draft of your inquiry report to your Validation Group to make it as strong as possible before submitting it for accreditation, if you want your work to be recognized for accreditation.

We suggest that you produce a 4–6,000 word on your professional inquiry that includes an evidence-based explanation of your educational influences in your own learning, in the learning of others and in the learning of the social formations that influence your practice and understandings. Before submitting it to your Validation Group you should check to see that you have:

i. Researched a good quality educational question related to your own professional practice in a way which has enhanced your educational knowledge?

ii. Explained your professional learning in a way which has appropriately integrated knowledge from other sources?

iii. Demonstrated your ability to identify your concerns, action plan, act and gather data to enable you to judge the extent to which you are living your educational values through your practice?

iv. Considered how your inquiry might help to improve your educational practices and/or those of others.

In presenting your account to your Validation Group and for accreditation you should bear in mind, Connelly's and Clandinin's (1990) point about validity criteria for narrative inquiry. This is still relevant today in 2022:

> We think a variety of criteria, some appropriate to some circumstances and some to others, will eventually be the agreed-upon norm. It is currently the case that each inquirer must search for, and defend, the criteria that best apply to his or her work.

Connelly, F. M. & Clandinin, J. (1990) Stories of experience and narrative inquiry. *Educational Researcher*, 5, 2–14.

In terms of evidence-based explanations, you can access a large number of these explanations in the webpage on Making Public The Embodied Knowledge of Master Educators at https://www.actionresearch.net/writings/mastermod.shtml. As you browse down the titles, we think that you will see something of interest to you and that this might be useful to you in generating your own living-educational-theory.

If you wish to develop your inquiries into a Master's degree you might find the following ideas on validation, rigour and using the ideas of others helpful in enhancing the scholarship and rigour of your contributions to educational knowledge. We also draw attention to the importance of creating a Culture of Inquiry and of educational conversations which express the mutual rational controls of critical discussion within a research community, as a research method in inquiries of the kind 'How do I improve what I am doing?'

2.10 Validation, Rigour and Using the Ideas of Others

While the number of people in the group is not an absolute, between three to eight peers usually form a Validation Group. It is a number that has pragmatically worked for developing in-depth conversations that focus on strengthening the validity of an explanation. The key idea is that individuals can help each other to strengthen the validity of an explanation by offering ways of strengthening the explanation. This is what Popper (1975, p. 44) is meaning by the exercise of the mutual rational control of critical discussion in strengthening the objectivity of an explanation through intersubjective testing. We can do this together by engaging in educational conversations.

For example, Jackie's Validation Group for her doctoral inquiry was constituted by Jean McNiff, (Internationally published author on Action Research) Tom Russell (Professor from Queens University, Kingston, Ontario), Linda Grant (from the Ontario College of Teachers), Professor Andre Dolbec, Peter Moffatt (Director of Education of the Grand Erie District School Board) and Jack Whitehead (Jackie's PhD supervisor at the University of Bath. (Delong, 2002, p. 173, transcript and video 23/02/97). In selecting your Validation Group of between four and eight peers it is wise to select people who understand the importance of offering (critical) responses that will help you to improve the quality of your explanation in terms of its comprehensibility, evidence, analysis and clarity of the meanings of values (see below). In a Master's programme, it is not wise to go longer than six weeks before submitting some draft writings on your inquiry to your Validation Group. This prevents you from just gathering data, without analysis, and suffering from data overload when you come to analyse your data.

In terms of validation, we like Martin Forrest's writings on 'The validation group as a conversational research community', from his MEd Dissertation (see pages 83–86 of

http://www.actionresearch.net/writings/jack/cycle3.pdf).

Martin explicitly draws on action reflection cycles in generating his living-educational-theory as an explanation of his educational influences (Appendix One).

A Validation Group can contribute to enhancing the rigour and validity of an explanation of educational influence, by focusing on responding to a practitioner-researcher's explanation of educational influence, in relation to four questions from the researcher:

i. How can I enhance the comprehensibility of my explanations?
ii. How can I strengthen the evidence I use to justify my explanation?
iii. How can I deepen and extend my understanding of the socio-historical and sociocultural influences in my practice and understandings?
iv. How can I enhance the authenticity of my explanation in the sense of showing that I am living my values as fully as I can as explanatory principles in my explanation of educational influence in learning?

There are two ideas that guide the workings of such a Validation Group. The first idea is from Karl Popper who emphasises that the objectivity of statements lies in the fact that they can be inter-subjectively tested through the mutual rational controls of critical discussion. The idea of inter-subjective testing is focused on our subjectivities as we respond to each other's ideas usually in conversation. Popper's ideas allow us to understand a necessary relationship between objectivity and subjectivity, rather than see them in opposition or as mutually exclusive:

> Now I hold that scientific theories are never fully justifiable or verifiable, but that they are nevertheless testable. I shall therefore say that objectivity of scientific statements lies in the fact that they can be inter-subjectively tested... I have since generalized this formulation; for inter-subjective *testing* is merely a very important aspect of the more general idea of inter-subjective *criticism*, or in other words, of the idea of mutual rational control by critical discussion.
>
> (Popper, 1975, p. 44)

The second idea is from Jurgen Habermas who claims that anyone acting communicatively is raising four validity claims. We have drawn on Habermas' ideas in the questions above while acknowledging the complexity of his language below:

> I shall develop the thesis that anyone acting communicatively must, in performing any speech action, raise universal validity claims and suppose that they can be vindicated. Insofar as he wants to participate in a process of reaching understanding, he cannot avoid raising the following – and indeed precisely the following – validity claims. He claims to be:
>
> a. *Uttering* something understandably;
> b. Giving (the hearer) *something* to understand;
> c. Making *himself* thereby understandable; and
> d. Coming to an understanding *with another person*.
>
> The speaker must choose a comprehensible expression so that speaker and hearer can understand one another. The speaker must have the intention of communicating a true proposition (or a propositional content, the existential presuppositions of which are satisfied) so that the hearer can share the knowledge of the speaker. The speaker must want to express his intentions truthfully so that the hearer can believe the utterance of the speaker (can trust him). Finally, the speaker must choose an utterance that is right so that the hearer can accept the utterance and speaker and hearer can agree with one another in the utterance with respect to a recognized normative background. Moreover, communicative action can continue undisturbed only as long as participants suppose that the validity claims they reciprocally raise are justified.
>
> (Habermas, 1976, pp. 2–3)

One of the early criticisms of a research question that included 'I', such as 'How do I improve what I am doing?' was that an explanation, of educational influence in learning that emerged, would be 'merely subjective' or 'anecdotal' with no scholarly or rigorous qualities or capacity for any form of generalisability. To meet these criticisms, we advocate the following processes of validation and methods of enhancing the rigour of the Living Educational Theory research.

2.11 The Validation Group as a Conversational Research Community

In this section, we share two examples of the validation process, one from Martin Forrest and the second from Peggy Kok. Full details of these examples can be seen in Appendix One and Appendix Two.

In his M.Ed. dissertation, 'The Teacher as Researcher', Martin Forrest (1983) describes how he used a Validation Group to test the validity of his account of the effectiveness of his in-service support with two primary school teachers. This support focused on two teachers, Carol and Sue, who were working in different schools. Carol taught five and six year olds and Sue taught eight and nine year olds. Martin saw that Carol's five and six year old pupils were developing historical understandings that Sue believed were beyond the comprehension of her eight and nine year old pupils. Martin believed that he could influence Sue's learning in a way that benefitted her pupils by convincing Sue that her pupils could develop their historical understandings at a higher level than Sue thought possible. Martin videotaped the pupils in Carol's classroom and showed Sue the tape to demonstrate that if the five and six years could develop this historical understanding it should be possible for Sue's eight to nine year olds to develop this understanding. Martin produced his first explanation of his educational influence in Sue's learning.

When Martin submitted this explanation of educational influence in learning to his Validation Group, he believed that he had produced an evidence-based explanation that was sufficient justification for the claims that he made in his explanation. His explanation focused on a claim that he had had an educational influence in the professional development of a Sue, in her primary school teaching. The explanation was focused on improving the learning and historical understanding of Sue's primary school pupils. Martin explained to the Validation Group that he had shown a video to Sue of Carol's pupils and that Sue then decided that she would see if her pupils could learn those aspects of the curriculum that she had not thought possible. Sue worked with her eight to nine years and satisfied herself that her pupils could learn those aspects of the curriculum that she had thought were too advanced for her pupils. Martin explained his influence in Sue's learning in terms of working on the learning of her pupils to develop historical understanding that she had not thought to be possible before seeing the video of Sue' pupils.

However, the Validation Group did not accept that the evidence Martin produced was sufficient to justify his claim. Having listened to their reasons, Martin accepted their responses and continued with his inquiry. Martin focused on the data that he would need to produce in the evidence that the Validation Group explained that they needed to see to be convinced of the validity of Martin's explanation of educational influence in Sue's learning.

In a subsequent Validation Group Martin satisfied the group that he had produced an explanation of educational influences in learning that was sufficiently supported by the evidence.

The questions below are concerned with making explicit the criteria we use to judge improvement and with judging the effectiveness of one's own actions in relation to improvements in the quality of learning. Such questions appear to be fundamental in many of our inquiries. In Living Theory research, it is important to recognise the importance of educational conversations that focus on learning and evidence-based explanations. In the second Validation Group, the evidence that Martin provided convinced the group that his claims were valid in relation to his answers to his questions:

Martin's questions

1. How can we know that an improvement has taken place in the school classroom?
2. What criteria do we use to judge whether an innovation has led to an improvement in the quality of learning?
3. In the context of my work as an inset tutor, how effective am I in my role as a disseminator and supporter of innovation?
4. What evidence is there to support my claim to be helping teachers to improve the quality of their children's learning?

The questions were concerned with providing criteria for judging improvement and with trying to identify evidence of improvement of a kind which would satisfy the Validation Group.

Some writers, such as Richard Winter (1989) prefer to focus on rigour, rather than validity.

2.12 Rigour and Using the Ideas of Others

Peggy Kok explains below how she uses Winter's six principles of rigour to strengthen her explanation of educational influences in her own learning (see pages 76–82 at http://www.actionresearch.net/

writings/jack/cycle3.pdf). The six principles are those of reflective and dialectical critique, risk, collaborative resource, plural structure, theory practice and transformation. Peggy begins with the plural structure of her report before focusing on reflexive critique, dialectical critique, risk, multiple resource and theory practice transformation. (Appendix Two)

***

As we tutor and work with students from international contexts we have become aware of the importance of recognising and responding to cultural differences. For example, we have become increasingly aware that not all cultures emphasise the importance of educational inquiries in which the student asks questions. We are increasingly aware of the importance of checking with students to see how the language we use has been understood, or misunderstood. For example, Peggy says in her report above:

> I had not imagined that the words I had interpreted as instructions were possibly just suggestions which I did not have to obey.

We recognise the importance of working within the motivational and energy flowing values of Cultures of Inquiry. We seek to create and sustain such cultures within our individual educational relationships and communities of practice. We will now stress the importance of Living Theory communities of inquiry and practice for sustaining our own motivations and the motivations of others.

2.13 Creating a Living Educational Theory Community

You can access the details of many local communities of Living Theory researchers from their living-posters below. The importance of belonging to a community of Living Theory researchers is that they contribute to the creation, sustaining and evolving of a Culture of Inquiry (Delong, 2002, 2013; Vaughan & Delong, 2019) that can enhance the global influence of Living Theory research with values of human flourishing. Such a Culture of Inquiry can be expressed within a Validation Group to help you to strengthen the validity and rigour of your explanations of educational influences in learning.

You can access the living-posters of each community from the homepage at: https://www.actionresearch.net/writings/posters/homepage2020.pdf

You could also create and share a living-poster of your own and from your own community with the help of the guidelines on 'How do Create and Share your Living-Poster.

One of the most impressive Living Educational Theory communities has emerged from the collaboration between four Irish researchers, Bernie Sullivan, Mary Roche, Catriona McDonagh and Máirín Glenn. These researchers were all awarded their doctorates from the University of Limerick for their Living Theory thesis between 2006 and 2007. Over the past 14 years they have worked together to form and sustain the Network Educational Action Research Ireland (NEARI). They submitted a successful proposal to form a Special Interest Group of the Educational Studies Association of Ireland (ESAI) on 'Values Based Practitioner Action Research' (VPAR). See their following note of the 12 May 2020, providing everyone with information and inviting us all to make suggestions on how to strengthen the NEARI community.

On 12 May 2020, at 13:18, NEARI people <info@eari.ie> wrote:

Hi everyone,

We would like to draw your attention to our report from our last fabulous NEARIMeet which was held online on 24 April 2020. If you follow this link http://www.eari.ie/2019/06/23/neari-at-carn-study-day-at-the-national-college-of-ireland/ you will get a flavour of what happened on the day.

We also launched our new ESAI Special Interest Group (SIG) there too. It is called Values Based Practitioner Action Research (VPAR) (see http://esai.ie/sigs-2020/) and it is an extension of NEARI. The SIG is a forum for action researchers and those who teach action research. The SIG recognises, supports or promotes research that is grounded in the researcher's values.

We would also like to remind you of our ongoing, thought-provoking conversations over in our discussion group area! All contributions are welcome! Similarly, if anyone wanted to make a contribution to our Resources Page we would be delighted.

Also, if you would like to write up a short blog pertaining to your reflections on your action research, just send us an email and we would love to publish them on our web site.

Finally, if you can offer us any advice on how we might strengthen NEARI and make it more accessible, meaningful and useful for people, then please let us know.

BEST WISHES,

BERNIE SULLIVAN, CAITRIONA MCDONAGH, MÁIRÍN GLENN AND MARY ROCHE

Prolific writers, one of their publications, "Enhancing Practice through Classroom Research: A Teacher's Guide to Professional Development 2nd Edition", offers references, questions for reflection, case studies, and advice relating to data protection and storage. It provides an accessible introduction to understanding and improving teaching and learning through a process of reflection, research, and action. Divided into five parts, this self-study action research approach emphasises the positive aspects of enhancing practice and reflects how this can lead to higher levels of teacher autonomy and agency (McDonagh et al., 2019).

One gathering of a global community of Living Theory researchers took place on 27 June 2020. You can access the details of this gathering and the participants at: http://www.spanglefish.com/livingtheoryresearchgathering/index.asp

2.14 Creating Your Own Living Theory Community

You can access details of Living Theory communities by accessing details of NEARI and the Blue Water Action Research Group from the 2021 Living Poster's Homepage at: https://www.actionresearch.net/writings/posters/homepage2021.pdf

Both living-posters demonstrate the commitment of the Living Theory researchers to supporting each other's educational inquiries and those of others over many years.

2.15 Educational Conversations/Dialogue as Research

When Jackie works with her mentees, she uses the language of 'loving educational conversations'.

We believe that educational conversations and dialogue as research can be seminal to Living Educational Theory research since the dialogue generates, clarifies and synthesizes the concepts and processes in creating one's own living-educational-theory in a Culture of Inquiry. Jackie (2019) writes

> The ontological importance of conversation and dialogue in my relationships informs this approach to educational conversations as a research method. The nature of my influence can be seen through the videos and emails, embodied in a form of inquiry that focuses on dialogue. The conversations are important and legitimate research process whereby I am showing my educational influence with Michelle Vaughan. To me this is self-evident and not revolutionary, as Shotter (2011) says:
>
>> It is our spontaneous, embodied ways of seeing and acting in the world that we change… we change in who we 'are,' how we relate ourselves to our surroundings.
>
> But to say all of this is not to say anything very revolutionary, for such a form of 'research' is already a part of our everyday practices; it is only revolutionary to recognize that fact.
>
> (p. 191)

2.16 Dialogical Relationships in Cultures of Inquiry for the Creation of Living-Theories

In Vaughan and Delong (2019a), Delong writes:

> I believe that we can create a kinder, safer, more loving future by developing our loving educational conversations. Gadamer (1975) discusses the form of human interaction through dialogue:
>
>> …To conduct a dialogue requires first of all that the partners do not talk at cross purposes. Hence it necessarily has the structure of question and answer. The first condition of the art of conversation is ensuring that the other person is with us…. To conduct a conversation means to allow oneself to be conducted by the subject matter to which the partners in the dialogue are oriented.
>
> (p. 367)

> He tells us that conversation as an art form means that we do not talk at cross purposes and thus use a question-and-answer format. We need to ensure that we are on the same wavelength as our colleague and that the matter at hand is paramount. Gadamer (1975)

advises that a thinking person will search for everything in favour of an opinion, not for the weaknesses.

(p. 367)

Jackie writes: When I am coaching/mentoring others in creating their living-educational-theories, I make use of questions that I think will help them move on in their thinking, that will facilitate, not control, the conversation. I take care that the questions be small steps that encourage deeper thinking and yet not too long a stride so that they lose what they have accomplished or become afraid to take the next step. Questioning can be a means of controlling a conversation so I try to be fully cognizant that the questions or comments that I make in guiding the researcher are loving, educational and without prior judgement. Michelle Vaughan describes this "nice scaffolding" assistance (27/01/2019):

Michelle shares the supportive Living Theory research process.
Video 2.5. https://www.youtube.com/watch?v=fzawRc48YgQ&feature=youtu.be

> I said [to Jean] I don't know if Jackie knew that she was going to tell me to do all these things along the way but it felt like she had the next step for me planned and was just waiting for me to get somewhere so that I could take the next step. Because had she told me everything up front, I might have been overwhelmed about the process but it was a very nice scaffolding. And I said it really felt like the writing was a journey of self-discovery…

At the heart of our continuing commitment to support the generation of living-educational-theories and to enhance the global educational influence of Living Theory research with values of human flourishing is our sense of educational responsibility. We are relating this responsibility to the theme of the 2021 conference of the AERA on 'Accepting Educational Responsibility'. In Part Three, we will focus on a form of educational responsibility that includes the value of living global citizenship within a Culture of Inquiry that supports the generation and sharing of living-educational-theories in doctoral inquiries. This leads us into Part Four on extending the global influences of Living Educational Theory research as a global social movement.

Appendix

 # Martin Forrest's Use of Validation Groups

The first meeting of the Validation Group engaged in a lengthy discussion which ranged widely over a number of possible criteria of improvement; there were many conflicting points of view and many different pieces of advice were offered to the researcher. Two features stand out in this discussion: first, the expressed wish to try to pin down in fairly precise terms the nature of the improvement sought and think in terms of established educational research methods using experimental and control groups. Carol reacted strongly to the suggestion which came from several members of the group, that improvements might be measured in the conventional way:

> It reminds me of the old system of teaching children by the I.T.A. method and the traditional (method). How can you compare one group of five year olds to another group of five-year-olds. How can you compare the methods of teaching reading against completely different groups?
> (Taped discussion of first Validation Group meeting)

Carol's response shows up a key weakness in traditional methodology and encourages the search for an approach which takes account of individual differences in children and teachers.

The alternative methodology of an action research approach in which improvements are evaluated over a period of time was put forward as a totally different approach and one that was unfamiliar to most members of the Validation Group. She says:

> Suppose it's not a method where you compare. Suppose we don't look at it like that, suppose we say that as a teacher you have certain values, that you're trying to stimulate certain kinds of qualities in them and that's our main task, to try to understand how you as an individual are relating to these pupils, what you're doing, the

kind of problems you say you have, the solutions you've imagined… if you can actually hold up for public criticism the kind of relationships you have in the classroom with pupils and other people who can identify with the experiences and the problems you're having (we)can actually learn something about the process of improvement from you, because you've been through certain kinds of processes, that in itself is extremely valuable, because you're holding up for the first time to public criticism the actual process of education and in groups like this I think we'll be able to identify with each other.

(Jack Whitehead –taped discussion of first Validation Group meeting)

It was agreed that evidence would be collected in the form of audio and videotape recordings and, where appropriate, examples of children's work with a view to demonstrating improvement taking place over a period of two to three months.

Following the first Validation Group meeting, Martin discussed with the two teachers how the action research might be given a sharper focus, bearing in mind that the intention was not for the researcher to engage in a traditional form of educational research activity, but to monitor improvements taking place overtime in relation to the teacher's own educational values and to look at particular children in the class for particular improvements taking place. By the time of the second Validation Group meeting both Sue and Carol were well under way with their respective cycles of action and reflection. Martin had recorded a video of Sue's five and six year old pupils working in a way that Carol had stated earlier that she did not believe it possible for her eight and nine year olds to do. Watching the video of Sue's pupils prompted Carol to explore the possibility that her eight and nine year olds could engage in a higher level of learning than she initially thought possible.

Martin's Evaluation of the Solutions in Relation to Sue's Learning

The report Martin presented to the final Validation Group meeting explained his educational influences in Sue's learning and spanned the period from early February to late May.

In his explanation of his educational influence as a professional development tutor, Martin traced the history of one full action/

reflection cycle in which Sue attempted to resolve two particular problems that she had encountered in her work with historical artefacts. First, there was her need to establish effective ways of promoting the development in her children of lively inquiring minds and the ability to question and argue rationally. Second, there was her concern to provide opportunities for children to relate the artefacts to an historical context and in so doing to promote her other aims.

Sue's educational values may be said to have been negated (Forrest, 1983) in two particular respects: first, in relation to helping her pupils to develop lively inquiring minds, Sue felt that she had failed with the first artefact case to provide conditions which might most effectively promote a questioning discussion and rational argument among the children. This problem was resolved by implementing group work, and by the use of a 'feely box' in which pupils handled historical artefacts without seeing them in order to place them on a time line, to help sustain discussion.

Second, Sue had experienced a negation of her declared intention of helping the children to study each object in its historical context. On the one hand, she felt it important for them to speculate in an imaginative way and on the other she wished to introduce relevant source materials. With the first feely box, problems arose because Sue found difficulty in integrating the additional resources she had provided with the children's study of the artefacts. This difficulty arose partly from Sue's not knowing precisely what resources would be needed to back-up the artefacts. Furthermore, her own wish to share the children's ignorance in relation to the nature of the objects conflicted with her need as a teacher to be ready to tackle the next stage of development: the exploration of the historical context of each object. The long-term solution would be to produce supporting packs of two-dimensional resource material. The short-term solution was provided by the phased introduction of relevant resources supplies from the Polytechnic resources collection.

Sue – Modification of Practice in the Light of Evaluation

Martin's explanation of his educational influence in Sue's learning, presented to the Validation Group, represents one completed cycle of action/reflection by Sue and had incorporated within it a number of suggestions from Martin for modification of her practice. One suggestion related to seeing how far the children can work systematically on their own.

In the course of the third Validation Group meeting, Sue indicated that, as a result of seeing the videotape of Carol's five and six year olds and the extent to which they had learnt to work independently of the teacher, she would like to see how far her eight and nine year olds had now developed the ability to work autonomously as the result of the work she had been doing. "I would like to use the experience and just give them the objects without any help at all."

Accordingly, Sue planned two weeks after the final Validation Group meeting for the Martin to video record the whole class. Sue formed new groups of pupils, each working with a completely new object. Sue had thus embarked upon a new cycle, spurred on by her colleague from another school and taking into account the points which arose from her evaluation of the earlier implementation of work with artefacts.

In his evaluation of Carol's learning, Martin encouraged Carol to go beyond what she was mistakenly seeing as limitations in the children's capacities to learn.

Martin's Evaluation of Carol's Learning

Carol's educational values included her contention that it is important to try to get five to six year old children to appreciate some idea of time. Her belief in the importance of this may be said to have been negated by her perception of limitations in her children' understanding of time past. In discussion with Martin (as the professional development tutor and researcher), Carol voiced her doubts about helping children to sort out a 'sense of chronology.' Martin encouraged Carol to sort out a 'sense of chronology' with the historical artefacts of a Roman amphora an eighteenth century book and a cobbler's last. Carol overcame her doubts with a positive result.

A second way in which Carol's educational values may be said to have been negated is in relation to her aim of developing lively and inquiring minds. Here again, it was Carol's own perception of her children's limitations which formed a barrier. Carol felt that words of exhortation written by the Avon primary teachers 'Working Party' of which she had herself been a member, were less appropriate to her own much younger children; for example the report states:

> The exercise is likely to be more productive if, in the first instance, children are allowed to handle and discuss the object without teacher interference.
>
> (Avon Education Committee, 1982c)

Carol's conviction that such a technique was impossible with five and six year olds, at first seemed unshakeable, but her recognition that they may be "helped to do this through experience" is contained in her statement:

> It's like putting a maths card in front of a five year old and saying 'Try and work things out for yourself. They wouldn't be able to unless they'd had experience before.

Carol was prepared to try out the procedure and to see what happened, though she was clearly sceptical:

> .... I will give it a try just to prove the point.

The second Validation Group discussed the transcript of the children using their second artefact case in which Carol introduced the feely box and made some reference to the transcript of the subsequent discussion between Carol and the researcher. The documentation makes clear that Carol acknowledged that an improvement had taken place in relation to developing an enquiring mind as evidenced by their use of language. The language used by the children drew the following question from Jack Whitehead at the second meeting of the Validation Group:

> If we could get back to that point about criteria; on the first question, would everybody accept that kind of evidence if it was subjected to analysis of the relevant criteria of lively enquiring minds, the ability to question and argue rationally was evidence........?
> .... I've got a feeling for the first time that Martin might be able to justify that statement –it's on the last page (of the transcript) –"I wonder whether my Auntie Millie's auntie was born there."

Encouraged by the response of the children to the second artefact study case, Carol decided to withdraw from the discussion to an even greater extent when she came to use the third study case. This time she did not use the feely box but reverted to wrapping each object in paper. The proceedings were videotaped and the recording presented to the third Validation Group meeting for them to scrutinize. The Validation Group was clearly impressed, in particular, by the way the children approached each object in turn with very little help this time from their teacher.

JACK: "The last thing that impressed me most (with that shoe last) was the way, somehow, these children came to that conclusion through dialogue and discussion themselves. It was very impressive."

MARY W: "I just wanted to say I was very impressed by the evidence of lively enquiring minds…"

The researcher was asked by Jack to pick out the points in the early dialogues with Carol when she made plain her doubts about the childrens' ability to work in this autonomous way.

The following dialogue ensued:

CAROL: "You proved me wrong on this!"

JACK: I think that's quite crucial to Martin's work: I was very impressed at the way the children were arguing among themselves and I just felt here, when you say here on the bottom of the second page "they wouldn't be able to unless they had experienced it before"…. (reference to analogy with Maths workcard)…. what you've demonstrated here is that you were giving them that experience and they did argue rationally."

GROUP MEMBER: "You weren't giving them this before"

CAROL: "They'd actually progressed."

With regard to Carol's concern with developing in her children an understanding of time past as well as with regard to language development, one extract from the first Validation Group meeting, after Carol had used her first artefact study case, shows that Carol recognised the importance of using artefacts to overcome the severe limitations in children's understanding of time.

RON ADAMS: "What do you hope to achieve with these that you couldn't achieve in their absence?"

CAROL: "Well, it's a lot better to have the objects than photographs with this age. Such a lot of language has come out of it –I suppose I could have had language out of other objects –it's given them some insight into historical things. They've been very excited about them."

With the second and third study cases, very limited attention was paid to placing objects in their historical context and associating specialised vocabulary with the artefacts. However, with encouragement from Martin this level of specificity was gradually extended. For example, with the second box, Carol explained the use of a weaving comb and Martin's intervention enabled the children to place this object chronologically before a Roman mosaic.

Comments were made by members of the Validation Group on the evidence presented in the videotape of children showing some awareness of time. One of the objects discussed by the children was a leather-bound eighteenth century book.

One group member made the following point:

> It couldn't be a library book, because you couldn't keep a book out of a library as long as that: obviously they've got some concept of time, haven't they? Also, their idea of a Roman book which was a scroll, they obviously felt that, because there wasn't a suggestion that you could have the same things at the same time.

At the end of their study of each object in turn, Carol invited the group, on Martin's suggestion, to see whether they could arrange the objects in chronological order. The result was that they placed the Roman amphora as the oldest with the eighteenth century book as the next oldest (which, in fact, it was). The cobbler's last was placed at the other end of the time scale. Carol had videotaped this lesson.

Carol – Modification of Practice in the Light of Evaluation

The videotape was played back to Carol's class immediately after it had been recorded on a monitor with a large screen in the middle of the school hall. Several colleagues were among those who came to see part of the videotape at the end of afternoon school. Carol and her colleagues were impressed by the progress they observed in the children which they saw to be the result of their work with artefacts.

Since this written study has been restricted to the practice of two teachers, it has seemed unwise to be side-tracked into discussing the interest shown by other colleagues of the two teachers. At Sefton Park Infant's School, however, several teachers used the artefacts with their own children and followed Carol's work with interest. The Head showed a lively interest throughout.

Evaluating Martin's Role (as Professional Development Tutor and Researcher)

In their response to Martin's final draft report before its submission for Masters' accreditation, a member of the Validation Group stated:

> What I think I'd need to see in relation to your (question) No.2, are the teachers saying they actually lack something and that you're actually working with them to provide something they say they lack; this being used in the classroom with your pupils, and then trying to relate this to your No.1 which is then judging whether or not improvements have taken place in the quality of the pupils' learning.
>
> (Taped discussion of first Validation Group meeting)

Both Sue and Carol were questioned independently and on separate occasions by members of the Validation Group about the researcher's in-service role. With regard to the researcher's role of disseminating the innovation, in this case the use of historical artefacts, and in sustaining teachers in their own work as teacher researchers,

RON KING: "One change is that there wasn't much history taught and now there is!"

PETER: "That's a very important point."

(Taped discussion of second Validation Group meeting)

Support for Carol

JACK: "(Martin is claiming to have provided) in-service support and I think we've got to be able to demonstrate this, that yes, he has assisted in some sense improvements to take place in the classroom. Now I can cope with the first question (i.e. that improvements have taken place in the classroom); I'm still a bit hazy about the claim to know that in-service help is actually helping/"

MARY WILSON: "Carol thinks that the in-service help has been helpful … surely if we're looking at Martin's role

>   as an in-service teacher, in opening ... teachers to something they didn't know before, we saw this here and now we're sure."
>
> JACK: "That will in itself be evidence."
>
> MARY WILSON: "Sue is now going into the classroom to try the same things herself because her expectations have been raised and I don't think we need further evidence from the teachers."
>
>   (Taped discussion of third Validation Group meeting; Forrest, 1983)

Appendix

2

Peggy Kok's Use of Richard Winter's Six Principles of Rigour

The Plural Structure of My Action Research Report

The problem facing me is how should my accounts be organised for analysis? I cannot resist (the positivist in me is not yet dead) designing a structure that has a logical flow to it -analysis and interpretation of data, conclusion and recommendations.

Winter (1989) typifies a conventional report as:

> Linear, presenting a chronology of events, or a sequence of cause and effect; they are presented in the single voice of the author, who organizes evidence to support his or her conclusions, so that the report will seem authoritative and 'convincing' to readers.

> However, because the process of Action Research seeks "differences, contradictions, possibilities, questions, as ways of opening up new avenues for action....and situations cannot be reduced to a consensus, but must be presented in terms of the multiplicity of viewpoints which make up the situation" (Winter, 1989) an Action Research report has to be expressed in a different format.

Winter considers the appropriate format for an Action report to be a 'plural structure' which consists of "various accounts and various critiques of those accounts, and ending not with conclusions (intended to be convincing) but with questions and possibilities (intended to be 'relevant' in various ways for different readers)."

At this point of my report, I am still struggling with this report. It is difficult for me not to have the familiar research report framework to guide me along. It is a very painful experience for me not to have a skeleton to fill out my research efforts. How I wish I can write under neat headings like "Analysis and interpretation of data" and "Conclusion and recommendations."

How do I present the "dialectical, reflexive, questioning and collaborative form of inquiry" (Winter, 1989) that is action research?

How should a piece of action research be presented without using any positivistic framework and yet in the eyes of the world, measures up to the validity and reliability associated with scientific research?

Action research is a highly personal endeavour, so how could it have general applicability?

I find solace in the following part of Winter's discussion of plural structure, his fifth principle in the conduct of Action Research:

> ...One does not need to address explicitly a universal audience or to utter a statement in the form of a universal law in order for one's words to have a general significance:
> 'Significance' is, in a very important sense, in the mind of the beholder, as an interpretation which finds points of contact, of relevance, to which the beholder can relate.

I have all the data in my hands and the significant truths have already been extracted from the transcript of the discussion on my paper. I believe that amongst the people who read this action research report, there will be someone who will harmonise with the chords I struck within the structure of the situations I have presented in my diary, my paper and my analysis of my tapescript. Having said that I am convinced that my action research report so far has fulfilled the criterion of plurality of structure.

Logically, the analysis of my tapescript should be presented in the following paragraphs as it is the highlight of my report. I have relegated it to a position at the rear of this report not because it is unimportant but because at this point, a new concern has emerged: I am concerned now with whether my accounts will stand up to the scrutiny of those who:

> Cast doubt upon the value of small-scale inquiry carried out with minimal resources by people actively engaged in the situations they are investigating.
>
> (Winter, 1989)

For now, I urgently need to find the answers to my new inquiry. Therefore, the progress of this report from this point onwards will be to investigate if my action research efforts have been rigorous enough to stand against comparisons with scientific research.

To facilitate that investigation, I shall use five of Winter's (1989) "Six principles for the conduct of Action-Research" as criteria for judgement. The fifth principle, that of plural structure, has in my view been followed closely and have been discussed above. In the following paragraphs I shall use examples from my accounts to show that I have fulfilled each of the remaining five criteria. I shall use the data from the analysis of the tapescript (in Appendix D of my full report) to prove my case. It will be for my readers to judge and decide if they are in agreement with my interpretations and claims.

Principle No. 1: Reflexive Critique

Winter (1989) explains the first principle, that of reflexivity, in the following way:

The thesis of reflexivity begins by insisting upon modest claims: making judgements depends on examples from various personal experiences (not on representative samples of universally agreed categories). These examples can be analyzed, but no analysis will be complete or final, because inquiry will take the form of questioning claims rather than making claims. The result of the inquiry will thus take the form of a dialogue between writers and readers concerning possible interpretations of experience, rather than a single interpretation thrust upon a passive reader by a writer whose inquiry has resulted in certainty. It is this process of questioning claims which is itself a dimension of validity –not the only one but an important one.

Winter outlines the basic procedure of reflexive critique as follows:

1. Accounts will be collected, such as observation notes, interview transcripts, written statements from participants, or official documents.
2. The reflexive basis of these accounts will be made explicit, so that
3. Claims may be transformed into questions, and a range of possible alternatives will be suggested, where previously particular interpretations have been taken for granted.

In the paragraphs that follow, I shall give examples of reflexive critique present in my inquiry with reference to the discussion on the paper I presented.

Having presented the gist of my paper to the group using a diagram which I had earlier put on the blackboard, I assumed the role of 'tutor' with the task of leading the group and in Jack's words,

> ...to bring out of people here their own inquiries in relation to what you have written and to get some genuine questions coming which would be free and open, which will not be imposed as in skills training...

Analysing the tape for evidence that I had performed this role assigned to me, left me with a sense of dissatisfaction. I could not honestly say that I had been successful in managing the group in this way. Most of the time, I was concerned with clarifying, answering, giving examples, views -hardly what a good discussion group leader would be doing. However, it is not my inability to fill out the role 'assigned' to me that I was unhappy about. It was my realisation of my unquestioning acceptance of tasks given to me that woke me up to the fact that perhaps I should have made my feelings clear to people instead of complying ever so readily.

When Jack suggested that I took on the role of 'tutor' the day before the discussion, I was hesitant as I was doubtful if it was possible for me to simultaneously 'defend my paper' and take on the responsibility of charting the educational development of others. I did not voice my doubts strongly enough because Jack was the authority and I reluctantly agreed although I did say before I left him that I would have to 'play it by ear' in the session the next day. But the fact remains that when tasks are delegated or assigned to me by those in authority to do so, I do not ask questions nor try to exert any influence by stating my case. If there is a job to be done, it should be done and done well, don't ask -that has been my philosophy. On page 4 of the transcript (Appendix D of my full report), I stated emphatically that:

> ...somebody has to be right, somebody has to tell me what to do, and if somebody tells me what to do I will make sure that I will do it to the best of my ability. Even here. The assignments -Jack says, you do a paper on the nature of teachers' knowledge, I never questioned or said that I would not do it, I will do, even the first AR (Action Research) —"Peggy you prepare a lesson plan."

> I never questioned why, did you notice that: Jack, I never asked you why because you were the teacher and you said to do it and every step of the way he said, "do this, do this and do this" and I did it.

Here, I had made explicit a claim that I had been given orders to do things. This has consistently been my interpretation of such situations in which I perceive the other party as having more power than I. I would have lived with that belief probably for the rest of my life had it not been for Jan who remarked:

> That's an interesting perception of what's happened between you and Jack there because I don't perceive what's happened to me over the time that we've been together I have been told to do this, do this and do this and I have done them. I am not sure whether that's been true for you either because you perceived things that way.

That observation prompted me to ask Jack for confirmation and what he said was a revelation to me. He said:

> I think I did make suggestions but you took them as instructions.

I had not imagined that the words I had interpreted as instructions were possibly just suggestions which I did not have to obey.

Reflexive critique in this case has opened my eyes to the fact my conditioned responses to what I perceive as orders has deprived me of the freedom to explore possibilities and exercise choices which could result in better quality work.

Here Is Another Instance of Reflexive Critique in My Inquiry

The second most significant event in the discussion was my discovery that despite my consciousness of the fact that people's opinions should be valued and respected, I was observed to be rather undemocratic in an instance when I had the power to overrule the wishes of the majority. This observation was made by Jack when he said:

> You see, yesterday we were talking, and I was trying to suggest that your task today would be to bring out of people here their own inquiries in relation to what you have written and to get some genuine questions coming which would befree and open, which

will not be imposed as in skills training. But when you offered choice to us at the beginning I knew how difficult that was for you and then as soon as you got one person....(laughter). Because it was what you wanted to do.

(Appendix D, page 5)

Jack was referring to the choices I offered to the group at the start of the discussion as to how they would like to have the session conducted. One of the choices was that I gave a short presentation using a diagram I had previously put up on the board. The other choice was that people would just respond freely to what I had written in my paper. Although the majority in the group preferred free response, I eagerly sprang to my feet to give a presentation as soon as one person had indicated such a preference.

Jack's evidence was corroborated by Steve and Leslie:

STEVE: Because it was what she'd wanted to do. First piece of evidence she finds to support, she gets to the blackboard.

LESLIE: Yes, going to the blackboard would enable her to be the instructor again.

These comments confirmed the fact that I still very much wanted to hold on to the control that a teacher had. By going to the board, I could do what I had planned beforehand and to give information because only then was I confident that everyone would at least have grasped the gist of my paper. Although my actions were natural responses to the situation, I had not realised their effects on people in the group especially those whose wishes I had ignored not intentionally, but because I was "desperate to get to the board". Perhaps I could have asked the people who had wanted free response to my paper their reasons for their choice instead of just counting hands.

Reflexive critique – people questioning my behaviour and telling me how they have interpreted my actions has enabled me to be more sensitive and respectful of the expressed needs of others. It has made me aware that there are other viewpoints apart from mine.

Lastly, where reflexive critique is concerned, I feel I have to mention that I was totally oblivious to the fact that my use of the masculine gender practically throughout the paper I presented had in Moira's words dismissed "half the population…". I had not thought that using man as generic was anything wrong as back home, we do not fuss about such things. However, Moira's indignation and anger set me thinking about this issue of equality between man and woman and I begin to see the logic behind it. It is not just words we are quibbling over, it is the fight for recognition as equals that had made Moira angry and having been there to experience her response to the way I had chosen to represent man/womankind, awoken me to another reality that I had been aware of but did not give much thought to until now.

Principle No. 2: Dialectical Critique

This principle is based on the concept of 'dialectics' as "a general theory of the nature of reality and of the process of understanding reality…". On this basis, Winter proposes a method of analysis which helps the researcher decide what is significant from amongst the numerous possible interpretations one can come up with when one takes a step back and reflects upon them. In simple terms, 'dialectics':

> …Puts forward a coherent general theory both of the nature and structure of reality and also the process of analysing and understanding reality….dialectics gives us a principled basis for making selections. It thereby helps to contain our potentially vast amounts of data and interpretation within the practical limits (for example, time, resources) of practitioner research.

Using dialectics as an approach to analysing data entails an investigation of:

1. the overall context of relations which gives them a unity in spite of their apparent separateness, and
2. the structure of internal contradictions -behind their apparent unity -which gives them a tendency to change, in spite of their apparent fixity.

Was there dialectic critique in my inquiry?. I would say yes. I had assembled my thoughts, beliefs and feelings into a paper and what I had presented in that paper was a structure of my reality -my work background, the political climate that shaped and sustained my thinking, how that thinking had been influenced by what I had learnt about action research and the writing and thoughts of those for and against positivism and finally, how I managed to find a way to accommodate the new ideas I had been exposed to within my life's framework. This was the definition of the scope of my inquiry.

The contradictions were picked out by my peers in the discussion of my paper. I had openly supported social engineering because it was, to me, the only logical way for us as a young nation to survive and progress. At the end of the paper, I said:

> I have thoughts, ideas and knowledge that were not there before. Now I look beyond ostensibly invincible structures and see a way of making life within it more meaningful and valued. I propose to introduce change in teacher training slowly and given time and modest successes there may be a possibility where there can be cooperation between government and people in working towards reform in teaching training in the vocational and educational setting.

The first few questions that followed my presentation were:

> What would an implementation of these ideas do for your society as a whole?....What is your motivation really? Is your system, the existing system working so poorly in terms of (a)producing people with skills and (b)producing happy people, or satisfied people or people who are going to live a full and rich life or are there any shortcomings in any of those departments that you see that AR can ultimately improve?

Peter probably could not understand why I should now embrace the philosophy of Action Research when I had spent half of my paper glorifying the political system and economy of my country and even till the very end, I wrote:

> I accept the way my country is run and I give my government my fullest support and loyalty.

It could have appeared that I was holding two ideas at the same time where what might be more plausible would be to have one or the other but not both together. Though in thinking, I have moved into the realms of values as against structure and concern with the ends and not the means, in practice I have not really been transformed by what I have learnt and accepted through action research -democracy, justice, valuing people. The observations by the group set off contradictions in me. I want to be more humane, less mechanistic but all the ghosts of my past come to haunt me and to impose structures, order and control in the way I relate to the world and people. These contradictions are there and it will take some time and a lot of conscious effort on my part to resolve. I don't just feel that they are there, they were perceptively noted by Jan when she said: (Page 10, Appendix D):

> I think she has oscillated between two extremes....This term you have been going in a different direction that you were going in the last. And I am not sure what I am left with here except you are in a lot of contradictions because there is a lot there that is unspoken.

Steve shares similar feelings when he said:

> Yes, I got a feeling that there is no synthesis yet. You have stated the thesis and antithesis and in some sense you are leaving the synthesis somewhere in the future…
>
> (Appendix D, page 10)

These observations accurately describe the tension and contradictions within me from the time when I started to look for a focal point to build my paper around. With the completion of the paper I have released some of that tension in theoretical proposals but not in reality. Jack illuminated the group with the following explanation:

> …One of the central points about education and training is the point in which you are accredited, where judgements are made, where you are assessed. In relation to power and control that is where you begin to see how a system is organised….It may appear to be a throwaway line but I think it is very significant: "I do not care if I don't get and 'A' for this paper". I suppose, I think we all ought to care. If we feel that the quality of the work we've judged in relation to the criteria….Peggy's work itself justifies that judgement and we are in a set of power relations that might come to a different conclusion using the same criteria. Then it is what you do about it that the synthesis takes place. When she gets back to Singapore, she intends to do certain things. We'll only see the synthesis in action there.

I think I do not need to restate the obvious. The principle of dialectic critique was alive and kicking throughout my whole inquiry.

Principle No. 3: Collaborative Resource

The third principle –that of collaborative resource indicates:

> ...A process of simultaneously giving weight to the understandings contributed by all members, and at the same time a process of 'deconstructing' the various contributions so that we can use them as resources for 'reconstructing' new categories and interpretations.

Unlike positivistic research where the researcher is detached from those whom he observes, working collaboratively in action research means that:

> ...It is the variety of differences between the viewpoints that makes them into a rich resource, and it is by using this resource (the differences between viewpoints) that our analysis can begin to move outwards from its inevitably personal starting point towards ideas which have been interpersonally negotiated.

In the previous examples given to illustrate reflexive and dialectic critique, I have shown how through other peoples' questioning of my statements and actions that had resulted in a broadening of my mind towards certain things. Reflexive critique would have been impossible without the operation of the principle of collaborative resource. Without collaborative resource, I would have been much poorer in knowledge, probably living in ignorant bliss that much of what I believed in was unquestionably right.

Principle No. 4: Risk

This principle states:

> ...That initiators of research must put themselves 'at risk' through the process of investigation....the process is not merely one of exposure to refutation, but of exploring possibilities for transformation....In engaging in a process where the purpose is change (innovation at the level of practice and the development of new insights concerning practice) we are part of the situation which is undergoing change. We have no theoretical basis for exempting ourselves from the processes we set in motion, and we do not want to be exempt; on the contrary, we want to change because we want to learn as much as possible...

I think my inquiry has satisfied this criterion fully. Writing that paper for discussion was a 'risk'. I had consolidated my thoughts and views into 15 pages and I was prepared for people to question my claims, assertions, beliefs and proposals and to emerge from their scrutiny with a much wider and informed worldview. Although the discussion did not focus on everything I had written it had resulted in the crystallisation of some significant insights and realisations that benefited me educationally and professionally. If anyone in the group was at risk, it was certainly me. I still remember what Steve said to me at the end of the whole ordeal (presenting the paper and having it discussed). He said I was "very brave". There can be no bravery without the element of risk present.

Furthermore, towards the end of my paper, I had made some proposals on how I would change the face of teacher training. I have committed myself to black and white statements these plans of mine. It is done now and I am exposing myself to the risk that I may not be able to get these plans to materialise. In research done in the positivist tradition, all I needed to do was to make recommendations and apart from the risk that my report was not valid or reliable, I could rest easy once the report is out.

Principle No. 6: Theory, Practice and Transformation

Winter emphasises that:

> ...Theory and practice are not two distinct entities but two different and yet interdependent and complementary phases of the change process.

There are two action research inquiries contained in this report. The first one is ready for implementation. I have surveyed the theories produced a paper that is a synthesis of my thoughts and reading, gathered valuable insights through discussion with my peers and all that is left is to go back to my place of work and apply the theories to my practice to transform it. I can anticipate that the transformation will not be a smooth straightforward matter but that there will be a continual cause-and-effect relationship between theory and practice.

> ...theory, being based in practice, is itself transformed by the transformations of practice. Theory and practice do not therefore, confront one another in mutual opposition: each is necessary to the other for the continued vitality and development of both.

The second inquiry is just at the synthesis stage. It requires the validation of a collaborative group before implementation can take place. If I may project the course of development of this second inquiry, I would say that the outcome of a debate amongst my peers as to whether I have satisfied the six criteria of rigour inaction-research would be in the form of insights that would provide me with guidance in doing future action-research in a rigorous way.

My understanding of Action Research has deepened and I now have a structure to work with. It is a different structure from the one that I am familiar with but having acquired in theory how to build such a structure in conducting research, I am more confident of my ability to conduct such research when I am back at work in Singapore.

PART

3 Doctoral Level Inquiries

Part Three builds on Part Two to address the deeper, more complex requirements of those seeking to make an original contribution to knowledge through a doctoral thesis. In addition to building on Parts One and Two, Part Three recognises the demands on you, the practitioner-researcher, and your context, and the different requirements of a doctoral thesis in making an original contribution to knowledge. This recognition requires a development in the philosophical base of supervision from the tutoring in Part Two.

Organisation of Part Three:

1. Setting Stage for Study
    a. Why engage in doctoral research?
    b. Self-Concept/Awareness
    c. Transparency with family and employer
    d. Obstacles/Barriers/Constraints
    e. Support and Encouragement
    f. Living Theory Culture of Inquiry
    g. Critical Friends
    h. Supportive community
    i. Validation group
2. Developments in the Philosophical Base from Parts Two to Three
3. Master's to PhD: what's changed?
    a. Criteria for PhD
    b. Living Educational Theory Master's to PhD
    c. Other Master's to Living Educational Theory PhD
    d. Writing your doctoral research proposal and transfer report

DOI: 10.4324/9781003369158-5

i. Christine Jones' successful Research Proposal to Liverpool Hope University

ii. Christine Jones' successful Transfer Report to Liverpool Hope University

Christine Jones' successful Transfer Report to Liverpool Hope University

e. Range of different professional contexts and inquiries addressed by Living Educational Theory researchers

f. An Example of a PhD Ethical Approval

g. Programs of Study

i. Course Work

ii. Thesis

iii. Viva

4. Approximate Timelines and Schedule of Research
5. Available resources

a. Free libraries

b. Other texts

Let's begin with setting the stage.

3.1 Setting the Stage for the Study

a. Why engage in doctoral research?

To begin with, you need to consider your reasons for engaging in this research journey. There are three sides of the argument for making this decision: one is personal development – improving the self, the second is for professional development and the third is contributing to human flourishing. By far the greatest reason for the Living Educational Theory journey is the development of self. The process of articulating, describing and examining your values, critically engaging with the literature and creating your own theory of knowledge, your own living-educational-theory, is transformative. Moreover, the process does not end upon the accreditation of the degree; it becomes a way of living and being for the rest of your life with no rest from wanting to improve yourself and your practice.

The second perspective is focused on improving yourself and your skills and knowledge for your work and workplace. When your questions is "How do I improve what I am doing?", your research process includes focusing on an area of improvement, developing a research question and action plan for improving, taking action and collecting data for evidence of improvement, always asking, "how do I know?". This new knowledge will give you more confidence in your knowing and open up opportunities in the academic and job world. For example, in order to teach graduate programmes, most universities require a doctorate as a prerequisite.

The third reason is influencing others beyond yourself and others in proximity to extend your influence as a global citizen (Potts, 2019) and contribute to human flourishing (Reiss & White, 2013; Whitehead, 2008). Coming from privileged societies, it is incumbent on us to encourage and support others in less fortunate circumstances to thrive with the codicil that we must be respectful or non-colonising.

b. Self-Concept/Awareness

We find it is of great value to know yourself, your strengths, weaknesses and passions. If you are naturally self-disciplined, this process will go extremely smoothly; however, if you know that you need encouragement and support to sustain your work, you will need to build in those supports. We have found that most researchers need a Culture of Inquiry (Delong, 2002) with like-minded researchers and particularly, Living Educational Theory researchers, to maintain a steady progress towards the goal of completing your PhD in a timely manner. There is a very extensive and supportive Living Educational Theory community available to you for the asking. We include ourselves in that community as well as the members of the EJOLTs community who may be contacted through the Community Space at ejolts.net and from ejolts.editor@gmail.com.

c. Transparency with family and employer

There is no honey-coating the fact that this is a demanding process. You are adding a significant body of work to your life that will demand that you give up some activities that can be suspended for this period. You must consult with, be transparent with your family, friends, employer and colleagues. Not only do you want to preserve those very important relationships, but also, you will need their support through the process and their love when it is done.

What can you give up? It may take some time to analyse what activities can be side-lined for the approximately five-year period and picked up later. As an example, Jackie gave up the tending of her garden. Yes, it went wild but was recovered after the degree was attained. She also took a suspension from some committee work that was not aligned with her job as superintendent of education. Many social activities were curtailed.

It may also be a matter of timing. For parents with small children, it may be appropriate to wait until they are past the early years and need less parenting time. It may be a matter of a partner who can pick up some of the duties for that period of time, of taking on a timetable of workplace duties that is reduced or of arranging a four over five employment contract, where income is spread out over five years with one year free from work duties.

d. Obstacles, Barriers and Constraints

Control your research/Speak with your own voice

It may appear to go without saying but if you are following your passions, if you are serious and answering a question about your improvement and living according to your values, you will still find challenges and obstacles on the way. Therefore, ensure that what you are studying matters to you, not what is important to others, no matter how influential they are – it is your own living-educational-theory. It must be your voice that is speaking, not others speaking for you. Remember that the doctorate is evaluated on your originality of mind and critical judgment.

Getting stuck

Jack has had stellar success in the sense of the completion of 38 of the doctorates that he has supervised at the Universities of Bath and Cumbria. Thirty-three of these can be accessed at https://www.actionresearch.net/living/living.shtml together with another 32 Living Theory Doctorates accredited from different universities around the world. Among that group were many that struggled and took suspensions during troubled times in their job or with family crises. For example, Jackie's job was threatened with termination (Delong, 2002, p. 38):

> The six-month period of January to June 1998 was the start-up and downsizing of the administration. This was a time of great strain for me because I was the lowest in seniority with the exception of the superintendent on two-year secondment (although technically since we were all on personal contracts, seniority did not exist). Without the downsizing I would be demoted. My e-mail to Jack called *Black Day* on April 3,

1998, said: ***Three superintendents to go and I'm number three***. Fortunately, three accepted severance packages and I kept my job. It's important to remember that through all this chaos, the work of the schools and the school system continued with the usual demands on us to perform with care and competence.

In order to withstand pressure, Jack suggested taking a suspension for six months. At first, Jackie was appalled at the thought because it felt like failure, like giving in, but once she came to see that she could still think and write when time came available, the pressure was off to be totally productive and meet thesis deadlines. This release of pressure was just what she needed. After six months, she picked up and continued.

With the International students that Jackie has mentored, there have been 'stuck' times where getting 'unstuck' was a challenge. What strategies have helped with transcending this obstacle? Sometimes, it was as simple as consistent, persistent "loving them into learning" (Campbell, 2011). At others, it was a matter of analysing together what had been accomplished and what was still needed to finish. For the really 'stuck', it included going back to the fundamentals of what really mattered to the researcher, recording that in a SKYPE or Zoom meeting, uploading it to YouTube on 'Unlisted' and having them script their words for a new piece of writing. Jackie uses prompts like:

What would help you get over being stuck?

What really matters to you right now?

What part of what you have written already do you like?

Who could you share your burden with who could help?

Can you send me a paragraph describing the "stuck" feeling?

Do you need a deadline extension or suspension?

So far, Jackie has not experienced someone so stuck they couldn't finish their doctorate but there are several examples of coming 'unstuck'. First, Liz Campbell. Despite a supervisor that tried to direct Liz in a direction that was not of any interest to her and wasting her time for a year, Liz with the support of Jackie and the Living Educational Theory community managed to get back to her thesis on "Love in the classroom", bring her thesis to completion (Campbell, 2019) and graduate in February, 2019.

Second, Parbati Dhungana of Katmandu, Nepal with whom Jackie worked from the time of their meeting in Split, Croatia at the ALARA Conference in October 2019. With what appeared to be steady progress with the sharing of three Chapters of her thesis, came the following 21 November 2020 email:

> Regarding dissertation writing, I am stopped! I don't know what stuck me. As the three festivals end from today, I may get time and mood to continue it. Right now, I am blank and nothing to share with you.
> (Delong, personal email, 21.11.20)

That same day, Jackie wrote and Parbati agreed to meet on Friday, 27 November: "Hi, Parbati. If you want to, let's have a Skype chat after Wednesday to see if we can get you unstuck! Love, Jackie"

Parbati sent a 20-page document, part poetry, part drama and part narrative of her Chapter 4, written that day. Jackie asked her what had caused her to get 'unstuck' and she replied that Jackie's contacting her, encouraging her, and agreeing to meet made her think about what she could share and thus she wrote the chapter. On 28 November, she wrote:

> Dear Jackie,
> It was a really great time. I am feeling fresh and alive today. From tomorrow I am planning to continue with new energy. Thank you so much for being with me in my hard time. With love, Parbati.
> (Delong, personal email, 28.11.20)

Suspensions

One of the available strategies for you when you hit a very bad time in your life and need a 'release valve' is to request a suspension of studies so that you can get life back on the rails and feel energized again to return to your research and writing. When you are investigating your practice and values, it's nearly impossible to resist thinking about them and thus your work will continue on your question on some level but it may take a back seat to life's other demands. And you will probably write, collect data, makes notes about your practice and improvement but not at the same rate and degree or under the same pressure. Suspensions are quite common, usually for six months, but you can request a longer time if needed.

e. Support and encouragement
No matter how well-disciplined you are, the process of creating your own-living-educational-theory is a test of perseverance, tenacity and endurance. At times, it will lift you up and fill you with joy and at others, you will feel defeated and frustrated. To keep you moving forward with your wheels on the tracks, you will need support and encouragement from a Culture of Inquiry, critical friends, a supportive community and a validation group.

f. Culture of Inquiry
We have written a full description and explanation of a Culture of Inquiry for the creation of living-educational-theories in Part Two. You will need this space where you can feel safe and respected for your embodied knowledge and comfortable sharing your vulnerabilities. This Culture of Inquiry may be in person or virtual, may be spontaneous or sustained and may include as few as 2 and as many as 20 individuals. A spontaneous group may emerge out of the time allocated for course work, from a conference, from your workplace or with your supervisor. However, it may be necessary for you to take the lead and invite other researchers to join you in a location set aside for empathetic listening and appreciative inquiry. It's important to spend the time in the beginning to agree on meeting frequency, confidentiality (especially if video recording is involved) and building the relationships.

g. Critical friends
Your critical friends may be part of your living theory Culture of Inquiry or not. In any case, you will need one or more individuals who are willing from time to time to read, respond and discuss your research and writing. Expectations for the critical friend need to be set early in the process so that both of you are in agreement that the feedback requested will be accepted with an openness to criticism without it be viewed as a personal attack. Having said that, an appreciative response can be included in the critique and suggestions for strengthening the research. The more specific the responses from the critical friend, the more useful they will be for moving your work forward.

h. One critical friend might be knowledgeable about your field of inquiry (Healthcare); another, the expectations and process of a doctorate; another, a good editor.

i. Supportive community
We mentioned above the need to consult with your family and friends before you embark on a PhD. You will need their

encouragement and support. And when you say that you can't join them for some event, they will understand that for this period of time, you will need to focus your time and efforts on creating your own-living-educational-theory.

We have found that if you share the nature of your research and that you will need their help in wanting to improve your practice and in holding yourself accountable for living according to your values, most people are inspired by the approach and want to be involved.

j. Validation Group
In Part Two, we covered most of the information around a Validation Group of about five individuals with relationships connected to either your site of practice or your academic world. All they need to play this role is the time and willingness to help you, some expertise in either part of your thesis, (your work or academia), and an inquiring mind. The frequency of meeting in real time or virtually depends on when you need help in strengthening your research and their availability. In a Validation Group meeting, you will need to video record the session (with permission) or have someone to take notes since there will be so much valuable information for you to retain for reflection later. To retain the support of your Validation Group, you will need to respond to their review of your work so that they feel that you are listening, receiving and incorporating their suggestions. This is not to say that you must feel obliged to automatically make the suggested changes. It may be that this serves as an opportunity to pursue the ideas posed, challenge assumptions and sometimes, to defend your position. Drawing on Habermas' (1976, pp. 1–2) criteria of social validity, a Validation Group is often asked for suggestions on how to strengthen the comprehensibility, evidence, sociocultural and sociohistorical understandings and authenticity of the explanations of educational influences in learning.

Here is an example from Delong's PhD thesis:

Public presentation and accountability

a. Validation Groups:

I have searched for and found a number of opportunities for presentation of my research at given points in time and in search of informed responses. I have taken advantage of times when groups of academics have been in Ontario together for presenting papers for feedback and response and they have been very accommodating. The most committed of these groups has been my validation group which was established at the time of my research proposal in 1996. It consisted originally of Dr Tom Russell, Queen's University, Dr Linda Grant, Manager of Standards of Practice, Ontario College of Teachers, Dr Andre Dolbec, University of Quebec at Hull, Dr Jean McNiff, University of West England, UK, Dr Ron Wideman, Nipissing University, and Peter Moffatt, Director, Grand Erie District School Board. Dr Fran Squire, Project Manager, Ontario College of Teachers, Marg Couture, Executive Assistant ETFO, Darrell Reeder, Psychologist and Cheryl Black, Teacher and Vice-Principal, Grand Erie District School Board were added at later dates as willing volunteers.

> Issues of bias and distortion have been addressed by British researchers who have a longer tradition of engaging with problems associated with administrator research. Lomax, Woodward, and Parker (1996) establish the importance of validation meetings in which ongoing findings are defended before one or more "critical friends" who serve as a king of devil's advocate.
>
> (Anderson & Jones, 2000)

This validation process is clearly explicated by Michael Erben (1998a) in his reader on biography:

> The validation of such research (in fact, of any research) is based upon the degree of consensus among those for whom the investigation is thought to be of interest and relevance. The descriptions, organization, conclusions and formulations represented in the research receive their validation by an experienced group of peers who regard the study as significant, worthwhile and in concert with its aims.
>
> It is clear that one of the advantages of biographical research is that the variety that is the life of the subject will guide researchers against too rigid a view of methodology. As a number of methodologists have commented (e.g. Erickson, 1986); Wolcott, 1992) too concentrated a focus on research techniques can dull the

understanding of the relationship between method and purpose of the investigation. The useful comment of Geertz's that, 'man is an animal suspended in webs of significance he himself has spun' indicates the reciprocal, constitutive nature of object and subject (Gertz, 1973, p. 5). As such, the interpretive requirement is that the complex life-accounts of research subjects be studied, described and appreciated using as varied a repertoire of investigative approaches as would any cultural texts.

(pp. 4–5)

Jackie continues her Validation process: The Validation exercise occurred on three occasions. The first was held at the Act Reflect Revise Forum on 27 February 1997, when Jack convened my Validation Group to respond to "My Learnings Through Action Research." At the second meeting on 3 December 1998, I presented a paper, "Seeking An Understanding of Influence By Representing And Explaining My Life" to my Validation Group for reaction. The third validation group met on 17 February 2000 in Brantford at the Act Reflect Revise Conference IV to review my paper "My Epistemology of the Superintendency." At each meeting, I noted suggestions for improvement and made amendments to my writing and thinking so that each time there was evidence of improvement. Each session was audio or videotaped and transcribed. And while the group did not meet formally, I shared my "My Living Educational Theory: My Standards of Practice/Standards of Judgment" (2001) paper, with Cheryl Black, Jack Whitehead, Dr Michael Manley-Casimir and the Brock-Grand Erie masters group and received feedback that I have incorporated into this thesis. These papers are included in Part A of the Appendices.

In addition, for the 27 July 1998 Transfer Seminar I wrote a paper, made written responses to questions posed by Dr Hugh Lauder, Chair of the Research Committee at Bath, met with the Head of Graduate Studies and presented an oral seminar to the University of Bath Research Committee.

(Delong, 2002, pp. 314–317)

We move now to the developments in the philosophical base from Part Two to Part Three.

3.2 Developments in the Philosophical Base from Part Two to Part Three

The developments in the philosophical base from Part Two to Part Three is organised under the following sub-headings:

i. The standards of judgement
ii. The logic of an explanation of educational influence in learning

Our supervision of Living Educational Theory research inquiries is grounded, as in the previous Parts, in explorations of the implications of asking, researching and answering questions of the kind, "How do I improve what I am doing?". The development in the philosophical base of our supervision in Part Three is focused on the nature of an original contribution to knowledge in a Living Educational Theory research thesis. Hence, we clarify below the epistemology, or theory of knowledge, in supervision for the generation of an original contribution to Living Educational Theory research.

We think that it is worth emphasising that in the generation of their own living-educational-theory the researcher also generates their unique living-educational-theory methodology in the course of its emergence in the production of their living-educational-theory. Each unique living-educational-theory methodology can draw insights from other methodologies such as autoethnography, action research, self-study and narrative inquiry. We are emphasising this point to avoid the application of a pre-existing research methodology to the inquiry.

In producing an original contribution to knowledge, in the field of Living Educational Theory research, the researcher justifies the claim of originality in relation to existing knowledge in the field. This involves a critical and creative engagement with the existing knowledge in Living Educational Theory research and with the theories of other researchers and research methodologies that have been used in the generation of a living-educational-theory.

In generating a doctoral thesis, as an original contribution to knowledge in the field of Living Educational Theory research, it is important to recognise that we are focusing on the award of Doctor of Philosophy. In the award of such a degree by the University of Lancaster, UK, to Dr Arianna Briganti, the certificate specifies that the degree of Doctor of Philosophy is in International Development and Living Educational Theory. In our supervision, we focus on the contribution of the doctoral thesis to **Living Educational Theory** research, while recognising that the doctoral thesis can also make an original contribution to other forms or fields of knowledge. We share below the process of making a doctoral research proposal to a university as a necessary condition for researchers who wish to undertake doctoral research.

In our supervisions, we focus on enabling the researcher to generate their explanation of their educational influences in learning. The explanatory principles are the unique constellation of relationally dynamic values (see below) that the individual uses to give meaning and purpose to their practice. These are clarified in the course of their emergence in practice. In a doctoral thesis, the explanations must relate to the ideas of others in establishing its contribution to knowledge. This involves a critical engagement with these ideas. We are including the following reference to Michael Bassey (1991) because Bassey points to the dangers of inappropriate engagements with the ideas of others that he refers to as 'genuflecting', 'sandbagging' and 'kingmaking'. And an admonition, "The purpose of references should be to support the claim to knowledge of the paper, not the claim of the author to be well-read!"

We have stressed that a doctoral thesis is an original contribution to knowledge and this must be justified in the thesis. At the heart of justifying an original contribution to knowledge is its epistemology, in the sense of its theory of knowledge. We use three ideas to distinguish an epistemology. These ideas are the unit of appraisal, the standards of judgment and the logic in the contribution to knowledge.

The unit of appraisal is what is being judged. In Living Educational Theory research. The unit is the individual's explanation of their educational influences in their own learning, in the learning of others and in the learning of the social formations that influence practice and understanding. Because we think that this unit is clear and unambiguous, we shall concentrate on: (i) clarifying the standards of judgement we use in our supervision of the evolution of the explanations of educational influences in learning: the unique constellation of relationally dynamic values that constitute the explanatory principles in the explanations and the standards of judgement and (ii) the living logics that are used to judge the validity of a claim to be making an original contribution to knowledge. The logic of the explanation is the mode of thought appropriate for comprehending the real as rational. That is, it follows the rules of a logical argument and makes sense to the reader. The logic is important as it establishes the claim that the contribution to knowledge fulfils an explicit criterion of rationality while recognising that there are different forms of rationality (MacIntyre, 1988).

3.2.1 The Standards of Judgement

The standards of judgement we use to judge the validity of our claims to know our educational influences in learning are focused on the validity of the explanatory principles we use in our explanations of educational influence. At the heart of our explanatory principles are our understandings of the relationally dynamic values that constitute the values-laden nature of our educational relationships and educational influences.

3.2.1.1 Clarifying and Using Values as Explanatory Principles

To distinguish something as educational involves a judgement of approval and value. Ontological values are the values we use to give life its meaning and purpose. Each individual has their own unique constellation of such values. They are relationally dynamic in the sense that they are engaged in the continuous flow of the inquiry, "How do I improve what I am doing?". For example, values such as freedom, justice and responsibility are lived by many of the researchers we have supervised. These values are not independent of each other. Our freedom to do what we want can conflict with our responsibility to value the freedom of others. Our responsibility to support social justice can also conflict with supporting an individual's freedom to do what they want to do. In our own research we value being loved into learning (Campbell, 2011), Cultures of Inquiry (Delong, 2002) and academic freedom (Whitehead, 1993). Others we have supervised have used the following values as explanatory principles: social justice, care, compassion, loving recognition, respectful connectedness, exquisite connectivity, educational responsibility, guiltless recognition, societal reidentification, an inclusive, emancipating and egalitarian society, and international development. For example, Huxtable communicates her unique constellation of relationally dynamic ontological values:

> This thesis offers an original contribution to knowledge as a multimedia narrative. It communicates my ontological values of

a loving recognition, respectful connectedness and educational responsibility, and social values of an inclusive, emancipating and egalitarian society. I clarify meanings of my values, as they emerge within living-boundaries through the evolution of my living-theory praxis, to form explanatory principles and living standards of judgment in my claim to know my practice.

(Huxtable, 2012)

Because the meanings of such values are fundamental to a living-educational-theory, it is important to check with others that the meanings are clear and justified. For this reason the submission of explanations of educational influence, in which the values are used as explanatory principles, for strengthening in regular meetings of validation groups is so important. The validation groups enable the values to be clarified and justified in ways that can be comprehended and criticised by others, through the mutual rational controls of critical discussion (Popper, 1975, p. 44). Because of the importance of public criticism during the course of some five to seven years of part-time commitment, we advocate the submission of proposals for presentation to conferences such as the International Professional Development Association (IPDA), the Action Research Network of the America (ARNA), the Collaborative Action Research Network (CARN), the American Educational Research Association (AERA), the British Educational Research Association (BERA), Action Learning Action Learning Association (ALARA) and the Association of Teacher Education in Europe (ATEE). Each of these Associations has associated journals and we advocate the submission of both proposals and papers to these conferences and journals. This gives the researcher the opportunity to test out their ideas in public forums over the course of their research and provides evidence to support one of the criteria for a doctoral thesis that it should contain matter worthy of publication, but it may not be presented in a form ready for publication. Accepted papers for publications can be included as Appendices in the doctoral thesis to support this criterion.

The ontological values we use to give our lives meaning and purpose, and that we use as explanatory principles in our explanations of educational influence, may not immediately come to mind as academic standards of judgment. Love, for example, as an explanatory principle, in the sense of loving what we are doing, is an ontological value embraced by many of the researchers we have worked with, including ourselves.

For example, Jackie stresses her dialogical way of being in explaining her educational influences in learning and the importance of 'being loved into learning' in her educational relationships. Both of us identify with Ortrun Zuber-Skerritt's point about building on love and working through local and global action to connect us with each other as human beings and with nature:

> ... I have argued that we need to shift away from the mindset of neoliberalism and reductionism dominating our present society and driving its obsession with consumerism, power and control. Instead we need a collaborative, participative and inclusive paradigm built on love and working through local and global action to connect us with each other as human beings and with nature. Society needs to be renewed by making a shift from the negative energy of fear, competition, control and war to the positive energy of faith, love, hope and creativity. Clearly, we need to conceptualize and practice not just learning conferences but Loving Learning Conferences.
> (Zuber-Skerritt, 2017, p. 224)

Continuing on this topic of love, Skolimowski (1994) lists some of the main characteristics of a participatory research program and points to love as the deepest form of participation:

Love is the deepest form of participation.
Where there is love there is participation.
Loveless participation is an anaemic involvement.
To participate is the first step to loving.
(p. 159)

We recognise that the inclusion of love within a research program may be too much for minds trained in the rigors of objectivity. Yet, we both recognise the importance of love in loving what we are doing. Lohr's (2006) doctoral thesis on "Love at Work" uses Love as an explanatory principle and living standard of judgment. We also identify most strongly with the way Cho (2005) focuses on the work of Freire (1998, p. 22) where love in an educational relationship enables both student and teacher to preserve the distinctiveness of their positions by turning away from one another and towards the world in order to produce knowledge through inquiry and thought. We mentioned this in Part Two and think that it bears repeating:

> ...love means the pursuit of real knowledge, knowledge that is no longer limited to particular content passed from one to the other, but rather knowledge that can only be attained by each partner seeking it in the world. To put this differently, knowledge is by definition the inquiry we make into the world, which is a pursuit inaugurated by a loving encounter with a teacher. With love, education becomes an open space for thought from which emerges knowledge.
>
> (Cho, 2005, p. 95)

We find that multimedia narratives with digital video for clarifying and communicating meanings of embodied expressions of ontological values such as love and encourage students to do the same. In an article (Whitehead, 2013), Jack focused on the use of a multimedia narrative to communicate the meaning of the expression of embodied values of loved into learning with Jacqueline Delong, Liz Campbell and Cathy Griffin:

> We do not want to overload you with all the material in the following video, but we hope that you will access minutes 11:14 to 12:33 of Jackie, Liz and Jack in a conversation about our inquiry and presentation for the American Educational Research Association
>
> (p. 14)

Video 3.1. Loved into Learning A
http://www.youtube.com/watch?v=5MPXeJMc0gU
During minutes 11:14 to 12:33, the conversation consists of:

> Jack: Your phrase, loved into learning ... you experienced this being loved into learning with Jackie and possibly some of the other participants on the master's programme. [Liz is nodding and smiling.]
>
> Jack (11:34): Could I just check that? It seemed very important because I don't think Jackie and myself have focused on Jackie's influence in those terms, yet it seemed really important to you that you had experienced that loved into learning that you were able then to communicate, I think, to your own students.
>
> Liz (12:01): That's exactly the point I was trying to make, Jack, and I have written about it before in different pieces in my master's and in something I did in your class, Jackie.

Jackie: Yes. Liz: I don't know if I actually called it loved into learning, but that is my concise way of explaining what happened. I was introduced to the idea of being loved into learning in a conversation where Cathy and Liz explained Jackie's influence in their learning for their master's degree in terms of being loved into learning.

Video 3.2: Loved into Learning B
http://www.youtube.com/watch?v=qcDSqryJ6Jg

The image at 1:35 minutes of the 9:45-minute clip above is taken where we are talking about being loved into learning. If you move the cursor backwards and forwards around 1:35 minutes you may experience the empathetic resonance (Huxtable, 2009) of Liz's, Cathy's, Jackie's and Jack's energy-flowing value of being loved into learning.

To communicate our embodied expressions of meaning, we need both the visual data showing the expressions above and our linguistic expression of being loved into learning. Liz and Cathy also brought into Jackie's awareness the quality of loving into learning they experienced in Jackie's tutoring (Whitehead, 2013, pp.14–15).

Jack needed a relationally dynamic value that grounded his educational relationships within social formations. Joy Mounter (2019) provided this relationally dynamic value in her understanding of ~i~we~I~us~ relationships:

> ~i~we~I~us~ relationships as a relational value used as an explanatory principle in explanations of educational influence in learning.
>
> ~i~we~I~us~ as a relational value is key to understanding my thesis and a thread that permeates each aspect of my original contributions to knowledge. Explored in-depth in chapter three, as the reader you will see the thread evident throughout each chapter. Living Educational Theory as a form of self-study research holds the practitioner, their practice and the educational influences they have in a place of shared mutuality, refining ontological values as life-affirming energy and standards of judgement (Whitehead, 2012). Living Theory as a research methodology engenders a sense of community at its heart through the very nature of the research, as you look at your influences in your own learning, the learning of others and the social formations you are part of. Social validity and rigour is also ensured through Popper's (1975) view that objectivity is grounded in intersubjective criticism and drawing from Habermas' (1976) questions to ensure the social validation.

Living Theory is synonymous with my sense of relationships needed within a researching community.

I have developed my understanding of ~i~we~I~us~ through the African understanding of Unbuntu. Tutu (2012) describes this relational dynamic, between self and being part of something bigger, relationships within community as, "I need you, in order for me to be me; I need you to be you to the fullest." I also draw on and develop the research of Whitehead and Huxtable (2015) who discuss how the 'I' in self, is 'distinct, unique and relational', which exists in an 'inclusive, emancipating and egalitarian relationship'. Huxtable (2012) further defines the "trustworthy, respectful, co-creative spaces," where the world of researchers practice, questions and values touch. This space is then represented as the tilde or ~ within i~we~i.

We use 'i' and 'we' to point to a relationship where individuals and collectives are neither subordinated nor dominant but exist in an inclusive, emancipating and egalitarian relationship.

We use ~ to stand for living-boundaries (Huxtable, 2012): trustworthy, respectful, co-creative space, where individuals, collectives and the complex worlds of practice, knowledge and socio-historical cultures they inhabit and embody, touch.

(Huxtable & Whitehead, 2015)

My own thinking and sense of self is defined by Huxtable and Whitehead's (2015) relational 'i' and by my self-identity 'I', not as an egotistical 'I' Huxtable (2012), rather 'I' as in 'I am important, QUIFF, central to the learning theory the children developed, the importance of a sense of self (Mounter, 2008b) developed in community with relation to others.'

At the heart of our ontological values is a flow of life-affirming energy. Both of us recognise the importance of including a flow of life-affirming energy as an explanatory principle and living standard of judgement in our understandings and communications of the ontological values we use as explanatory principles in our explanations of educational influences in learning. We accept Vasilyuk's (1991) point about the importance of such energy in his 'Energy Paradigm':

Conceptions involving energy are very current in psychology, but they have been very poorly worked out from the methodological standpoint. It is not clear to what extent these conceptions are merely models of our understanding and to what extent they can be given ontological status. Equally problematic are the conceptual links between energy and motivation, energy and meaning, energy and value, although it is obvious that in fact there are certain links: we know how 'energetically' a person can act when positively motivated, we know that the meaningfulness of a project lends additional strength to the people engaged in it, but we have very little idea of how to link up into one whole the physiological theory of activation, the psychology of motivation, and the ideas of energy which have been elaborated mainly in the field of physics.

(Vasilyuk, pp. 63–64)

We understand that each individual has their own unique constellation of energy-flowing values that they use as explanatory principles and living standards of judgement in evaluating the validity of their claims to be making a contribution to educational knowledge. Each one of us, in our Living Educational Theory research needs to find an appropriate form of representation for communicating our meanings to others. We identify with Boland's understanding of spirituality as a relation between the individual and the cosmos. We would add that our expression of spirituality in our supervisory relationships is accompanied by the expression of our life-affirming energy:

I here take spirituality as something separate from religion. Religion (for me) is a defined system of belief or worship (see Thayer-Bacon, 2017). This is not what I am talking about. I use the term spirituality here to define the link between the human being and what I would call the cosmos.

(Boland, 2020, p. 4)

You may be able to identify and understanding our meanings of a flow of life-affirming energy at 1 min 25 seconds of the following clip from a supervisory conversation between Jackie and Jack.
Video 3. Life-affirming energy
https://www.youtube.com/watch?v=w2kdOfRKFYs
The context was a supervision session at the University of Bath in which Jackie was presenting a redrafted Abstract to Jack for her doctoral thesis. The phone rang, Jack answered it and commended the wisdom of the caller in relation to his research. On returning to Jackie, Jackie responded with the question, "I don't think that you will acknowledging my wisdom will you?" Jack's immediate response

was "No"! This evoked the explosion of laughter between us shown on the clip that is expressing the flow of life-affirming energy that we express in our educational relationships and research and need to include in our explanations of educational influences in learning.

In justifying a claim to have made an original contribution to knowledge, we have focused on the importance of defining the unit of appraisal as the explanation given by the individual to explain their educational influences in their own learning, in the learning of others and in the learning of the social formations that influence practice and understandings. We have also focused on the importance of clarifying and communicating the relationally dynamic constellation of values that are used as explanatory principles in the explanations of educational influences in learning. We now turn to the importance of the logic of the explanation in the sense that logic is the mode of thought that is appropriate for comprehending the real as rational (Marcuse, 1964, p. 105).

3.2.2 The Logic of an Explanation of Educational Influence in Learning

Because there are different logics that underpin different views of rationality, we encourage Living Educational Theory researchers to distinguish between propositional, dialectical and participatory, or living logics. First, propositional logics can be framed as a statement that can be either true or false; it must be one or the other, and it cannot be both. As an example, in propositional logic the statements, 'I am free/I am not free', cannot both be true simultaneously. Contradictions are, however, the nucleus of dialectics and have focused disagreements over 2,500 years between formal and dialectical logicians. We agree with Marcuse (1964) when he says that propositional logic conceals the dialectical nature of reality:

> In the classical logic, the judgement which constituted the original core of dialectical thought was formalized in the propositional form, 'S is p.' But this form conceals rather than reveals the basic dialectical proposition, which states the negative character of the empirical reality.
>
> (p. 111)

In answering his question, "What is Dialectic?", Popper (1963) rejects dialectical claims to knowledge as, *"without the slightest foundation.*

Indeed, they are based on nothing better than a loose and woolly way of speaking" (p. 316). He demonstrates, using two laws of inference, that if a theory contains a contradiction, then it entails everything, and therefore, indeed, nothing. He says that a theory which adds to every information which it asserts also the negation of this information, can give us no information at all. *A Theory which involves a contradiction is therefore entirely useless as a theory* (p. 317).

We disagree with this point that Popper makes about contradiction because we experience ourselves as living contradictions in our inquiries, "How do I improve what I am doing?" in the sense that we hold together, in our experience, some of our ontological values together with their negation. We understand that Popper is referring to linguistic statements and accepts Aristotle's Law of Contradiction that claims that two mutually exclusive statements cannot both be true simultaneously. In Living Educational Theory research, living contradictions are included in explanations of educational influences in learning, Ostensive expressions of meaning that communicate such embodied experience, are combined with linguistic statements to communicate the meanings of explanations of educational influences in learning that include contradictions.

In embracing living contradictions, in the logic of our explanations of educational influences in learning, we have been influenced by the ideas of Ilyenkov (1977) in his work on dialectical logic, where he asks, "If any object is a living contradiction what must the thought (statement about the object) be that expresses it":

> Contradiction as the concrete unity of mutually exclusive opposites is the real nucleus of dialectics, its central category. On that score there cannot be two views among Marxists; but no small difficulty immediately arises as soon as matters touch on 'subjective dialectics', on dialectics as the logic of thinking. If any object is a living contradiction, what must the thought (statement about the object) be that expresses it? Can and should an objective contradiction find reflection in thought? And if so, in what form?
>
> Contradiction in the theoretical determinations of an object is above all a fact that is constantly being reproduced by the movement of science, and is not denied by dialectics or by materialists or idealists. The point that they dispute is something else, namely: what is the relationship of the contradiction in thought to the object? In other words, can there be a contradiction in true, correct thought?
>
> (p. 313)

In the generation of our living-educational-theories we use insights from both propositional and dialectical theories. However, when explaining educational influences in the learning of social formations, we need to go beyond both of these forms of rationality in developing our participatory or living logics.

Our participatory/living logics have much in common with Thayer-Bacon's (2003) relational perspective of knowing:

> My project is one of analysis and critique, as well as redescription. What I offer is one pragmatist social feminist view, a relational perspective of knowing, embedded within a discussion of many other relational views. In Relational "(e)pistemologies," I seek to offer a feminist (e)pistemological theory that insists that knowers/subjects are fallible, that our criteria are corrigible (capable of being corrected), and that our standards are socially constructed, and thus continually in need of critique and reconstruction. I offer a self-conscious and reflective (e)pistemological theory, one that attempts to be adjustable and adaptable as people gain further in understanding. This (e)pistemology must be inclusive and open to others, because of its assumption of fallible knowers. And this (e)pistemology must be capable of being corrected because of its assumption that our criteria and standards are of this world, ones we, as fallible knowers, socially construct.
>
> (2003, p. 7)

The concepts of a relational perspective of knowing knowers/subjects are fallible, that our criteria are corrigible (capable of being corrected), and that our standards are socially constructed, and thus continually in need of critique and reconstruction, resonate with us in that they help us explain our relational ways of knowing and our uncertainty about standards of knowing and judging.

Following these developments in the philosophical base from Parts Two to Three, just to reframe the chapter, we focus on:

4. Master's to PhD: what's changed?

    4.1. Criteria for PhD

    4.2. Living Educational Theory Master's to PhD

    4.3. Other Master's to Living Educational Theory PhD

    4.4. Writing your doctoral research proposal

  i. Christine Jones' successful Research Proposal to Liverpool Hope University

  ii. Writing your transfer report
    Christine Jones' successful Transfer Report to Liverpool Hope University

 4.5. Range of different professional contexts and inquiries addressed by Living Educational Theory researchers

 4.6. An Example of a PhD Ethical Approval

 4.7. Programs of Study

  i. Course Work

  ii. Thesis

  iii. Viva

5. Approximate Timelines and Schedule of Research
6. Available resources

 6.1. Free libraries

 6.2. Other texts

Next, we address what's changed from your Master's to a PhD degree, give an example of a proposal, a transfer report and an ethical approval. This is followed by programs of study, timelines and some resources.

3.3 Master's to PhD: What's Changed?

There are a number of changes in moving from a taught master's to a doctoral research programme. The commitment of time is important. Because a living-educational-theory is based on practice, the course work for a master's takes a minimum of a year and the dissertation can be completed within one year. The course work and thesis for a doctorate can take a minimum of five years of part-time research. This is because a Living Educational Theory research doctorate is grounded in the educational workplace practices of the researcher and includes the generation of an original contribution to knowledge.

 Supervision for a doctorate is different from tutoring for a master's programme. A doctoral supervisor must have the competence to supervise a doctoral thesis to successful completion. This usually means that at least one of your supervisors should be competent to supervise a Living Educational Theory research programme. You can find that such supervisors have been acknowledged in the doctoral theses at https://www.actionresearch.net/living/living.shtml. If you are having problems finding an appropriate supervisor, you could contact members of the Editorial Board of the Educational Journal of Living Theories from https://ejolts.net/editorial, for advice.

Over more than five years of part-time research for a doctorate, you are likely to find a supportive community of Living Educational Theory researchers is of great help in sustaining your motivation for your inquiry. You could share your inquiries with individuals and communities who participated in the first International, Living Educational Theory Research Conference:

http://www.spanglefish.com/livingtheoryresearchgathering/index.asp

You could check out their contexts and research interests from the living-posters at:

https://www.actionresearch.net/writings/posters/participants2020conference.pdf

You may also contact people who may be interested in helping you with the formation of a validation group or with developing proposals for presentation at conferences such as those of The Action Research Network of the Americas (ARNA), The International Professional Development Association (IPDA); The Collaborative Action Research Network (CARN); The British Educational Research Association (BERA); The American Educational Research Association (AERA); The Association of Teacher Education in Europe (ATEE); The Action Learning Action Research Association (ALARA). Each of these organisations publish papers in their own affiliated journals and provide you with the opportunity to develop a research presentation at a conference into a submission for consideration for publication in a journal.

3.3.1 Criteria for PhD

The criteria used by the examiners of a doctoral thesis, appointed by a university, usually include an original contribution to knowledge, a critical engagement with relevant literature, a coherent research methodology and material worthy of publication although it need not be presented in a form that is ready for publication in the thesis.

In a Living Educational Theory doctorate the original contribution to knowledge is focused on the explanation of educational influences in the researchers' own learning, in the learning of others and in the learning of the social formations that influence practice and understanding. These explanations are values-laden and each Living Educational Theory researcher has their own unique constellation of relationally dynamic values that they use as explanatory principles in their explanation of educational influence in learning.

In terms of the methodology, used in a Living Educational Theory thesis, it is important to recognise that this methodology is generated in the course of the inquiry rather than being pre-specified and applied in the inquiry. This methodology is clarified and communicated in the course of its emergence in the inquiry in practice.

3.3.2 Living Educational Theory Master's to PhD

For researchers who are moving from a Living Educational Theory Masters to a PhD programme, the transition can be seen as part of continuous process in the generation of a living-educational-theory. If you are such a researcher, you could immediately focus on the writing of a research proposal for a doctorate (see the illustration of Chris Jones' proposal below).

3.3.3 Other Master's to Living Educational Theory PhD

For researchers who are moving from a Master's using another methodology to a Living Educational Theory PhD, the writing of a Living Educational Theory doctorate proposal requires a transformation in thinking. The transformation is focused on grounding the doctoral inquiry in questions of the kind, "How do I improve my practice?". The grounding of a research proposal in your 'I' as a practitioner and researcher, rather than in the conceptual theories of other people, does require a willingness to make the decision that is fundamental to the generation of a living-educational-theory. Polanyi (1958) has described the decision of Personal Knowledge, "I must understand the world from my point of view, as a person claiming originality and exercising his personal judgement responsibly with universal intent" (p. 327).

For those wishing to register for a Living Educational Theory doctorate from a traditional master's programme, we recommend Parts One, Two and Three of this book.

Next, we share an example of a proposal and a transfer report.

3.3.4 Writing Your Doctoral Research Proposal

In writing a doctoral research proposal, it is wise to be aware of which Universities you are likely to submit your proposal to. Each University will have guidelines on what they are expecting in a research proposal that are available from their webpage. They will also provide details of the areas of research they are wanting to supervise and have expertise in.

All universities are wanting to support doctoral research programmes that make an original contribution to knowledge. Hence, your proposal should define a clear question with a section on the originality and significance of the contribution to knowledge you wish to make. You should be clear about the methodological approach you intend to take. In a Living Theory research inquiry, it is important to acknowledge that a living-educational-theory methodology emerges in the course of generating a valid explanation of educational influences in learning. This living-theory-methodology draws insights from existing methodologies such as self-study, action research, narrative inquiry and autoethnography. You should also provide details of the literature in the field that you will creatively and critically engage with.

You can evaluate your own proposal by asking:

- Have I positioned my research (approximately 900 words) through discussing the texts that I believe are most important to my research in way that demonstrates my understanding of the research issues and points to my original contribution to knowledge?
- Have I described clearly my research design and methodology (approximately 900 words) that will structure my research together with specific methods that I intend to use? Does my research design include a definition of my subject matter that gives some indication of the originality of the research as a contribution to your field of inquiry? Does my discussion of methodology include the overall approach with the reasons for using this approach?
- Have I provided the reader of my proposal with a clear understanding of the context in which my research is located and with specific details of the individuals and groups I will be researching with?
- Have I referred to the ethical guidelines I am following, for example, those of the British Educational Research Association? These are available from https://www.bera.ac.uk/publication/ethical-guidelines-for-educational-research-2018

An initial registration at a University for an MPhil/PhD programme requires an accepted research proposal before supervisors can be appointed. This can take several months. Having said this, it is wise to have a supervisor in mind. After registration is completed, research begins. A transfer report will be submitted some two to three years into a five-year part-time research programme when the PhD registration is confirmed. Because of the practitioner nature of creating a living-educational-theory, most programmes are part-time. The qualities of a successful transfer report are considered after the following successful research proposal from Christine Jones. First the proposal.

i. **Christine Jones' successful Research Proposal to Liverpool Hope University**

"How do I promote inclusion through living my values and developing living standards of judgement to which I hold myself accountable?".

The successful proposal was organised as follows:

- Context/Background
- Research Focus, rationale and draft research questions
- Research Methods
- Methodology
- Contribution to Knowledge
- References
- Supporting Statement
  You can access the proposal at:
  http://www.actionresearch.net/writings/jones/chrisjonesproposal.pdf

ii. Writing your Transfer Report

Christine Jones' successful Confirmation/Transfer Report to Liverpool Hope University.

Title - How Do I Promote Inclusion by Living My Values and Developing Standards of Judgement to which I Hold Myself Accountable (Working title of Thesis)

This paper is submitted as part of the process of confirming my PhD registration

Introduction

I am a practitioner-researcher enquiring into my practice. At present, I am a Statutory Special Educational Needs (SEN) manager working within the Education Inclusion Service. At the time of my inquiry, significant changes are taking place which are having a huge impact on the public sector and consequently, Local Authority Children's Services in which I work. In 2010, the Coalition Government came into being, and since then we have seen the introduction of schools becoming Academies and Free Schools developing, with responsibilities being placed more with schools than Local Authorities. In the world of Special Educational Needs, a world in which I have spent my career, the biggest changes within the last thirty years are being introduced by the government and these are to take place over the next few years.

The Local Authority in which I work is making a financial cut of thirty million pounds over the next three years. Subsequently, this is having an impact on the Children's Services and Education Inclusion Service of which I am a part with a significant reorganisation taking place over the coming year. It is within these national and local changes that I am undertaking my inquiry.

This paper clarifies my research to date and it has been organised in line with the guidance on the university's PhD Confirmation Event:

- Aims of my Inquiry
- Literature Review
- Methodology
- Interim Findings and Outcomes
- Proposed Structure of Thesis
- Bibliography
- Appendices

You can access the confirmation/transfer report to a PhD registration at:

http://www.actionresearch.net/writings/jones/chrisjonestransfer.pdf

We move now to looking at the possible range of Living Educational Theory inquiries.

3.3.5 Range of Different Professional Contexts and Inquiries Addressed by Living Educational Theory Researchers

We now provide you with the details and access to Doctoral theses to show the range of different professional contexts and inquiries addressed by Living Educational Theory researchers. You can access the full range at https://www.actionresearch.net/living/living.shtml. These include:

i. Inclusive and Inclusional Empowerment
ii. International Development Practice
iii. Enhancing Cosmopolitanism
iv. The work of a community volunteer
v. Public Health
vi. Enhancing Economic Independence
vii. Environmental Activism
viii. From Engineer to Co-Creative Catalyst
ix. Moving Beyond Decolonisation
x. Improving a multi-professional and multi-agency healthcare setting
xi. Improving health visiting support
xii. Presencing aesthetic and spiritual being

Because of constraints of space, we have only included below the full Abstract for:

i. International Development Practice
ii. Enhancing Cosmopolitanism
iii. The work of a community volunteer

iv. Public Health
v. Engineer and a Co-Creative Catalyst in generating organizational change

We have pulled out five examples of Living Educational Theory PhDs to show a range of sites of practice, inquiries, professions, countries and contexts. The first, from Arianna Briganti in international contexts including Afghanistan, shows the generation of a living-theory of international development with the values of human flourishing of the relationally dynamic values of empathy, social and gender justice, outrage, responsibility, love for and faith in humanity and dignity.

1. https://www.actionresearch.net/living/ABrigantiphd.pdf
   Ariana Briganti's (2020) doctorate on My living-theory of International Development. University of Lancaster.
2. https://www.actionresearch.net/writings/keizer/keizer.pdf
   Anne Keizer-Remmer's doctorate on – Underneath The Surface of Cosmopolitanism: In search of Cosmopolitanism In Higher Education. University of Humanistic Studies, Utrecht, the Netherlands, 2017.

> Writing a doctoral thesis is a puzzling endeavour. It is like embarking on an expedition with a fair idea about the destination, the route to follow, and the duration of the journey. One starts out with a more or less coherent itinerary, clear stops on the route, and a well-defined end in mind – only to find out that it has seemingly autonomously evolved into a completely different expedition; it develops as it goes along and becomes something one has neither anticipated nor planned. In my case, I set off on a quest to find cosmopolitans, but instead encountered myself as a "living contradiction" (Whitehead, 2000, p. 93). As such, this exploration has benefited from a metamorphosis from a post-positivist rationalistic plan to 'prove something' into a participant-led socio-analytic visual study – one that is embedded in an account of a reflective practitioner (Schön, 1983, 1987) as she grapples with cosmopolitanism as an inspirational moral concept for professional higher education. How did this endeavour develop? During my career as a teacher, trainer, consultant, and supervisor it had often struck me how students would overestimate their own capacity to understand, communicate, and work with the culturally Other…

The third, from Bruce Damon, is focused on research that is grounded within community relationships in South Africa with values of mutual respect; equality and inclusion; democratic participation; active learning; making a difference; collective action; and personal integrity.

3. https://www.actionresearch.net/living/damons/damonsphd.pdf
   Bruce Damon's doctorate on – A Collaboratively Constructed Process Model For Understanding And Supporting The Work Of The Community Volunteer In A Community School. 2017 Nelson Mandela Metropolitan University, South Africa.

   The fourth, from Elizabeth Wolvaardt, is grounded in a higher education context in South Africa, with values of care and agency.

4. https://www.actionresearch.net/writings/wolvaardtphd/Wolvaardtphd2013.pdf
   Elizabeth Wolvaardt's Doctoral Thesis, Over the conceptual horizon of public health: A living theory of teaching undergraduate medical students, 2013 University of Pretoria.

   The fifth, from Graham van Tuyl, shows how an educational journey, from being an Engineer and a co-creative catalyst, can have inclusional and transformational influences in organisational change.

5. https://www.actionresearch.net/living/gvt.shtml
   Graham Van Tuyl's Doctoral Thesis, From Engineer To Co-Creative Catalyst: An Inclusional And Transformational Journey, 2009 University of Bath.

   We move now to ethical approval.

3.3.6 An Example of a PhD Ethical Approval

A necessary condition for the acceptance by a university of a research proposal is that the research has ethical approval. You can access Arianna Briganti's successfully completed Research Ethics Application to the University of Cumbria at:

http://www.actionresearch.net/writings/cumbria/cumbriaethicsapproval.pdf

Here are sections 14 and 15 from the full ethical approval document to show the kind of detail that is needed to answer questions on "How will participants be recruited and from where? Be as specific as possible" and "'What procedure is proposed for obtaining consent?"

Doctoral Level Inquiries

14. **How will participants be recruited and from where? Be as specific as possible.**

I will involve those who are part of my practice as a development worker – colleagues, practitioners and beneficiaries from around the world. I will ask them to be involved in my research via email or in person. I will be interviewing them in person (when possible since my research focus on an international activity), via Skype or by using online-questionnaires. Email correspondence is also a means for collecting data. The participants will be able to choose freely whether to take part or not.

15. **What procedure is proposed for obtaining consent?**

I know the vast majority of the people who will be part of my research well, since they have been, and still are, part of my professional life. Hence my aim is to ensure my research maintains an ethical approach to gaining consent and to fully respect them and their opinions on the matters we discuss throughout my research. However, I'm aware of ethical boundaries arising from the fact that we all belong to different cultures and we have different ways of looking at, and understanding, research. The majority of the beneficiaries I work with do not view research as a priority. This is probably because they are often struggling for survival in countries where their basic human rights are neglected. I don't want to, and I will not, violate the cultural boundaries that might lead them to deny consent. Many of those people, particularly women, may not be comfortable with videoing our conversations; many are more likely to prefer to talk informally within the privacy of their own homes and would consider it a lack of respect if I took notes or asked them to fill in a survey. Some are illiterate and in many cases we don't share a common language, so an interpreter would be needed. This is normally a trusted person or family member. However, I have to make the scope of my research clear to the interpreter, and that no harm is intended to those who take part. On the one hand, the presence of the translator (when needed) eases communication and helps me in obtaining consent.

This is why I will use my intercultural competences to explain (mainly orally) what my research is about; and I will have to explain clearly the aim of the research itself to both the beneficiaries and the interpreter. I am also aware that I am in a position of power since I have been working with those people for quite some time and they might consider me as a 'highly respected person'. In many countries, it is not acceptable to say no to such a person, thus I'm extremely careful that their consent is not solely motivated by cultural norms, which could cause them personal discomfort. I aim at always being transparent about that in order to ensure, they as feel as possible to refuse to be part of my inquiry. In the past, what has proved favourable to the beneficiaries' interest (which is my priority) is to guarantee anonymity by using pseudonyms and avoid showing faces while recording. I will always stress that participants are free to withdraw at anytime (this is stated also in the participant consent form), and that I will use video recording or photography if permission is granted to me in writing. Often, the only thing I can do is to take field notes after the conversations to avoid cultural clashes.

In particular, in Afghanistan women do not feel comfortable in being recorded, so I spend time in explaining why I am advocating the use of recording. However, I also clarify that the recording is not compulsory and that we can have our discussion off-camera. Sometimes women agree to being recorded but don't want their faces to be visible.

I engage in the following:

I, both verbally explain my research and provide an easy-to-read synopsis of my research translated into their local language;

I ask all the direct participants in my research to fill in a consent-form explicitly (translated into their local language, if necessary) asking for their consent to use the gathered data. The consent-form will explicitly explain they have the right to anonymity and can withdraw at any time. The participants often give me their oral consent, according to their cultural norms, which endorses an oral agreement more than a written 'contract'. According to those norms it would be culturally insensitive to insist on signing a 'contract', which might be perceived as a lack of trust on my side. In order to avoid this, I accept when participants decide to seal our 'agreement' orally. Trust is at the base of my work as a development practitioner and I don't want to jeopardise my trust relationship with the participants;

I ask for the participants' feedback on the data I collected and my written exposition to ensure that everyone feels transparently represented in my research;

3.3.7 Programs of Study

3.3.7.1 Course Work

Some universities expect students to take courses while others, such as UK universities, do not. For example, Concordia University in Canada, has the following degree requirements:

Fully-qualified candidates are required to complete a minimum of 90 credits.

12 credits – Required Courses
EDUC 806 - Quantitative Methods (3 credits)
   EDUC 807 - Qualitative Methods (3 credits)
   EDUC 808 - Reporting Research (3 credits)
   EDUC 809 - Advanced Issues in Education (3 credits)

9 credits – Elective Courses
12 credits – Comprehensive Examination
   EDUC 890 - Comprehensive Examination (12 credits)

9 credits – Doctoral Proposal
EDUC 891- Doctoral Proposal (9 credits)

48 credits – Doctoral Dissertation
EDUC 895 - Doctoral Dissertation (48 credits)

And, here is a doctoral program at Trent University in Ontario, Canada:

The PhD in Interdisciplinary Social Research (IDSR) builds on Trent University's world-class reputation in interdisciplinary scholarship in the social sciences. With a combined emphasis on social inquiry, interdisciplinary research and professional scholarship, the IDSR PhD provides a theoretical, methodological and experiential training ground for the development of leading scholarship that builds understanding of key social, material and environmental issues facing societies, both historically and in the present day.

Program Features/Highlights

- Doctoral program providing **interdisciplinary and transdisciplinary** approaches to examining complex social issues both historically and in the present day.
- Establish pathways into academic and professional research positions in public, private and civil society sectors, including **education and caring professions, business and management, and the social sciences**
- Mentorship, interdisciplinary and **experiential learning opportunities** with a range of faculty from Trent's social science programs, professional schools and research centres

- Graduates from the program will be positioned to provide **advanced research capacity and leadership** among a wide range of social and professional fields.

Interdisciplinary Social Research PhD website
Program Options
- PhD
- Thesis based program
- Full-time or part-time studies
- Four years of full-time study to complete
- January, September and May program intake

Admission Requirements
- Master's degree in social sciences or a related discipline with at least A- (80%) overall
- A minimum A- (80%) standing on their Master's degree course work
- Demonstrated aptitude for theoretical inquiry and applied scholarship
- An area of intellectual and research interest consonant with the emphasis and aims of the program
- Students are encouraged to identify a faculty member they have determined as a good fit to act as a supervisor. Ideally, prospective students will have made contact with that faculty member in advance of submitting their plan of study and this faculty member has agreed to support the application.

In this program, we understand there is an open book comprehensive exam.

Comprehensive Exam

It is important to note that many universities do not include a comprehensive exam in their requirements. We draw here, from the University of British Columbia (UBC) website, for an example of an exam requirement:

UBC Calendar: http://www.calendar.ubc.ca/vancouver/index.cfm?tree=12,204,342,617

Doctoral Students
From the University of British Columbia Calendar:

> A comprehensive examination [is] normally held after completion of all required coursework. It is intended to test the student's grasp

of the chosen field of study as a whole, and the student's ability to communicate his or her understanding of it in English or in French. The student's committee will set and judge this examination in a manner compatible with the policy of the graduate program concerned. Programs should make available to students a written statement of examination policy and procedures. The comprehensive examination is separate and distinct from the evaluation of the doctoral dissertation prospectus.

Recommended Guidelines For Graduate Programs' Comprehensive Examination Statement

Although all doctoral students in the Faculty of Graduate and Postdoctoral Studies are required to successfully complete a comprehensive examination before being admitted to candidacy, the nature of the examination may vary significantly from graduate program to graduate program. It is important that graduate programs develop and make available to all new doctoral students (and faculty) a written statement clearly outlining their policies and procedures for the examination including; purpose, timing, examination format, examination committee, scope, criteria for evaluation and adjudication.

This document provides details about many of the topics that need to be covered in the program's statement of policies and procedures for the comprehensive exam. The objective is to help ensure that there is consistency in the nature of the comprehensive examination from student to student within a program, absence (and perceived absence) of bias, and overall fairness. The examination must be an academically useful tool and to be consistently of the highest academic standard.

PURPOSE OF EXAM

Clearly outline the purpose of the examination, including an assessment of whether the student has developed:

- strong analytical, problem-solving and critical thinking abilities
- required breadth and in-depth knowledge of the discipline
- required academic background for the specific doctoral research to follow
- potential ability to conduct independent and original research
- ability to communicate knowledge of the discipline

TIMING

- Specify timing of the comprehensive examination, including the earliest and latest dates by which the comprehensive examination must be completed.

- Inform students of the specific dates of their examination so that they have adequate time to prepare. This is crucial because of the importance of the examination and consequences of failure. The examination should be held reasonably early in the program. Students should not spend an unreasonable length of time preparing for it.

- Specify prerequisites for the examination. For example, clarify whether all coursework, laboratory rotations, seminars, etc. must have been completed prior to the examination and whether the examination is the final step before advancement to candidacy.

Examination Format

Clearly state the format of the examination. The format should be consistent for all doctoral students within a particular graduate program. The following list provides some of the more common examination formats used in achieving the purpose of the exam. Some graduate programs combine two or more of these formats or provide an option of more than one format to their students.

Comprehensive exams can include:

- oral examination of the student's knowledge of the field of study
- oral examination of student's knowledge of a series of previously assigned research papers or research topic(s)
- student prepares a research grant proposal which forms the basis of an oral examination (this proposal must not be the dissertation research proposal)
- written examinations
- take-home examination
- student prepares an extended research paper(s)
- student prepares an annotated bibliography
- student develops a syllabus for a course

3.3.7.2 Thesis

The assumed writing-up process is sequential in that the chapters emerge in sequence and subsequent to the data collection and analysis with the abstract written last. What we have found is that the process is messier than that and generally is not in any sequence. It is more likely that you will move in and out of chapters and make notes and attach tabs as they occur to you. It is an interesting exercise to observe how you are making meaning of your research and how the thesis emerges as that is as distinctive as your own-living-theory methodology.

All of the Living Educational Theory doctoral researchers we have worked with, have made a mistake when preparing their thesis for submission. They all believe that they have completed their thesis for submission when what they have done is to produce their first complete *writerly* draft. By this we mean that they have clarified for themselves the nature of their original contribution(s) to knowledge. Before the thesis is submitted, it needs transforming into a *readerly* text in which the aim is to communicate clearly the originality of the thesis to an examiner or other reader. The transformation involves focusing on the original contribution to knowledge that has emerged in the course of the production of the writerly draft. The nature of the originality needs foregrounding in an Abstract and in an Introduction that describes the organisation of the thesis. Each Chapter should begin with a paragraph or two that clarifies the contribution that each Chapter makes to the thesis as a whole.

Here is Pat D'Arcy's (1998) Abstract in which Pat states clearly what she does in her thesis and the claims to originality that she is making. Pat produced 13 drafts of her Abstract before she was satisfied that it communicated the essence of her thesis:

THE WHOLE STORY...

ABSTRACT OF PHD SUBMISSION

PAT D'ARCY

In this thesis I investigate the nature of written responses made to stories in an educational context, which can be characterised as aesthetic transactions with a text [Rosenblatt, 1938, 1978, 1985]. My research develops Guidelines designed to elicit such personally meaningful responses from teachers to pupils' stories as well as from pupils to the stories they read. I map those features which characterise the engaged and appreciative responses that I both made and received from primary and secondary teachers and consider in what respects they may be educationally valuable. I also consider how such responses could offer a form of meaning-related, interpretive assessment for the work of pupils as story writers and story readers.

This thesis also tells the story of my journey as an educational researcher. It acknowledges the mistakes I made, the confusions I grappled with and what I discovered in the course of my investigation about myself as an educator and about the values that underpin my thinking which sustained the whole enterprise.

I offer this thesis, therefore as an original contribution to the nature of engaged and appreciative responses made by teachers as well as by pupils in the field of story writing and story reading…

I also offer it as an original contribution to educational knowledge - the process of coming to know - as I have sought to construct my developing perceptions as a living educational theory. (Retrieved from https://www.actionresearch.net/living/pat.shtml)

When inserting video recordings, it is wise to keep them short and specific to the point being made and include a transcript of the dialogue. Responses to your validation group will assist you to keep on track and make revisions as you go.

3.3.7.3 Viva or Oral Exam

Purpose and examiners

Viva literally means 'viva voce' or with the living voice and thus the viva examination is the verbal defence of your thesis. Your thesis demonstrates your skill at presenting your research in writing. In the viva or oral examination, you will demonstrate your ability to participate in academic discussion with research colleagues. The purpose of the viva or oral examination is to demonstrate that the thesis is your own work, confirm that you understand what you have written and can defend it verbally, and investigate your awareness of where your original work sits in relation to the wider research field. It establishes whether the thesis is of sufficiently high standard to merit the award of the degree for which it is submitted and allows you to clarify and develop the written thesis in response to the examiners' questions.

You will have two examiners, with your supervisor auditing. An internal examiner will be a member of academic staff of the University, usually from your School/Department but not one of your supervisors. An external examiner, invited by your supervisor, will be a member of academic staff of another institution or occasionally a professional in another field with expertise in your area of research.

Preparation

Preparation for the viva or oral exam usually starts some three to four months before the viva. It is usual for a viva to be arranged some six to eight weeks after submission to give examiners the opportunity to read, judge and to write and circulate their preliminary reports to each other.

The question we initially focus on is "What is your thesis?". This usually creates some hesitation and confusion if this is the first time that the researcher has faced this question. At this point, it is wise to read the Abstract as this contains the answer to the question, "What is your thesis?"

At a viva, the candidate is usually given the opportunity to introduce their thesis and the contents of the Abstract can be drawn on to focus on the context of the research, the originality of the research and its methodology. In the viva, for a Living Educational Theory research doctorate, it is wise to have practiced a response to questions about methodology. This is because Living Educational Theory research does not apply a pre-existing methodology to the research. A living-educational-theory methodology emerges in the course of the generation of a living-educational-theory.

In preparing for a viva, it is wise to have practiced responses to questions about your critical engagement with the ideas of others. This helps you to position your research as both an original contribution to the field of your inquiry and as drawing insights from some of the most influential and relevant ideas of the day.

Examiners often give candidates the opportunity, towards the end of a viva, to respond with any reflections they might have on the viva. If you believe that some of your ideas have not been given due attention in the questioning, you should raise this at this point.

In the unlikely event that you feel that the viva has not been appropriate in examining your thesis, you must be prepared to express your concerns in writing to the Chair of the examination board as soon as you can after the examination and talk over with your supervisor the correct procedures offered by the University to register your complaint.

Issues and concerns

While not usual, Jackie was able to audit another viva that Jack was examining which she found to be very helpful and calming for her own viva. To have experienced the environment allowed her to envision herself in the context and have a sense of the questions that might arise. In her viva, when asked about her reference to Lyotard and to what degree she was on inside of all of his work in her viva, she replied that she had not studied all of Lyotard's (Lyotard, 1986) work because she found that much of the literature was useful in giving her the language to explain her own theorising. With Lyotard, it was his explanation that postmodernists create rules after they have taken actions which resonated with Jackie's way of being, in that she tried out ways of teaching or leading or administering and then created the policy to explain it.

Jack arranged for and received permission for the audio-recording of Jackie's viva which gave her data for future reflection and research. That viva went very smoothly with some minor editing required. It does not always proceed that smoothly as in the case of Ari Briganti where the questioning was often off topic and challenging to the extent that at the end of the viva, Ari did not understand that she had passed and would be awarded her degree!

3.4 Approximate Timelines and Schedule of Research

Stage One: Beginning the process

a. Choosing a supportive university and supervisor/s
   This can take several months to a year, depending on factors such as whether they can be found in your own region or country, the nature of your area of study, and the number of part-time programs available. Needless to say, finding a supportive supervisor will enable you to have an enjoyable, productive research experience and avoid a great deal of stress and heartache.

b. Application-three months

c. MPhil/Transfer/Confirmation Process
   A Master of Philosophy is a degree between a Master's and a doctorate that prepares the student for the PhD process and is available in the UK, Nepal and a few other countries. An alternative preparation and confirmation process is the Transfer report and seminar. The confirmation timeline is three months and the Transfer seminar and varies from 18 months to three to four years.

d. Doctoral Proposal with Ethical Review
   Takes about three months.

Stage Two: Writing the thesis

a. Framing a Question
   You will start with a working title but the question will change as you conduct the research and the final question is only solidified when writing the thesis.
b. Living Educational Theory Methodology
   Living Educational Theory Methodology provides the basis while drawing on other theories to create your own living-educational-theory methodology.
c. Data collection/analysis
   Data collection and analysis may take months or years but it is continuous throughout the process. It is part of analysis and writing at regular intervals through the doctoral journey and not just at the writing up stage.

Stage Three: First full draft/Thesis for submission

d. Writing up the final chapters
   You think that you are almost finished writing up almost a year before the actual submission when you have a first full draft of the thesis; editing takes much more time than expected and can take up to a year.
e. Abstract (300 words)
   The abstract is continuously evolving as the research is emerging but is one of the last pieces of writing since it is a short summary that concisely reports the aims and outcomes of your research so that readers know exactly what the thesis is about.

3.5 Available Resources

a. Free libraries:
   While most students have access to university libraries, those who don't might access public repositories such as,
   https://z-lib.org/
   https://core.ac.uk
b. Other texts:
   The Authentic Dissertation; Alternative Ways of Knowing, Research, and Representation by Four Arrows (Don Trent Jacobs) (2008)

This text is an excellent resource for researchers looking at alternative ways of representing their knowledge. The author has selected "brief dissertation stories that ...are authentic" and "are, in essence, spiritual undertakings and reflections that honor the centrality of the researcher's voice, experience, creativity, and authority" (p. 1). He points out that:

In the journal *Academe*, published by the American Association of University Professors, Lovitts' 2005 article, "How to Grade a Dissertation," described the conclusions of 276 faculty members at ten research universities who collectively had sat on nearly 10,000 dissertation committees, across the sciences, social sciences, and humanities. I highlight their conclusions about dissertations that the faculty rated as 'excellent.' Keep in mind that the research revealed that outstanding dissertations 'were very rare', a problem I hope will be rectified when more scholars begin to reach the goals stated above and express them in their work. These findings are relevant to legitimate concerns about the rigor of work that is arts-informed, storied, autobiographical, critical, anti-oppressive, ecologically situated, or indigenous-oriented. In fact, my reading of their determinations leads me to conclude that a dissertation has more potential to be rated as "excellent" if it moves in the directions that the stories described in this book reveal.

- There is *no set formula* that leads to excellence.
- Outstanding dissertations *defy explication*.
- Faculty "said such dissertations display a richness of thought and insight and make an important breakthrough."
- Such dissertations are a *pleasure to read*.
- "The faculty members [describe] students who produce outstanding dissertations as very creative and intellectually adventurous."
- The dissertations "leap into new territory and transfer ideas from place to place."
- The dissertation writer "used or developed new tools."
- The dissertation pushes the discipline's boundaries and opens new areas or research.
- Outstanding students typically *think and work independently*

(p. 3)

The book is arranged as if the researchers are presenting at a conference and cover topics that range from Indigenous ways of knowing to poetic inquiry and visual art to drama, dialogue and performance.

Warren Linds, co-editor of the 2001 text (Hocking, Haskell, Linds, 2001), *Unfolding Bodymind: Exploring Possibility Through Education*, concludes his presentation with:

> For example, there is one effect on my own teaching that I hadn't anticipated. I now ask my students to pay attention to their experiences in class and to write about them. I ask them to engage in reflective writing, but to start with description about what happened, then to engage in critical analysis. To me, writing this way is an important aspect of academic and practical work that hasn't been paid attention to very much in works on action, or participatory research. There is a difference between merely noting that an experience occurred or that you had a particular response to something, and thinking about how you responded to an experience, why you had a particular response, and what you learned from the experience and your response to it (pp. 173–174).

We now move to Part Four focused on Global contributions of Living Theory researchers to human flourishing and their work as global citizens.

PART

Living Our Educational Responsibilites As Global Citizens

Part Four builds on Parts One to Three in that it moves outwards to address the work being done world-wide in the Living Educational Theory social movement. This work requires a development in the philosophical base from our focus on the professional development of educators for master's and doctoral degrees, to fulfilling our educational responsibilities as global citizens (Potts, 2019; Potts et al., 2013), and citizen scholars (Delong, 2020b; Harper et al., 2020; Vaughan & Delong, 2019). As global citizens and citizen-scholars we are working with others from countries such as Africa, India, Malaysia, Canada, USA, UK and Israel in engaging in the international mentoring of Community-based Living Educational Theory research.

4.1 Developments in the Philosophical Base

The development in our philosophical base between Parts Three and Four is focused on changes in our economic security and the expression of our educational responsibilities as citizen scholars and global citizens.

During our work and research in Parts One to Three we were in paid employment, responsible to our contracts of employment with our employers. Jacqueline was employed as a Superintendent of Schools at the Grand Erie District School Board in Ontario, Canada and Adjunct Professor at Brock University. Jack was employed as a Lecturer in Education at the University of Bath, UK. Our work and research were focused on the application and development of a Living Educational Theory Research approach to the professional development of teachers. Our commitments to the development of Cultures of Inquiry were constrained by the organisational boundaries of the Universities and a District School Board.

Our work and research in Part Four has not been influenced by contracts of employment. In 2021, we are both receiving occupational pensions from our workplaces and state pensions that give us economic security to pursue activities in our productive work that we believe are worthwhile and that help to give our lives meaning and purpose with values of human flourishing.

Hence, the developments of our philosophical base in Part Four are focused on what we understand as our educational responsibilities as citizen scholars rather than as paid employees. We are now focusing our educational responsibilities in generating, sustaining and developing Cultures of Inquiry for Living Educational Theory Research with values of human flourishing. Our purpose is to spread the educational influences of Living Educational Theory Research through these contributions to the generation and sustaining of Cultures of Inquiry. In making this contribution, we accept what Maxwell (2021) refers to as the two great problems in learning.

The first problem is learning about the universe, and about ourselves and other forms of life as a part of the universe. Maxwell refers to this as knowledge-inquiry. We can see the successes of science and technology in contributing to resolving such problems of learning in the two rovers that have landed on Mars by the USA and China in 2021. We can also see its success in the production of effective vaccines that are being used to treat the pandemic of Covid-19 in 2021.

However, we agree with Maxwell that knowledge-inquiry has failed in contributing to the second great problem of learning. This learning is focused on how to create a genuinely civilised, enlightened, wise world. In 2021, this failure can be seen in the violence between citizens within and between different countries through the world. As we write, a ceasefire between Israeli and Hamas, in Gaza, has just been established following over 4,000 rockets being fired into Israeli from Gaza, killing some 12 Israelis with retaliatory fire from Israel killing over 200 Palestinians.

In our support for a Living Educational Theory Research, Culture of Inquiry in Part Four, we explain how this is contributing to resolving this second problem with what Maxwell refers to as wisdom-inquiry. Included within our explanation are our values of being citizen scholars and exercising our educational responsibilities is the recognition that our unique constellation of values are relationally dynamic. Hence, our use of these values as explanatory principles, means that our explanatory principles are relationally dynamic. This is perhaps best illustrated by what Delong means by her relational way of being. This is expressed in her educational relationship with the participants in the 2021 American Educational Research Association Symposium on "Accepting Educational Responsibility: Building

Living Theory Cultures of Educational Inquiry in global contexts." You can access the details of the Symposium, with papers, slides and brief video introductions from the participants at: https://www.actionresearch.net/writings/aera21/2021aerasymposiumfull.pdf

It is also illustrated by Jack's work as Extraordinary Professor in Community-Based Educational Research at North-West University in South Africa. He is also working with academic staff at Durban University of Technology and Nelson Mandela University who are seeking to live as fully as possible the relational dynamic values of an Ubuntu way of being.

We have organised Part Four into the following sections:

a. What is our meaning of educational responsibility as global citizens
b. EJOLTs as a vehicle for extending the Living Educational Theory social movement
c. Our contributions to previous Action Learning and Action Research conferences and publications
d. The contributions of other international Living Educational Theory researchers
e. Living Educational Theory in Cultures of Inquiry as Global Professional Development
f. International educational mentoring by creating Cultures of Inquiry around the globe
g. Digital Visual Data and Dialogue as Methods
h. Researching supportive supervisors, communities and universities
i. Addressing and avoiding colonisation
j. The role of social media in the Living Educational Theory social movement
k. Implications of our 'Educational Responsibility' as citizen scholars for the Living Educational Theory movement

4.2 What Is Our Meaning of Educational Responsibility as Global Citizens?

We see educational responsibility expressed in educational relationships. In these relationships the educational practitioner, as a self-study researcher, expresses an educational responsibility towards the other in generating valid, evidence-based explanations of their educational influences in the learning of the other in contributing to Cultures of Inquiry and in living, as fully as possible, the value of global citizenship. Please note that we do not say an educational responsibility **for** another. We express our educational responsibility **towards** the other, rather than for the other, to stress the individual's responsibility for themselves.

Following our contributions to a Symposium at the 2021 American Educational Research Association (Delong et al., 2021), we developed these ideas, in relation to equity and our responsibility as global citizens, at the 2022 Symposium at AERA on

"Cultivating Equitable Education Systems for the 21st Century in global contexts through Living Educational Theory Cultures of Educational Inquiry" (Delong et al., 2022):

Full video of 90 minute symposium plus 15 minute pre-session conversation at: https://youtu.be/4h_rRDqIJJ8

We include digital visual data to communicate the meanings of our embodied expression of our values-laden, educational responsibilities as global citizens. We include these data to show how to clarify and communicate the meanings of the embodied and ontological values that distinguish our educational responsibilities as global citizens. We do not shy away from including love within these values as we love what we are doing in education. These values are used as explanatory principles and standards of judgement in explanations of educational influences in our own learning, in the learning of others and in the learning of the social formations that influence our practice and understandings. We provide evidence below from universities around the world that living-educational-theory accounts, understood as valid, values-based explanations of educational influences in learning, have been recognised as contributing to global, professional knowledge bases.

Because of the importance of clarifying and communicating the meanings of the expression of our embodied values as global citizens, here is an example of the kind of digital visual data we use to communicate the meanings of our embodied values-laden, educational responsibilities as global citizens. Because a flow of energy is involved in everything we do, we emphasise the importance of flows of life-affirming energy in our educational practices and relationships. The example is a 1 minute 26 second video clip from an hour's supervision session between Jackie and Jack. Jackie had been working on a redraft of the Abstract for her doctoral thesis. Jack had explained a few days before that the initial draft of the Abstract was not clear in terms of Jackie's original contribution to knowledge. In the first 30 seconds of the clip, Jack is explaining why he now feels that the Abstract is appropriate.

We would like you to watch the clip and focus on 30–43 seconds in which we are both, through the laughter, experiencing what we are meaning by a flow of life-affirming energy. If you move the cursor backwards and forwards around 43 seconds, this is where we are expressing the mutual resonance of our flows of life-affirming energy.

https://www.youtube.com/watch?v=w2kdOfRKFYs

In our values-laden expressions of our educational responsibilities as global citizens, we express such flows of life-affirming energy. This energy also flows with the value of 'being loved into learning' (Campbell, 2011, 2019). Here is how Jackie presented ideas on being loved into learning at the 2015 Conference of the Action Research Network of the Americas (Delong, 2015):

> ...To engage participants in experiencing the nature of being loved into learning in a living-culture-of-inquiry for creating a living-theory of one's own life... show how the use of multi-media and multi-screen SKYPE conversations are enabling us to 'pool' our life-affirming and life-enhancing energies...

We also identify with Cho's (2005) analysis of love in educational relationships where love means the pursuit of real knowledge, knowledge that is no longer limited to a particular content passed from one to the other, but rather knowledge that can only be attained by each partner seeking it in the world. As Cho points out, drawing on the work of Freire (1998, p. 22), student and teacher turn away from each other and towards the world in order to produce knowledge through inquiry and thought.

The first 30 seconds of the video above, shows both of us focusing on the Abstract to Jackie's doctoral thesis, to clarify its original contribution to knowledge. What follows the flow of life-affirming energy between 30 and 43 seconds, through the laughter, is a return to the knowledge generation which results in the following excerpt for Jackie's successfully completed doctorate on "How can I improve my practice as a superintendent of schools and create my own living educational theory?":

> One of the basic tenets of my philosophy is that the development of a culture for improving learning rests upon supporting the knowledge-creating capacity in each individual in the system. Thus,

I start with my own. This thesis sets out a claim to know my own learning in my educational inquiry, "How can I improve my practice as a superintendent of schools?"

Out of this philosophy emerges my belief that the professional development of each teacher rests in their own knowledge-creating capacities as they examine their own practice in helping their students to improve their learning. In creating my own educational theory and supporting teachers in creating theirs, we engage with and use insights from the theories of others in the process of improving student learning.

The originality of the contribution of this thesis to the academic and professional knowledgebase of education is in the systematic way I transform my embodied educational values into educational standards of practice and judgement in the creation of my living educational theory. In the thesis, I demonstrate how these values and standards can be used critically both to test the validity of my knowledge-claims and to be a powerful motivator in my living educational inquiry.

The values and standards are defined in terms of valuing the other in my professional practice, building a culture of inquiry, reflection and scholarship and creating knowledge (Delong, 2002).

While the meanings of love in educational relationships and explanations of educational influence learning can be given different meanings by other individuals, we are heartened by Zuber-Skerritt's recognition of the importance of 'Loving Learning Conferences' in enhancing the spreading influence of the 'positive energy of faith, love, hope and creativity':

Society needs to be renewed by making a shift from the negative energy of fear, competition, control and war to the positive energy of faith, love, hope and creativity. Clearly, we need to conceptualise and practice not just learning conferences but Loving Learning Conferences (Zuber-Skerritt, 2017, p. 224).

We see that the positive, relationally dynamic, values include those explicated by Briganti (2020) in her living-theory of international development in which she holds herself accountable for living her values of human flourishing as fully as possible:

My thesis is focused on the relationally dynamic values of empathy, social and gender justice, outrage, responsibility, love for and faith in humanity and dignity. The originality lies in their use as explanatory principles in my explanation of my educational influence in my own learning, in the learning of others and in the learning of the social formations that affect my practice as a development professional (p. iii).

The significance, for the social movement of Living Educational Theory researchers, is its grounding in the practice of individual practitioner-researchers as they generate their own living-educational-theories as explanations of their educational influences in learning, in inquiries of the kind, "How do I improve what I am doing?" and "How do we improve what we are doing?". The explanations include an evaluation of previous learning in making sense of the present together with an imagined possibility of a future that is not yet realised.

In his paper on "Contributing to moving action research to activism with Living Theory research" Jack analyses practitioner-research that focuses on the communication of meanings of relationally dynamic values in educational conversations in the generation of living-theories by activist scholars that carry hope for the flourishing of humanity (Whitehead, 2020d). It explains how a Living Educational Theory researcher, as an activist scholar, can engage with and hold themselves accountable for contributing to Cultures of Inquiry that support living values of human flourishing as fully as possible.

In developing and researching a Living Educational Theory research approach, to enhancing the educational influences of Cultures of Inquiry with values of human flourishing, that include global citizenship, it is necessary for practitioner-researchers to imagine the future and to project themselves into its creation with others. At the heart of this process is, accepting an educational responsibility for projecting ourselves into this imagined future as global citizens.

In such projections, we recognise the importance of forming alliances in spreading the global educational influence of Living Educational Theory research with values of human flourishing, as global citizens. We now outline more details of the importance of forming alliances in a global social movement of Cultures of Inquiry with Living Educational Theory researchers, in living-global citizenship.

We are contributing to a global movement of Living Educational Theory researchers. This includes our commitment as individual educational practitioners to project ourselves into the creation of a future that has not been realised yet, but which is informed by the value of living-global-citizenship. This value has been clarified and communicated elsewhere (Coombs & Potts, 2012; Coombs et al., 2014; Potts, 2012; Potts et al., 2013).

In our engagement with Living Educational Theory research as a process, we generate and share our living-educational-theories as a product. We are now focusing on our educational responsibility to live as fully as possible the value of global citizenship in enhancing the educational influence of Living Educational Theory research in a global social movement.

4.2.1 Living Global Citizenship

Mark Pott's (2012) focused attention on the ideas of living-citizenship and living-global citizenship in his thesis on "How can I Reconceptualise International Educational Partnerships as a Form of 'Living Citizenship'?" (Potts, 2012). The idea of using living-citizenship as an explanatory principle in Living Educational Theory research was reinforced by the paper on "Bringing Living Citizenship As A Living Standard Of Judgment Into The Academy" (Coombs & Potts, 2012). Here is the Abstract:

Abstract

Living citizenship emerging from reflection on an international educational partnership makes a unique contribution to the field and importantly fulfils the AERA (2012) aim of improving educational practice for the public benefit. The BERA professional user review of 2003 asks: How do we learn to become good citizens? Members of the 5x5x5 = Creativity project team, suggest:

"A democratic society depends on everyone taking responsibility and contributing what they can, which is possible only when each of us feels we belong and are seen as uniquely creative, capable and self-determining individuals" (John & Pound, 2011, p. 1).

This paper explores the conceptual framework of 'Living Citizenship' as a means for developing international continuing professional development (i-CPD) through action research projects. The research focuses on video-cases that present findings from the development of an international educational partnership between two schools in England and South Africa. Adapting Whitehead's (2005) living educational theory approach to action research, 'Living Citizenship' supports and problematises international educational partnerships' through the influence of enabling participants' as critically active citizens. Such pro-active fieldwork links the values and objectives of social justice and knowledge exchange to proffering educational change within authentic i-CPD professional learning environments.

Potts et al. (2013) clarified these meanings further in a paper on "Developing Cultural Empathy And The Living Global Citizenship Agenda: The Social Role And Impact Of Technology In Supporting Global Partnerships". Coombs et al. (2014) deepened their understandings of living global citizenship in their book on "International Educational Development and Learning through Sustainable Partnerships: Living Global Citizenship".

At the heart of our educational practices are our values of living global citizenship with educational responsibility. Hence, we need to clarify our meanings of educational responsibility.

In terms of accepting an educational responsibility as educators, educational researcher and global citizens, we agree with Biesta's (2006) point about the responsibility of the educator:

…We come into the world as unique individuals through the ways in which we respond responsibly to what and who is other. I argue that the responsibility of the educator not only lies in the cultivation of 'worldly spaces' in which the encounter with otherness and difference is a real possibility, but that it extends to asking 'difficult questions': questions that summon us to respond responsively and responsibly to otherness and difference in our own, unique ways (p. ix).

In Living Educational Theory research, we do not see educational practitioners to be confined to the institutions of schools, colleges or universities. In Living Educational Theory research an educational practitioner is any individual who: accepts an educational responsibility for seeking to improve what they are doing with values of human flourishing; is researching their attempts to improve their practice, to influence the educational influences of others and the social formations that influence practice and understandings; is making public their explanations of educational influences in learning through such forums as the Educational Journal of Living Theories (EJOLTs). You can see some recent developments of community-based Living Educational Theory Research in the living-posters of members of the communities of practice at North-West University:

https://www.actionresearch.net/writings/posters/nwu22.pdf
Nelson Mandela University:
https://www.actionresearch.net/writings/posters/nmu22.pdf
Durban University of Technology:
https://www.actionresearch.net/writings/posters/dut22.pdf

4.3 EJOLTs as a Vehicle for Extending the Living Educational Theory Social Movement

As founder members, in 2008, members of the Editorial Board and published authors in the Educational Journal of Living Theories (EJOLTS), we are committed to the scope and commitment of EJOLTS:

The Educational Journal of Living Theories (EJOLTS) is committed to publishing living-educational-theory accounts of practitioner-researchers from a wide range of global, social, cultural and professional contexts. We welcome submissions from all engaged in Living Educational Theory research) researchers who wish to contribute rigorous and valid accounts of their living-educational-theories to improving educational knowledge. EJOLTs offers distinctive, stimulating opportunities for creativity, learning and spreading knowledge of educational influences in learning; learning which carries hope for the flourishing of our individual and collective humanity.

The journal focuses on the living-educational-theories of practitioner-researchers. Researchers generate their living-educational-theories as their values-based "explanations for their educational influences in their own learning, the learning of others and the learning of social formations" (Whitehead, 1989) in the process of researching questions such as, "How do I improve what I am doing". The values at the heart of Living Educational Theory research (often shortened to Living Theory research) are the life-enhancing values that are relational and ontological, in the sense that they give meaning and purpose to the lives of individuals and groups. They are values that carry hope for the future of humanity, such as love, freedom, justice, compassion, courage, care and democracy. (Homepage of EJOLTs at https://ejolts.net/)

As an on-line Journal EJOLTs permits and encourages the use of digital visual data as evidence in explanations of educational influences in learning. Such data enables the clarification and communication of the embodied expressions of the meanings of values as these emerge through practice. Such ostensive expressions of meaning are accompanied by lexical definitions of the meanings of values to communicate as clearly as possible the meanings of the values that constitute the learning as 'educational'.

4.4 Our Contributions to Previous Educational, Action Learning and Action Research Conferences and Their Publication

As our activities become more sharply focused on our educational influences as citizen-scholars, we emphasise the importance of working within communities as we contribute to Cultures of Inquiry. We continue to stress the importance of recognising and contributing to the educational influences of Cultures of Inquiry because sociocultural and sociohistorical influences form the social contexts in which our practice can be located. Because an important component of educational learning is extending one's cognitive range and concerns, we offer the following insights from presentations at an international Living Educational Theory Research Conference and to ARNA, CARN, ALARA and AERA, so that readers can see if these ideas help to extend their own cognitive range and concerns:

i. First International Living Educational Theory Research Conference hold on the 27 June 2020 with the details at:
   http://www.spanglefish.com/livingtheoryresearchgathering/index.asp
ii. Action Research Networks of the Americas (ARNA), the Collaborative Action Research Network (CARN) and the Action Learning Action Research Association (ALARA).

These contributions include:

Whitehead, J. (2019) The action learning, action research experiences of professionals - *ALARj* 25(1): 11–27. A keynote presentation to the tenth World Congress of the Action Learning Action Research Association with the theme of "The Action Learning and Action Research Legacy for Transforming Social Change: Individuals, Professionals, and Communities' Developments, Organizational Advancements, and Global Initiatives", 18 June 2018 in Norwich University, Vermont, USA. Retrieved 28 January 2020 from https://www.actionresearch.net/writings/jack/jackkeynoteALARA.pdf

Delong, J. D. D., Huxtable, M., Rawal, S. & Whitehead, J. (2019) An interactive symposium paper for the CARN/ALARA Conference 17–19 October 2019 in Split, Croatia with the theme:

'Imagine Tomorrow: Practitioner Learning for the Future'. Imagining tomorrow in the generation of living-educational-theories with learning for the future. Retrieved 5 May 2021 from https://www.actionresearch.net/writings/jack/JDD2019split.pdf

Whitehead, J., Delong, J. & Huxtable M. (2017) Participation and Democratization of Knowledge: Living Theory Research for Reconciliation from ARNA 2015-ARNA 2017 A presentation at the 2017 Conference of the Action Research Network of the Americas 12–16 June 2017 in Cartagena, Colombia. Retrieved 28 January 2020 from https://www.actionresearch.net/writings/jack/jwjddmharna070617.pdf

In the following two papers, we address international audiences as part of our contributions to enhancing the educational influences of Living Educational Theory research in generating, sustaining and evolving Cultures of Inquiry with values of human flourishing.

Delong, J., Whitehead, J. & Huxtable, M. (2019) Where do we go from here in contributing to 'The Action Learning and Action Research Legacy for Transforming Social Change?'. *ALARj* 25(1): 65–73. Workshop presentation at the 2019 ALARA Conference in Norwich University, Vermont, USA. Retrieved 28 January 2021 from https://www.actionresearch.net/writings/jack/jddjwmhalarj19.pdf

Abstract: The workshop brought together researchers who are engaged in action learning/action research inquiries of the kind, "How do I improve what I am doing and live, as fully as possible, my values that carry hope for the flourishing of humanity?" Participants comprised researchers physically present in the room, those present through SKYPE and those who have a virtual presence in the form of their living-posters at http://www.actionresearch.net/writings/posters/homepage020617.pdf.

This workshop focused on living-theory accounts created by educational practitioner researchers, including those engaging as AL/AR practitioners, which are contributing to a legacy for transforming social change. The living-theories used in the workshop included those accredited for doctoral degrees in different universities around the world. The workshop demonstrated the communicative power of multi-media narratives with digital visual data to clarify and communicate the meanings of embodied expressions of values that carry hope for the flourishing of humanity. Ideas, critically and creatively engaged with included current social theories such as de Sousa Santos' (2014) ideas on 'epistemicide'. These ideas were used to show how Western academic reasoning and epistemology can be understood and transcended in the generation of the living-educational-theories of individuals, grounded in their experiences and contexts.

Whitehead, J., Delong, J., Huxtable, M., Campbell, E., Griffin, C. & Mounter, M. (2020) Self-study in elementary and secondary teaching: A living theory approach, in Kitchen, J., Berry, A., Bullock, S., Crowe, A., Taylor, M, Guojonsdottir, H. & Thomas, L. (2020). *2nd International Handbook of Self-Study of Teaching and Teacher Education Practices*. Rotterdam, The Netherlands: Springer. Available from: https://www.actionresearch.net/writings/jack/STEPchpt4june2020.pdf (Accessed 28 January 2020)

Abstract: In this chapter we present examples of Living Theory research, a form of Self-Study, which show teachers, teacher educators and administrators researching to improve their teaching and the educational experience of students and contributing the knowledge they create in the process to a professional educational knowledge base. We clarify the relationship between education and educational research and show how Living Theory is distinguished within other forms of Self-Study research. Consideration is given to the opportunities and challenges of promoting this approach, and other forms of Self-Study research, as ways to improve practice in schools. We show the development of ideas since Whitehead's contribution 14 years ago, in 2004, to the first International Handbook of Self Study on, "What counts as evidence in self-studies of teacher education practices?". Our emphasis in this chapter is on practising educators, their professional development and gaining academic recognition for the embodied knowledges of Master and doctor educators.

Here is the abstract for our accepted proposal for a symposium presentation on "Accepting Educational Responsibility: Building Living Theory Cultures of Educational Inquiry in global contexts" at the April 2021 Conference of the American Educational Research Association with the theme of "Accepting Responsibility", with Jacqueline Delong (Canada), Shivani Mishra (India), Parbati Dhungana (Nepal), Michelle Vaughn (Canada) and Jack Whitehead (UK).

The contributors are all exploring the implications for improving their educational practices and contributing to educational knowledge of accepting educational responsibility in building Living Theory Cultures of Educational Inquiry in their local and global contexts. They are participating in a global social movement of educational researchers this is engaged in asking, researching and answering, "How do I, individually and in cooperation with others, enhance the difference Living Educational Theory research can make in a community concerned with extending human flourishing?" Each researcher is moved by unique constellations of values that are used to explain their educational influences in their own learning, in the learning of others and in the learning of the social formations that influence their practices and understandings.

You can access the successful proposal, papers, powerpoint slides and video-clips at: http://www.actionresearch.net/writings/aera21/aerasym2021.pdf

4.5 The Contributions of Other International Living Educational Theory Researchers

In this section, we share the work of Living Educational Theory practitioner-researchers across the globe. We include Mark Potts' Conversation Cafes that have been replicated by Swaroop Rawal in India. We include Swaroop Rawal's creation of the Life Skills curriculum, and her influence with Shivani Mishra at Sardar Patel University in India in the teaching of Master's social work students and in the rural areas of India and in refugee camps with Pakistani children. We include Arianna's Briganti's work in the development of a living-educational-theory of international development and the prize-winning work of the charity, 'Nove Onlus' in supporting a women's taxi-driver cooperative in Afghanistan.

i.. Mark Potts on Living Citizenship and Democracy Cafes:
You can access Mark's website on Living Citizenship at: http://www.livingcitizenship.uwclub.net/index.html. Mark explains how his website is based on the Zulu idea of Ubuntu and is dedicated to celebrating how we contribute to improving the lives of others.

You can access Mark's living-poster at https://www.actionresearch.net/writings/posters/mark20.pdf. Mark describes how he is living his values as a member of Salisbury Democracy Alliance, promoting deliberative Democracy Cafes and Citizens' Assemblies and as a volunteer for the Samaritans.

This 1:31 minute video https://www.youtube.com/watch?v=Qk1FMHJ0ojY explains Mark's work on democracy cafes.

ii. Swaroop Rawal and Shivani Mishra on life-skills education at Sardar Patel University in India.
Swaroop Rawal is working with Shivani Mishra at Sardar Patel University. In her living-poster at

https://www.actionresearch.net/writings/posters/swaroop20.pdf Swaroop describes life skills education as:

Life skills education is a decisive approach to break the cycle of poverty, abuse, and oppression of the vulnerable and the marginalised. It is a form of education which has the power to transform societies.

On her living-poster Swaroop also explains why she does what she does:

Why do I do what I do....Because I believe that a high-quality education is one of the most effective ways to reduce inequalities in society. I see my work as a support to all children, as a way to make their world a better place in which to live, to help the children to overcome adversity and become resilient, to learn how to face the problems they have to deal with in their young world, to empower them so they can grow into well adjusted adults. These are lofty goals but they are at the heart of what I am trying to achieve.

You can access Swaroop's doctorate on 'The Role Of Drama In Enhancing Life Skills In Children With Specific Learning Difficulties In A Mumbai School: My Reflective Account' from http://www.actionresearch.net/living/rawal.shtml

iii. Arianna Briganti on a living-educational-theory of international development and the charity 'Nove Onlus'

While we drew attention above, to the following values identified by Arianna Briganti (2020), in her living-educational-theory of international development, we think that they are worth repeating because of their significance in spreading the influence of Living Educational Theory research as a global movement with values that carry hope for human flourishing:

My thesis is focused on the relationally dynamic values of empathy, social and gender justice, outrage, responsibility, love for and faith in humanity and dignity. The originality lies in their use as explanatory principles in my explanation of my educational influence in my own learning, in the learning of others and in the learning of the social formations that affect my practice as a development professional. (p. iii)

Arianna Briganti is a founder member of the charity 'Nove Onlus' and continues to support its work as Arianna continues to live her values as fully as possible. In 2020, the MedFilm Festival awarded her the Koiné prize to Nove Onlus for the 'Pink Shuttle' project aimed at women in Kabul – see:

http://www.ansamed.info/ansamed/en/news/sections/generalnews/2020/11/17/medfilm-festival-awards-koine-2020-prize-to-nove-onlus_50aac46b-10d4-40b4-96c7-4354d9d3c9fc.html

The prize was awarded to Nove Onlus for:

...Its "Pink Shuttle" project, an initiative that saves women in Afghanistan from a life nearly exclusively destined for domesticity. The project uses minivans driven by women with other women aboard to help them find dignity in training, work, and skills, and gives back the right to freedom of movement in the Afghan capital. "This prize is very important, because it comes from a Festival that has always promoted intercultural dialogue and comes during a particularly tense situation," Nove President Susanna Fioretti told ANSAmed. Fioretti is intimately familiar with Afghanistan, where the war began 40 years ago and hasn't ended since.

For our contribution to female emancipation on site, it's sufficient to say that while in 19 years 3,732 driving licences have been issued to women in the province of Kabul, in four years 245 women have gotten a licence thanks to Nove Onlus courses.

Fioretti said. "Pink Shuttle solves the problem of female mobility in full respect of the local culture, because the minivans are driven by women and used to transport women to their destinations, which would have otherwise been impossible to do alone," Fioretti said. In fact, in Afghanistan women must always be accompanied by men to avoid various types of violence. The project currently has four drivers and another ten in training, while the minivans have increased from two initially to six currently, the last four having come from South Korea. Fioretti thanked OTB – Only The Brave Foundation, among the main sponsors of the association, which has nine members who work pro bono after having had experience in development cooperation in various agencies and countries.

The Pink Shuttle project will turn itself into a business run directly by Afghan women. Thanks to the training centre instituted by an accord signed with the Afghan Ministry of Women's Affairs, between October 2014 and February 2020 more than 2,500 female students attended one or more free training courses in English, computer sciences, professional cooking, driving school, or job orientation.

Fioretti said that Nove Onlus works on numerous projects for the most vulnerable groups – women, the disabled, children – in various countries, Italy included. (ANSAmed). (ANSA).

4.6 Living Educational Theory in Cultures of Inquiry as Global Professional Development

We have shared throughout our vision of Living Educational Theory in Cultures of Inquiry as Professional Development. In this section, we take a moment to make the connection between our intent to contribute to human flourishing by living our values more fully and by encouraging others to do so, too. We recorded a dialogue on this model for professional development using Living Educational Theory Research in Cultures of Inquiry. It is a more concise version of the 11 Points that follow:

Video 2. Jackie Delong and Jack Whitehead dialogue on A Living Educational Theory Research approach to professional development
https://www.youtube.com/watch?v=SXgMTZO4Nys (Whitehead, 2021)

In the introduction to this video at 00:19 to 1:34, Jack Whitehead says the following: This approach is a form of professional practitioner self-study research which generates valid accounts of your values-based explanation of your educational influence in your own learning, in the learning of others and in the learning of social formations. An author's life affirming and life-enhancing values as you live and work recognising resolving contradictions as far as you can, need to be explicit.

Framing a Living Educational Theory in Cultures of Inquiry approach to professional development

The Living Educational Theory in Cultures of Inquiry approach focuses on values-based research. Because we share so many common values and understandings, it opens the door to sharing different cultural experiences and intercultural education. Access to the internet has meant that we can meet our fellow practitioner-researchers creating their own living-educational-theories to share our concerns, provide encouragement, support, and resources any time, given the time differences. We learn about other ways of seeing the world and how we can help each other improve it.

Evidence for the recognition of different cultural experiences and academic traditions in a Living Educational Theory Research in Cultures of Inquiry approach to professional development can be accessed in the presentations on enhancing equity in networks of education in the 2022 Symposium at AERA (Delong et al., 2022). In the 2022 papers, you will see that, within our Living Educational Theory Culture of Inquiry, we have deliberately worked to integrate Eastern Wisdom Traditions and Western Critical Academic Traditions so that all voices are valued and heard:

Focusing our educational responsibilities in generating, sustaining and developing Cultures of Inquiry for Living Educational Theory Research with the values of human flourishing, we accept what Maxwell (2021) refers to as the two great problems in learning: the first problem, learning about the universe, about ourselves and other forms of life as a part of the universe. Maxwell refers to this as knowledge-inquiry. We can see the successes of science and technology in knowledge-inquiry. However, we agree with Maxwell that knowledge-inquiry has failed in contributing to the second great problem of learning, focused on how to create a genuinely civilised, enlightened, wise world.

A wise world would encourage and support teachers' professionalism through a Living Educational Theory in Cultures of Inquiry approach and contribute to resolving this second problem with what Maxwell refers to as wisdom-inquiry. Included within our explanations are our values of being citizen-scholars and exercising our educational responsibilities, is the recognition that our unique constellation of values is relationally dynamic. Hence, our use of these values as explanatory principles, means that our explanatory principles are relationally dynamic. Based on the results of this research, we advocate for the creation of living-educational-theories in Cultures of Inquiry using dialogue as a research-method with visual data, and for intercultural education for improving teacher professionalism for the future and for human flourishing.

For the complete explanation of these concepts, see Delong's 2022 article: https://ejolts.net/node/387

4.7 International Educational Mentoring by Creating Cultures of Inquiry Around the Globe

In this section, we review our work with Living Educational Theory research colleagues around the globe as activist citizen-scholars (Whitehead, 2020d). Initially, we connected with individual practitioner-researchers as a result of first meeting after a conference presentation, either on-site or virtually. Following up on that meeting, we have created sustained Cultures of Inquiry and individually or together have conducted Living Educational Theory research, written papers, published articles and presented at conferences with them. We worked with an international group of scholars, Shivani Misrahi, from India, Parbati Dhungana, from Nepal and Michelle Vaughan, from USA to present a symposium at the virtual AERA 10 April 2021, sharing our 'educational responsibility' as global citizens. We share some of these loving educational relationships and our contributions to the Living Theory social movement and to human flourishing.

In her quest to live her values as a living global citizen, Jackie ruminated on the nature of her role as 'a guide on the side' and the struggle she had in finding the right words to describe what she did to encourage and support individuals to create their own living-educational-theories. She rejected words like 'supervisor' and 'tutor' which, despite how kind and considerate the supervisor is, carry a power endowed by the institution and therefore constitute a power relation. The relational dynamic suggests a 'superior knowledge' (Polanyi, 1958). Another word, 'coaching', is used in the purview of sports and athletes but is also used in the work of a Life or Self-Improvement Coach where an experienced person assists a client to achieve their personal, business or professional goals. Sigrid Gjotterud (2009) uses the language of "guiding practice" (p. 70).

The word 'mentor' carries connotations of a workplace where a new employee is assigned a 'mentor' who will counsel him on the way things work in the organisation and again suggests a greater knowledge and responsibility for the smooth transition for the newcomer. Yamamoto (1988) changed her mind on that as he says,

> Inasmuch as "mankind's greatest achievements are the products of vision" (Dubos, 1968, p. 238), a mentor helps the person under his or her care to see beyond oneself and become more fully human. At the same time, mysteriously, the mentor is being helped to fulfill further his or her own human potential.
>
> (p. 188)

Nyanjom (2020) reiterates this concept of co-learning so that both mentee and mentor learn in the relationship.:

> The learning gained by mentors can be transformative in nature, directly affecting and enhancing mentoring practice (Castanheira 2016; Daloz 2012; Ghosh and Reio 2013; Langdon 2014; Rekha

and Ganesh 2012; Wyre, Gaudet, and McNeese 2016), and the knowledge gained from the process can lead to new understandings and innovative ways of enhancing practice.

(p. 243)

When both members of the mentoring relationship are valued for their equal contribution to the relationship, symbiosis occurs and both members reap the reward of the relationship. As Yamamoto (1988) describes, it is the recognition of the other individual, the experience of being seen that has an impact far beyond what the message or advice may be:

> What is sought is not praise, reward, or pity, all of which are an accounting for past deeds. Rather, it is regard-an acknowledgment of one's personhood as well as trust in what is and is to come-that is desired.
>
> (p. 184)

We share three of these loving educational relationships.

a. Michelle Vaughan, Associate Professor, Florida Atlantic University

First, Jackie reviews evidence from working and learning with Michelle Vaughan and shares their first meeting, supporting Michelle to create her living-educational-theory, their co-learning, Michelle's continuing influence in her doctoral programs and an example of life-affirming energy through "empathetic resonance".

Since the ALARA Conference in Norwich, Vermont in 2018, Jackie has openly made herself available to mentor individuals wanting to create their own-living-educational theory. At that conference, between our meeting at a workshop that we presented and June of 2019, Michelle Vaughan and Jackie created a culture of inquiry in which Michelle created her own living-educational theory and had it published (Vaughan, 2019). Liz Campbell coined the phrase that describes Jackie's way of teaching as "being loved into learning" (Campbell, 2011). Others have expanded that language. Michelle's language to describe Jackie's way of being in creating the Cultures of Inquiry was, "not bringing your ego into it" (Vaughan & Delong, 2019): https://youtu.be/wjm13drYVQc (Delong, 2021c)

When Jackie shared with Michelle the 'loved into learning' language, Michelle responded by describing her way of being that encouraged her research as "not bringing your ego into it":

> It's something about you not bringing your ego into it which I think allows the love to flow through. So, if you really want to have somebody feel that emotion, I think you approach a lot of these relationships without ego and that is, in my experience, rare in higher education...
>
> (p. 73)

Michelle goes on to say that the roles of mentor and mentee have been reciprocal in nature, offering both of them space to learn, grow and improve their practice,

> I am hopeful that in Jackie mentoring me to see beyond myself and become more fully the person I was meant to me, I am simultaneously helping to fulfil her own potential as I serve in my role as the mentee...
>
> (ibid. p. 78)

Michelle continues to build a culture of inquiry in her doctoral classes at Florida Atlantic University, USA. Michelle described the way she worked as the way in which Jackie asked her to explain what she would focus her energy on moving forward with her living theory. Michelle said that she thought that there was a natural next step that occurred in her practice, the application of her living-theory to her practice will continue to see her create a space where the connections she had with her students were first and foremost, not second. Not content first and then let me see if she can make a connection, but connection first and then content second, so she thought that there was a reshifting in that pyramid and that was in her practice. But she thought also there was a next step in her as an advocate of the field because she felt that she had been enriched by the process similarly to how Jackie had been a shepherd for her: she wanted to also be that person for others. Even though she felt that she was certainly a novice in this game, she was happy to learn alongside people.

She shared that community was what she was looking for and felt that people were ready to look at themselves. She thought that people were more openly looking inwards and have been looking inwards forever, but that it is more of a dialogue about why and how we do things and what things we struggle with and we want to be able to create a safe place for students to do that... the role that this plays is really about planting your feet firmly and knowing who you are so that you can be aware of when you are not who you are and know that that is toxic for you and find a way to find a safe place. She wanted to create a place where values were valid and the conversations matter and it's not secondary. (Vaughan, 2019, pp. 73–74)

In this video clip, Michelle says that she imagines Jackie "like a fairy godmother with all these lives that you are touching." Here is Jackie's reaction! If you put your cursor on the red line of the clip and just move it back and forth, I think you can see the life-affirming energy in both of us in the process called, "empathetic resonance" (Delong et al., 2013, p. 79): https://www.youtube.com/watch?v=ZO0ZE1C74lI

Jackie and Michelle presented a workshop in Montreal in June 2019 at the ARNA conference. In addition, Jackie and Michelle worked collaboratively to research and write an article that was published in December, 2019 (Vaughan & Delong, 2019).

a. *Parbati Dhungana, PhD student, now graduated, and Master's teacher at Kathmandu University, Nepal*

Second, Jackie shares her educational relationship with Parbati, Dhungana. Parbati's research focuses on working with a rural community in Nepal where the resources are limited including teacher professional development. She worked with her colleagues and the school community to build more collaboration, ownership and pride and, in the process, came to recognise her central value as "Living Love". Jackie met Parbati Dhungana in person at the CARN Conference in Split, Croatia in October, 2019 at a session presentation (Delong et al., 2019). Accepting her offer to support practitioner-researchers intending to create their own-living-educational-theory, Parbati and Jackie met regularly on SKYPE and recorded their meetings. By June of 2020, Parbati had created her own living-educational-theory and published her "'Living love': My living-educational-theory", (Dhungana, 2020) article in EJOLTs. She has made considerable progress in the writing up of her doctoral thesis and here is describing how she created a culture of inquiry in the rural school community:

https://youtu.be/-XRbDTF5a6s
07:41–9:18 (Delong, 2021e)

I realize that I created environment a safe environment: I have understood it as an aesthetic environment, an aesthetic learning space; that is, I worked with clearing the space making open space so that everybody can talk, share. And I use different means like sometimes pictures, sometimes I use video…

Parbati brought Living Educational Theory into her Master's class and started a culture of inquiry group. She recognised the importance for building that safe, democratic culture of inquiry space is her willingness to be vulnerable:

https://youtu.be/UyJY0o4794I
25:01–26:20 (Delong, 2021f)

Jackie: You're enjoying the process. That's what it should be!

Parbati: Yeah I'm enjoying; I'm learning a lot, I think. The next part of my learning is because of my class and I'm also taking the class as my research, as my self-study and whenever the question comes into my mind, I link with my class and then it is an amazing journey for me. It's a very exciting time. The next thing I explore is a very powerful component in my research that I have never talked about in my research field but whenever I talk about love and care and I might have been thinking 'vulnerability' but that was the very source root of my loving and caring because I was very vulnerable at that moment and because of that, I could be loving and caring.

At 36.54 Parbati describes a Culture of Inquiry group that she has created to help other researchers. At 37.21–37.49, she expresses how necessary their Culture of Inquiry is to her:

> I was inspired from you and it was very important because like some people don't need it; they don't want it because they work internally but some, like me, cannot do that. We need somebody to speak with, somebody to care and interact with so that we can understand better.

While Jackie has mentored Parbati, they have learned together to understand cultural differences, the nature of Cultures of Inquiry and to make explicit their values as explanatory principles.

a. Shivani, Mishra, Department Head of Social Work at Sadar Patel University, India

Third, Shivani Mishri and Jack first met at Manchester University, UK where both were presenters and Jack followed up with encouraging

Shivani to submit an article to EJOLTS. Jackie met Shivani through Swaroop Rawal, a member of the EJOLTS community, when Shivani submitted an article for review and was advised to get assistance with making the article ready to publish. Shivani says that she was so angry at the time that she vowed that she would never submit another article, but after working together, she will reconsider! In early 2021, Shivani asked Jackie to read her draft paper for our symposium for the AERA 2021 conference. She responded via email and Shivani asked if they could talk on SKYPE on 21.01.21. Here is part of their dialogue showing Jackie checking that she was helping and not colonising:

30:08–32:27

https://youtu.be/M3KSt2FWJmk

Jackie: I have a request for you. What I am doing as I mentor you is to try to be very careful that I am being helpful but I am not leading you. Do you understand? I never want to be colonising. I never want to be making you feel that you are doing something that you don't want to do. Do you understand what I am saying?

Shivani: Yes. Let me tell as of now you never make me feel me bad.

Jackie: Yes, but you need to tell me.

Shivani: The point is that: let me agree. I know my two limitations. First It takes me a time to articulate myself and my work on paper I am in the learning process. I have never done a paper in qualitative research. I'm a strong quantitative researcher, dealing with numbers. For the first time I am understanding these feelings and how to express your feelings.

Second basically, I am a very calm person but a very shy person to be honest. If I feel I can talk, go on; if not I never talk with the people. So you will also find in my paper. I hardly talk with the people. This is my nature. This is what you found in my paper.

So you are not leading me not earlier and now also, let me tell you honestly. You also don't need to feel that I am dependant on you. Initially, yes, I am dependent because I have read your papers and I want to learn from you. Moment you feel I am over dependent on you, you can cut me. I am trying my best so you don't feel I am so dependent in the future.

Jackie: Perfect!

Shivani's paper describes and explains her very courageous act of working with pre-school children using Life Skills. She was willing to be vulnerable and live her values in that she, a senior manager and university professor, joined the pre-school student teachers in the field working hand in hand with them to find ways to improve the quality of education for the young children. She shares in her AERA 2021 (Mishra, 2021) paper that as a junior in her university, she felt that she could not live her value of democracy but now as a senior leader she feels the educational responsibility to ensure the curriculum and teaching is democratic and she needs to listen to the students:

Shivani: This I learned from life skills training and also learned to understand my values of democracy and respect and these values are now my standards of judgment. (p. 12)

Jack's chapter (Tidwell et al., 2009) acknowledges the influence of students:

> I too have acknowledged the educational influences of the students whose research programmes I have had the privilege and pleasure of supervising. For the award of a doctorate there must be evidence, recognized by the examiners, of originality. This can be expressed as originality of mind or an original contribution to knowledge. I have learnt something highly significant for the growth of my own educational knowledge from each doctoral researcher.
>
> (p. 8)

4.8 Digital Visual Data and Dialogue as Methods

In addition to action research/self-study modes of inquiry, we will share two methods used in the most significant aspects of our data collection and analysis processes: a. Dialogue as research method; b. Digital visual data. Digital visual technology is used to "bridge divides of economic capital through digitally-mediated education that connects rural and urban students to rich educational resources outside the classroom walls." (Tierney & Renn, 2012, p. 2).

a. Digital Visual Data
Whitehead in Farren, Whitehead and Bognar (2011) sets the stage for using visual data,

> I am claiming that the forms of representation that dominate printed text-based media cannot express adequately, in the standards of judgment and explanatory principles of academic texts, the embodied values we use to give meaning and purpose to our lives in education.
>
> (p. 16)

Jackie and Michelle share their co-learning experience: The visual digital recordings have been seminal to the development of our thinking and reflexivity because we have been able to review the "loving educational conversations" recordings stored on YouTube. When we are viewing and listening to the conversations, we can see and hear the nature of the relationship, whether we are living our espoused values and/or what might be involved in improving ourselves or the relationship. In this ARNA 2019 clip from Vaughan and Delong (2019, p. 83), Jackie and Michelle discuss the use of visual data in their lives:

https://youtu.be/rD11P3C6yfo

(Delong, 2021a)

Michelle writes: Visual data can also play a role in capturing non-verbal communication and an exchange of life-affirming energy that is unable to be recorded when looking at a transcript of a conversation. It is these nonverbal cues that are often so important in building trust and encouraging the members of a culture of inquiry, whether micro or macro, to grow in their thinking and independence. The clip below has already been shared to illustrate the use of vulnerability and connection as core values of facilitating Cultures of Inquiry. However, view the clip again with a different lens (I suggest turning the sound off), watch closely as I frequently look to Jackie for 'validation checks.' In the span of this three-minute clip, I visually check-in with Jackie 20 different times. As a new researcher in the field and one of Jackie's mentees in our own micro culture of inquiry, I have relied on her guidance through my own growth. Here, for the first time, I am presenting to a group of others about Living Theory research and Jackie allows me to share at length, giving me positive energy and nods and smiles of encouragement to help me find my footing. Without the use of video, this data would not have been captured and I believe it adds an important element to the story of mentorship and facilitation (Vaughan & Delong, 2019, p. 83).

While recording, selecting clips and transcribing video data is time-consuming, we find such love, hope and joy (Liz's values that we share) in experiencing again the empathetic resonance in the conversations. We found that there was a plethora of raw data that requires editing and, in that process, we experience the art of finding themes in a personal inquiry.

Marshall says that images and concepts around which she organises her inquiry can arise from a variety of sources, but when they 'appear' they can have an intensity which makes her recognise them as powerful or invest them with such power:

> They serve as organizing frames for my self-reflection and for taking issues further conceptually and in practice. Typically, they have been repeated in more than one setting. Sometimes I will be encouraged because they have resonance for other people as well as me, but sometimes this is unimportant.
>
> (Marshall, 1999, p. 4)

Visual data is used extensively to describe and explain the subtleties of explaining one's values, the nature of one's influence and the meanings of loved into learning, dialogue as research method and Cultures of Inquiry. A method of 'empathetic resonance' (Delong, 2010; Whitehead & Huxtable, 2010) using digital technology is introduced to clarify the meanings of the expression of embodied values and life-affirming energy that contribute to the explanatory principles of educational influences in learning.

Through the visual data, we are highlighting the methodological importance of Jackie's dialogic way of being and through her educational conversations and dialogues she is clarifying the ontological values which are the standards of judgment that she uses as explanatory principles in her educational relationships with colleagues, Shivani Mishri, Parbati Dhungana, and Michelle Vaughan. Within the methodology is the explication of the life-affirming energy that practitioner-researchers experience, describe and explain primarily through the use of visual data which is more attuned to the comprehension of this vital human interaction, especially the use of "empathetic resonance".

b. Dialogue as Research Method

When Jackie shares the nature of a Culture of Inquiry (Delong, 2002) and extends the language to include "living Culture of Inquiry" (Delong, 2019), she does so in the sense that it is a relationally dynamic space that is changing and evolving each time it is created. For this culture to emerge, she proposes that time be committed to creating this inclusive space where researchers can feel safe and comfortable to reveal their vulnerabilities, so that they can describe and explain the nature of their educational influence in their learning, in the learning of others and in the learning of social formations through their values as explanatory principles as they create their own living-educational-theories. From David Bohm (1996), we acknowledge that:

> While we don't have 'rules' for the dialogue, we may learn certain principles as we go along which help us – such as that we must give space to each person to talk. We don't put that as a rule; rather we say that we can see the sense of it…
>
> (p. 13)

Because of Jackie's dialogic way of being, she has found that "loving educational conversations" (Vaughan & Delong, 2019) with colleagues, critical friends, and students have become part of dialogue as research method for her and that visual data are essential to deepening and conveying her thinking (Delong, 2020b). In mentoring others to create their own living-educational-theories, the dialogic processes inherent in email and, especially, Zoom and Skype video recordings, enable her to clarify her thinking and enable others to do the same (Delong, 2019; Vaughan, 2019; Vaughan & Delong, 2019). When we have respect for the "narrativity of experience", we can "promote empowered practitioners" (Anderson & Page, 1995):

> Discussions should not be concerned so much with how we structure our programs or content for a knowledge base, but rather with how we choose the processes we use to engage with practitioners around the knowledge base that they already possess.
>
> (p. 133)

In Jackie's continuing quest to deepen her understanding of the influence of dialogue as method, in a 26 January 2021 email conversation, Jackie wrote to Máirín Glenn:

Hi, Máirín. I have been thinking about how you 'measure' influence. It's a given that we often don't ever know or don't know for many years the nature of influence but I still need to do the investigation.

Máirín responded: Mmm… I agree about influence. Sometimes it's just as a result of an accidental meeting with someone, someone you just happen to bump into, that you realised that you have had an educational influence on their lives. Sometimes, of course, people just write to you and so on…

At EJOLTs and some other similar places, we already know the power of dialogue. However others are not aware of this, so much. I think your paper is actually ground-breaking because it names dialogue as an actual research tool. This is so important for all kinds of research – not just Living Theory – because it finally 'allows' researchers, from all hues of research, to actually state that they are going to use dialogue as a research method. It somehow gives people permission to take time to talk to colleagues about their work and their thinking about their work. It justifies taking time to engage with critical colleagues about research. Dialogue can now be named in research papers as an appropriate research tool, citing Delong 2020b of course!

There's also something about including dialogue in the pedagogy of Living Theory that's crucial. I think college lecturers are under massive pressure to be productive and to be seen to be productive – and sitting down to talk to people is very low on their list of priorities. If dialogue is seen to be a key research tool, they may feel more inclined to try it out. (personal email, Delong 261021)

We both feel that this is an important facet of Living Educational Theory research and often overlooked as a rigorous and viable research method.

4.9 Researching Supportive Supervisors, Communities and Universities Through Expanding Boundaries in the Living Educational Theory Social Movement

What we have always done has enabled individuals to generate their valid explanations of their educational influence in their own learning and in the learning of others. In order to influence others educationally, we need to have the ontological security, focused on our own capacities to assist and support people generating their own living-educational-theories.

In Jackie's work, as she mentors practitioner-researchers around the globe to create their own living-educational-theories in Cultures of Inquiry, she is expressing her passion to make the world a better place, a better way of being. She has the advantage of not being grounded in institutions, so she is able to mentor others, love them into learning (Campbell, 2011) and take the "slow approach" to action research. As Máirín Glenn (2020) says:

> Engaging in a slow approach to action research allows researchers to reflect on their identity, their values as well as their ontological and epistemological commitments- factors of the utmost importance in research in practice.

In the living-poster, Jackie expresses her intentions to improve her practice as a mentor and as a global citizen (Potts, 2019) and answer the question, 'How am I contributing to the Living Educational Theory research social movement by creating Cultures of Inquiry for mentoring practitioner-researchers to create their own living-educational-theories?'

When Jackie taught the Brock Master's cohort, the boundaries were defined with that experience and process. What she has done since then, which comes out in this living-poster, is to extend the sense of her boundaries. So, whereas the boundaries earlier were provided by being a superintendent of schools, she is now responding much more as a global citizen connecting, for example, with Michelle Vaughan at Florida Atlantic University, and Parbati Dhungana in Nepal at Katmandu University. She is still using her values and insights but the boundaries within which she is working have extended into this global context.

Her interest is in mentoring, providing support and encouragement and 'loving them into learning' for Michelle and Parbati. Now she is working to connect these researchers and their conversations together. Her latest living-poster above was posted on 27 June 2020 Living Educational Theory Research Gathering website, where people could then connect with her in this global response to the work of others as she spreads the influence of Living Educational Theory research. The first International Living Educational Theory research conference clearly answers one of her questions:

> Have I shown how raising the voices of Living Educational Theory researchers in the contexts of Canada, Nepal, USA, and South Africa has contributed to the extending global influences of Living Educational Theory research with values of human flourishing in educational conversations?

For information on this virtual conference, see
http://www.spanglefish.com/livingtheoryresearchgathering/index.asp.

4.10 Addressing and Avoiding Colonisation

While the process of dialogue as research involves recording and analysing the interchange between us and global citizen-scholars, it also involves checking for meaning and risks involved. "Intercultural translation" is de Sousa Santos' (2014) alternative both to the abstract universalism that grounds Western-centric general theories and to the idea of incommensurability between cultures and calls for an "ecology of knowledges", a rich intermingling of diverse and complementary (and sometimes conflicting) understandings. He sees the two as related and accounting for the destruction and assimilation of non-Western cultures by Western modernity. Whitehead (2016) writes:

> For Santos intercultural translation consists of searching for isomorphic (similar form or structure) concerns and underlying assumptions among cultures. It includes identifying differences and similarities, and developing, whenever appropriate, new hybrid forms of cultural understanding and intercommunication. These new hybrid forms… may be useful in favouring interactions and strengthening alliances among social movements fighting, in different cultural contexts, against capitalism, colonialism, and patriarchy and for social justice, human dignity, or human decency.
> (p. 91)

With this in mind, we make a point of asking the mentees to inform us if at any time we are 'guiding' or 'leading' them too much and becoming colonising. In an interview,

> Senator Murray Sinclair, a member of the Ojibwe First Nation, Manitoba's first Indigenous judge and former chief commissioner of the Truth and Reconciliation Commission, has dedicated his life to highlighting the power of conversation as a means of educating Canadians about a more complete version of their country's history.

In response to the question, "How can we begin to decolonize our society?", he says:

> We all have to recognize that we are part of a heritage and ongoing reality of colonialism. Oftentimes, we have been influenced to such an extent that we often don't even know that we're discriminating or being discriminated against. We must question what we've been taught …
> (Moore, K. & Wahiakatste, D-D., 2021)

In a Skype conversation on 1 April 2020, Parbati shared the process of creating her own living-educational-theory with Jackie's mentoring.

Jackie writes: She said that she always felt that she could ask any question, show her vulnerability and felt supported and free to take her own direction. She said that she felt that Jackie's mentoring built her confidence. When asked if she ever felt colonised, she said that she never felt pressured to go in any direction she did not want to go. Furthermore, Parbati shared that she is basing her support of other students at the university on my model of creating a Culture of Inquiry and plans to teach that way when she finishes her studies. I asked her outright if she sensed any hierarchy in our relationship or if my "guiding practice" (Gjotterud, 2009) was gentle and helpful. She said that she had never found my influence to be controlling or colonising and she felt the way that I loved her into learning, actively influences the way she worked with me. She does say, however, that gender issues are prevalent in the patriarchal society of Nepal.

In our dialogue preparing for the AERA 2021 symposium, we talked in our Culture of Inquiry with Michelle, Parbati and Shivani about gender issues. With this paper, our colleagues and mentees have not only validated our claims to have influenced them in Cultures of Inquiry, but also helped us to understand our relational and dialogic ways of being, extended our understandings to include 'our relational ways of knowing' and gender equity as a value in 'Global Cultures of Inquiry':

https://youtu.be/9vEwOpwuiPA

(Delong, 2021h)

Parbati shares about Nepalese women not encouraging and helping other women in order to empower them:

17:46-21:18 So that is very completely different from the way Jackie has been doing to me. Particularly I feel a female can be empowering and supportive and she can understand in better way but in academia also female students and even female faculty members, they are not closely supporting other females.

In response, Shivani says that she can relate but that she has been fortunate as she has been mentored by Swaroop Rawal and now by me. Shivani 21.18:00–21:38 https://youtu.be/kxy4ul4a5uk

I always prefer that a female should be supported first by female. That is all required because we females are sailing on the same boats ... In my case, I am lucky because for the last three years I am in touch with Swaroop, mam, and Jackie is helping me out a lot.

There are obstacles and constraints in dialogue as research method: some of the issues that can constrain us: critical feedback, and gender and cultural differences. One of the barriers in supporting practitioner-researchers is the struggle to give critical feedback that is received as helpful, acceptable and not personal. Offering critique that might be valuable can be challenging. The intended message is not necessarily the one received by the student. This is even more challenging when the mentoring is written and given by e-mail than when it is delivered face-to-face. In order to try to establish a dialogue, we encourage the students to reply to the advice so that we might learn about the effect our message has on them. Marie Huxtable (2020) says that it is a fairly common problem:

> On the one hand there is resistance to introducing what might be construed as a note of discord into intellectual discourse, on the other hand no progress is made without it.
>
> (p. 212)

In a Skype dialogue with Parbati Dhungana, Jackie asked her outright if she sensed any hierarchy in their relationship or if her "guiding practice" (Gjotterud, 2009) was gentle and helpful. She said that she had never found Jackie's influence to be controlling or colonising and she felt the way that she loves her into learning actively influences the way she worked with her. She does say, however, that gender issues are prevalent in the patriarchal society of Nepal.

Her earlier research, Master's (Dhungana, 2007) and M. Phil. (Dhungana, 2013), was concerned with gender inequality and female subordination in literature and in society. In her *Educational Journal of Living Theories* article (Dhungana, 2020), she describes and explains her educational influence in own learning and in the learning of others as she explores her value of "living love" as her explanatory principle for improving her practice and creating her own living-educational-theory.

We have observed that female students will often receive criticism differently. In one incident, Dhungana's supervisor made some suggestions for readings and she felt that he was criticising her work. After Jackie talked with her about it, she realised that he was just trying to help and enjoyed reading the literature recommended. Shakeshaft (1995), is concerned with an androcentric nature, which she defines as "the practice of viewing the world and shaping reality through a male lens" (p. 140); and her earlier research (1987) indicated that:

1. Relationships with others are more central to all actions for women than they are for male administrators.
2. Teaching and learning is more often the major focus for women than it is for male administrators
3. Building community is more often an essential part of the women administrator's style than it is for the man (Donmoyer et al., 1995, p. 146).

It bears some thinking, assessing and reflection on the nature of Jackie's mentoring and its influence on human flourishing. There do seem to be some patterns. One is that each time that she presents at conferences and offers to work with practitioner-researchers creating their own-living-educational-theories, one individual accepts her offer and in a Culture of Inquiry goes on to create and publish her living-educational-theory whether in an article or in a doctoral thesis. This action seems to address Zuber-Skerritt's (2017) intent, "by making a shift from the negative energy of fear, competition, control and war to the positive energy of faith, love, hope and creativity. Clearly, we need to conceptualise and practice not just learning conferences but Loving Learning Conferences" (p. 224).

4.11 The Role of Social Media

4.11.1 Twitter

The @ sign is used to call out usernames in Tweets: "Hello @twitter!" People will use your @username to mention you in Tweets, send you a message or link to your profile. A hashtag is any word or phrase immediately preceded by the # symbol. When you click or tap on a hashtag, you'll see other Tweets containing the same keyword or topic.

In a response from Swaroop Rawal to Jacqueline Delong about Swaroop's use of Twitter, Swaroop sent back the following link and details: https://twitter.com/YoSwaroop/status/1257311776158347267?s=20
Swaroop Rawal on Twitter

"Day 1 #Renascence A new beginning. Living theory research begins with the researcher telling stories of what is important to them;

a brief biographical story to help them clarify their values; beliefs to recognise their embodied; acquired knowledge. See https://t.co/Q321mdl4XDhttps://t.co/eg8VOW5YGd"
twitter.com

We had about 6.3K impressions for this tweet – with 767 media view for this video...

https://twitter.com/YoSwaroop/status/1259492015118544897?s=20
We had about 6, 707 impressions 767media views for this tweet - https://twitter.com/YoSwaroop/status/1259492777328390145?s=20

4.11.2 Facebook

Facebook started in the USA as a way for some college students to stay in touch when they had left campus. It has evolved since then to become one of the largest social networks in the world. You can get a Facebook as follows:

1. On the Facebook homepage at https://www.facebook.com/ click on New Account and enter in your first name, last name, email address, password, birthday and gender.
2. Click the 'Sign Up' button. If all of your information is correct, you will be sent a verification email to the address you provided.
3. Open the verification email. It may take a few minutes for the email to get delivered. Click the link in the email to activate your account.

You can access and contribute to the Facebook page for the Educational Journal of Living Theories at. https://www.facebook.com/ejolts.

You can access and contribute to the Facebook page on Living Theory Research at:
https://www.facebook.com/groups/425250191585772/

4.11.3 LinkedIn

LinkedIn claims to be the world's largest professional network. Since December 2016, it has been a wholly owned subsidiary of Microsoft. As of February 2021, LinkedIn had 740 million registered members from 150 countries. LinkedIn allows members to create profiles and 'connect' to each other in an online social network which may represent real-world professional relationships. Members can invite anyone (whether an existing member or not) to become a 'connection'.

You can print off the details of how to join LinkedIn from: https://www.digitalunite.com/node/2062/printable/print

Here is a LinkedIn post I received from my twitter account about a webinar I addressed on the 5 June 2021. The poster for the event is included after the Twitter post to show the kind of information you can share through Twitter.

4.11.4 Use of Webinars and ZOOM

Here is an email Jack received about a Webinar, organised by the University Malaysia. The flyer was circulated using social media and the presentation took place virtually using the social media application ZOOM

> Thank you so much for agreeing to share your ideas with educators in Malaysia. I have consulted my colleagues in Malaysia, we would like to suggest a special webinar via ZOOM titled "A living educational theory approach to action research and pedagogical practices" (please suggest changes if you want). The suggested date and time are as follows:
> Date: **23 June 2020** (Tuesday)
> Time: **14:00 +1 UK** (21:00 +8 Malaysia)

Jack Whitehead speaking on "A living educational theory approach to action research and pedagogical practice." A Webinar on "Action Research on Pandemic Pedagogy" in Malaysia on the 20 June 2020.

4.11.5 The Use of ZOOM in Gathering Data on Conversations, Questions and Responses in the CHAT Facility

The use of social media applications such as ZOOM is enabling presentations to take place virtually that could not take place because of financial constraints in travelling and being accommodated at the physical located. The CHAT facility is enabling participants to share emails, responses and questions that can be taken up immediately by a speaker or at a later time, as the CHAT facility can be saved and referred to. Perhaps one of the most important innovations permitted by the social media is the gathering of data that shows the relational dynamic between communities of practitioner researchers. Each individual has a unique constellation of values that they use as explanatory principles in explanations of educational influences in learning. These relationally dynamic values are expressed within the contexts of communities of practice such as those illustrated below in a screenshot from a ZOOM webinar.

4.11.6 Using the Internet to Spread Information On

- **The living-posters of communities of practice**
  As the most influential social media application of the last 40 years, the internet offers the opportunity to communicate ideas from communities of practice to a global audience.

  See, for example, the homepage of living-posters at https://www.actionresearch.net/writings/posters/homepage2021.pdf

- **The Educational Journal of Living Theories (EJOLTs)**
  On the homepage of EJOLTs, you can see listed the connections with social media:
- Educational Journal of Living Theories Facebook
- Educational Journal of Living Theories Twitter
- Educational Journal of Living Theories Gmail
- Educational Journal of Living Theories RSS
- Home
- Current Issue
- Archive
- Published Papers
- Abstracting & Indexing
- Publication Ethics
- Impressum

Living Educational Theory Research: Doing Educational Research Differently

- **The Network Educational Action Research Ireland**
  http://www.eari.ie/2021/05/07/notes-from-the-spring-vpar-nearimeet-online-17-april-2021/

4.12 Implications of Our 'Educational Responsibility' as Citizen Scholars for the Living Educational Theory Movement

Each of those individuals influences her circle of influence (Covey, 1989) by living according to their values, expanding the Living Educational Theory social movement and creating Cultures of Inquiry with their groups so that others can be supported to create their own living educational-theories and see a better way of living and loving. Michelle Vaughan calls this "the ripple effect" (Delong, 2020b, p. 85; Vaughan & Delong, 2019). In addition, each of the mentees learns to see the symbiosis in the co-learning that comes in the mentoring process. Jackie feels not only the self-enhancing, life-affirming energy that comes in the sharing of experiences and knowledge but also the joy and pleasure of contributing to the public sharing of the lived values and renewed excitement and confidence of the mentees. Jackie also has a sincere desire to improve her mentoring and asks her mentees for feedback on how to improve:

> Mentors who desire to guide another's learning and development must, therefore, focus on enhancing their mentoring attributes. Becoming an effective mentor requires a conscious and purposeful effort at developing the requisite competencies (Orland-Barak and Hasin 2010). The objective of becoming better can be achieved by developing through conscious, deliberate, and continuous learning.
>
> (Nyanjom, 2020, p. 243)

The Living Educational Theory research methodology is scientifically significant as a research process where practitioner-researchers use their energy-flowing values as explanatory principles to explain their educational influence on themselves, on others and on social formations where they live and work. Methodological inventiveness (Dadds & Hart, 2001) derives from the use of dialogue and digital visual data as research method (Delong, 2020b) and draws from a variety of methodologies including narrative inquiry, self-study, and action research. Each of us has used methodological inventiveness to create our own living-educational-methodologies which evolves during the course of the research over time. For both of us, it is research that has evolved as post-doctoral work over 20 years.

Each of the contributors to our AERA 2021 symposium experienced a "sustained Culture of Inquiry" (Vaughan & Delong, 2019) for creating living-educational-theories within the symposium group. With their own values, they have taken that epistemology into their sites of practice to enhance their influence. The values that we share that inspire our writing include love, vulnerability and care. Reflecting on the contributions of the members of the symposium, we can see each individual's commitment to improving their world albeit that they come from vastly different parts of the world, different perspectives (social, economic, spiritual, cultural), different contexts and different experiences. If our Culture of Inquiry could more broadly influence our world, it would bring about a focus away from economic rationality and a focus on life-affirming energy, energy-flowing values and human flourishing.

If each of us, as citizen scholars could create Cultures of Inquiry for the engaging and inspiring of others to live their values based on "True North principles" (Covey, 1989; Covey et al., 1994), create their living-educational-theories and, with a 'ripple effect' (Vaughan & Delong, 2019), improve our 15% (Morgan, 1988; 1993) of the world, our combined contributions to human flourishing would be significant. We believe that the world is changed one person at a time with each individual in their 'Circle of Influence' (Covey, 1990), like social media waves, influencing others to do the same. At the heart of this influence is the decision taken by Delong (2002) to being with a claim to know her own learning in her educational inquiry:

> One of the basic tenets of my philosophy is that the development of a culture for improving learning rests upon supporting the knowledge-creating capacity in each individual in the system. Thus, I start with my own. This thesis sets out a claim to know my own learning in my educational inquiry, 'How can I improve my practice as a superintendent of schools?'
>
> (Abstract)

Planning for 2021AERA Symposium on the 08–02–2021
https://youtu.be/SG3k3qc_0hY
(Delong, 2021i)

This video of our planning for the 2021 AERA Symposium is included to highlight the importance of educational conversations in generating our contributions to knowledge with the generation and sharing of our living-educational-theories.

We have also focused on our 'loving educational conversations' as symposium presenters where the living expressions of our energy-flowing values are only weakly communicated by value-words such as love, vulnerability and care. Communicating the meanings of our energy-flowing values enables us to unite in answering one of the questions asked by the organisers of the 2021 AERA annual conference: "How can we unite with practitioners, with scholars across other academic fields and disciplines, and with other citizens beyond academia to strategically address complex social and educational problems?" Within the energy-flowing values evident in this Culture of Inquiry of symposium contributors, we see the commitment to contribute to human flourishing. Michelle's answer is:

> This question itself calls for the need to make meaningful connections outside of our immediate circles. I propose that meaningful connections can be made through the conscious commitment to build Cultures of Inquiry that can address the complex social and educational problems we face. As each individual within a Culture of Inquiry identifies their own personal values, a diversity of thought and experiences weave together to provide space for conversation, dialogue, and, most importantly, trust to explore the complicated issues we face. Acknowledging that we each have values that are unique to us and that those values create a lens in which we navigate the world is an important step to having dialogue (and studying that dialogue) that builds a strong Culture of Inquiry. It is interesting to note that there are consistent themes that run across the work of each member of this symposium. Core values of love, vulnerability, and care show up in explicit and implicit ways in much of the work we each do in our spheres of influence. Perhaps these values also play a role in what we should be considering as educationally responsible moving forward.
>
> (Vaughan, 2021)

Shivani shares the risk she took as she committed to working democratically with early childhood students, taking the training and teaching the young children Life Skill Education (Rawal, 2006) alongside the student teachers in their field practice in a rural school in Gujarat, India. She recognised her "living contradiction" (Whitehead, 1989) as she articulated her value of democracy and commitment to student learning and recognised her teaching as negating both. Once she improved her practice, her research showed that after she included the voices of the students and taught them more responsively, their learning improved thus creating her own living-educational-theory. Within a Culture of Inquiry with the encouragement and support of Swaroop Rawal and Jackie Delong, she came "to understand my living-educational-theory and my educational responsibilities" (Mishra, 2021, p. 15).

Parbati, shares the meanings of the value-words from the Nepalese culture which is particularly important in helping to avoid any colonising tendencies we might have in 'imposing' the meanings of our value-words through the medium of English. In developing our Culture of Inquiry, we are living the spiritual value, interconnectedness… we are connecting and collaborating with others so that we can connect with ourselves and experience love or oneness and joy. (Dhungana, 2021) It seems we all are on our spiritual journey! When she was not assigned a teaching module at her university she decided that to improve her practice and live her values more fully, she would volunteer her time to create a Culture of Inquiry for students and

> Thus, taking educational responsibility is satvic when we continuously live our values influencing self, other, and the social formation (Whitehead, 1989) with the aim of fulfilling the common good of citizen-scholars.

In our dialogue on 8 February 2021, in the clip above, we shared our common values of love, vulnerability and caring within our respect for each individual's unique values. Jack remarked that he thought our community reflected Socrates concept of 'the One and the Many' in the Phaedra (Plato, 1910). We talked at length, too, about our fears of colonising the other, especially with the controlling effect of the English language which can limit the capacity of ESL researchers to share their research. Having said that, we have all worked to raise our consciousness of this issue and make it explicit in our dialogue.

We do intend to infer that the Living Educational Theory social movement (Whitehead, 2019) has the potential and our sincere desire to improve our world one individual at a time. To do this we need to influence others to a create Culture of Inquiry, a safe and democratic space, where practitioner-researchers are encouraged and supported, "loved into learning" (Campbell, 2011), and feel free to share their vulnerabilities and create their own living-educational-theories. The epistemology of Cultures of Inquiry includes 'dialogue and digital visual data as research methods'. Vaughan (2021) asks: Are we teaching with love, vulnerability, and caring? Are we leading with love, vulnerability, and caring? And, lastly, are we researching from a place of love, vulnerability, and asking conference attendees to pause and reflect on how these values show up (or do not appear) in their own practice and scholarship. As we consciously shift to take on more responsibility in education, the role and important of these values has never been more necessary." (p. 15)

With the help of the digital video-data, we point to the relational qualities we express (as our life-affirming energy) as distinguishing a 'Global Culture of Inquiry' from the individual contributions, we are all making to our distinct and different cultures of our inquiries from within our national boundaries. We think that you will have seen our loving responses to practitioner-researchers who are working and researching from within cultural contexts with national boundaries, by engaging with them from within our relational qualities that distinguish our own contributions to developing a 'Global Culture of Inquiry' as activist citizen scholars.

Each individual's response to this question brings into this text the energy-flowing values that we individually and collectively believe carry hope for human flourishing from within our language and across our different contexts. It is our hope that our Culture of Inquiry with values of love, vulnerability and care can and will more broadly influence our world to bring about a focus away from economic rationality and a focus on life-affirming energy, energy-flowing values and human flourishing. As activist scholars, we are inviting you and other interested researchers to join us in our cooperative inquiry.

References

Anderson, G., & Jones, F. (2000). *Knowledge Generation in Educational Administration from the Inside-Out: The Promise and Perils of Site-Based Administrator Research.* Paper presented at Division A, AERA, in New Orleans.

Anderson, G., & Page, B. (1995). Narrative knowledge and educational administration: The stories that guide our practice, in Donmoyer, R., Imber, M. & Scheurich, J. (Eds.), *The Knowledge Base in Educational Administration: Multiple Perspectives.* New York: SUNY.

Bassey, M. (1991). Creating education through research. *British Educational Research Journal,* 18(1), 3–16. Presidential Address to the British Educational Research Association, 29th September 1991 in Nottingham. Available from: http://www.bera.ac.uk/files/presidentialaddresses/Bassey,_1991.pdf

Biesta, G. J. J. (2006). *Beyond Learning; Democratic Education for a Human Future.* Boulder, CO: Paradigm Publishers.

Bohm, D. (1996). *On Dialogue.* Schouten & Nelissen. Available from: http://sprott.physics.wisc.edu/Chaos-Complexity/dialogue.pdf

Boland, N. (2020). Lived spirituality: Exploring the richness of inner work. *Educational Journal of Living Theories,* 13(2), 1–20. Available from: https://ejolts.net/node/364

Briganti, A. (2020). *My Living-Theory of International Development.* Ph.D. Thesis, University of Cumbria, UK. Available from: https://www.actionresearch.net/living/ABrigantiphd.pdf

Buber, M. (1970). *I and Thou.* Edinburgh: T. & T. Clark.

Campbell, E. (2013). The heART of learning: Creating a loving culture of inquiry to enhance self-determined learning in a high school classroom. *Educational Journal of Living Theories,* 6(2), 45–61. Available from: https://ejolts.net/files/Campbell6%282%29_0.pdf

Campbell, E. (2019). *How Has Love Influenced Me as a Teacher Researcher, and Learner? A Narrative Inquiry into a Teacher's Abrupt Awakenings.* Ph.D. Thesis. Nipissing University. Available from: https://www.actionresearch.net/living/campbellphd/campbellphd2018.pdf

References

Campbell, E., Delong, J., Griffin, C., & Whitehead, J. (2013). Introduction to living theory action research in a culture of inquiry transforms learning in elementary, high school and post-graduate settings. *Educational Journal of Living Theories*, 6(2), 1–11. Available from: http://ejolts.net/node/211 (Accessed 20 January 2023).

Campbell, L. (2011). *Journey to the Otherway: How Can I Improve My Practice by Living My Values of Love and Joy More Fully?* M.Ed. Thesis. Brock University, Canada. Available from: http://www.spanglefish.com/ActionResearchCanada/index.asp?pageid=255602

Carr, W., & Kemmis, S. (1983). *Becoming Critical: Knowing Through Action Research*. Victoria: Deakin University Press.

Carter, K. (1993). The place of story in the study of teaching and teacher education. *Educational Researcher*, 22(1), 5–12, 18.

Cho, D. (2005). Lessons of love: Psychoanalysis and teacher-student love. *Educational Theory*, 55(1), 79–95.

Connelly, F.M. & Clandinin, J. (1990). Stories of experience and narrative inquiry. Educational Researcher, Vol. No.5, pp. 2–14.

Coombs, S., & Potts, M. (2012). *Bringing Living Citizenship as a Living Standard of Judgment into the Academy*. A presentation to the BERA conference, University of Manchester, 4–6 September 2012. Available from: http://www.actionresearch.net/writings/jack/coombspottsBERAPaper2012.pdf

Coombs, S., Potts, M., & Whitehead, J. (2014). *International Educational Development and Learning through Sustainable Partnerships: Living Global Citizenship*. London: Palgrave Macmillan. Available from: https://www.actionresearch.net/writings/jack/coombspottswhitehead.pdf

Corey, S. (1953). *Action Research to Improve School Practices*. New York: Teachers College, Columbia University.

Covey, S. (1989). *The Seven Habits of Highly Effective People*. New York: Simon & Schuster.

Covey, S. (1990). *Principle-Centered Leadership*. New York: Summit.

Covey, S. R., Merrill, A. R., & Merrill, R. R. (1994). *First Things First: to Live, to Love, to Learn, to Leave a Legacy*. New York: Simon & Schuster.

Creswell, J.W. (2007). *Qualitative Inquiry & Research Design: Choosing Among Five Approaches*. California, London, New Delhi: Sage.

Dadds, M., & Hart, S. (2001). *Doing Practitioner Research Differently*. London: Routledge/Falmer.

Damon, B. (2017). *A Collaboratively Constructed Process Model for Understanding and Supporting the Work of the Community Volunteer in a Community School*. Ph.D, Nelson Mandela Metropolitan University, South Africa. Available from: https://www.actionresearch.net/living/damons/damonsphd.pdf

D'Arcy, P. (1998). *The Whole Story*. Ph.D. University of Bath. Available from: https://www.actionresearch.net/living/pat.shtml

Delong, J. (Ed.) (2001). *Passion in Professional Practice: Action Research in Grand Erie*. Brantford: Grand Erie District School Board.

References

Delong, J. (2002). *How Can I Improve My Practice as a Superintendent of Schools and Create My Own Living Educational Theory?* Ph.D. Thesis, University of Bath, UK. Available from: https://www.actionresearch.net/living/delong.shtml

Delong, J. (2010). *Understanding Complex Ecologies in a Changing World: Engaging Educators in Representing their Knowledge in Complex Ecologies and Cultures of Inquiry*. AERA 2010 Conference Denver, Colorado. Available from: http://www.spanglefish.com/ActionResearchCanada/index.asp?pageid=225581

Delong, J. (2011). *Democratic Evaluation Bluewater*. [Video file]. Available from: https://www.youtube.com/watch?v=SShZFmETpkk

Delong, J. (2013). Transforming teaching and learning through living-theory action research in a culture-of-inquiry. *Educational Journal of Living Theories*, 6(2), 25–44. Available from: http://ejolts.net/node/213

Delong, J. (2015). *A Pedagogy of Loving into Learning in Living-Cultures-of-Inquiry*. Presented at the 2015 Action Research Network of the Americas Conference, Ontario Institute For Studies in Education, Toronto, Ontario, Canada, May 10, 2015. Available from: https://www.actionresearch.net/writings/arna/ARNAjdd260415.pdf

Delong, J. (2019). Dialogical relationships in living cultures of inquiry for the creation of living-theories. *Educational Journal of Living Theories*, 12(1), 1–22. Available from: https://ejolts.net/node/334

Delong, J. (2020a). *Jack4minutesjdd050620*. [Video file]. Available from: https://youtu.be/9VTciLigPGI

Delong, J. (2020b). Raising voices using dialogue as a research method for creating living- educational-theories in cultures of inquiry. *Educational Journal of Living Theories*, 13(2), 71–92. Available from: https://ejolts.net/files/4Jackie367.pdf

Delong, J. (2021a). *Michelle and Jackie at ARNA*. [Video file]. Available from: https://youtu.be/rD11P3C6yfo

Delong, J. (2021b). *AERA 2021 Symposium Planning020321*. [Video file]. Available from: https://youtu.be/4S0J9tzJYSs

Delong, J. (2021c). *Loved into Learning and Leaving Ego at the Door*. [Video file]. Available from: https://youtu.be/wjm13drYVQc

Delong, J. (2021d). *Empathetic Resonance*. [Video file]. Available from: https://www.youtube.com/watch?v=ZO0ZE1C74lI

Delong, J. (2021e). *Parbati on Building a Culture of Inquiry*. [Video file]. Available from: https://youtu.be/-XRbDTF5a6s.

Delong, J. (2021f). *Parbati Shares her Willingness to be Vulnerable Parbati and Jackie 120121*. [Video file]. Available from: https://youtu.be/UyJYOo4794I

Delong, J. (2021g). *Shivani and Jackie Reviewing Shivani's Paper30:08–32:27*. [Video file]. Available from: https://youtu.be/M3KSt2FWJmk

Delong, J. (2021h). *AERA 2021 Symposium Planning020321*. [Video file]. Available from: https://youtu.be/9vEwOpwuiPA

Delong, J. (2021i). *Planning for 2021aera Symposium on the 08-02-21*. [Video file]. Available from: https://youtu.be/SG3k3qc_0hY

References

Delong, J., Griffin, C., Campbell, E., & Whitehead, J. (2013). The significance of living-theory action research in a culture of inquiry transforms learning in elementary, high school and post-graduate settings. *Educational Journal of Living Theories*, 6(2), 78–96. Available from: https://ejolts.net/files/Delong_at_al6%282%29_0.pdf

Delong, J., Huxtable, M., Rawal, S., & Whitehead, J. (2019). *An Interactive Symposium Paper for the CARN/ALARA Conference 17–19 October 2019 in Split, Croatia with the Theme: 'Imagine Tomorrow: Practitioner Learning for the Future'*. Imagining tomorrow in the generation of living-educational-theories with learning for the future. Available from: https://www.actionresearch.net/writings/jack/JDD2019split.pdf

Delong, J., & Whitehead, J. (2011). *Transforming Educational Knowledge through Making Explicit the Embodied Knowledge of Educators for the Public Good.* A paper presented at the 2011 American Educational Research Association Conference in New Orleans, USA. Available from: http://www.spanglefish.com/actionresearchcanada/documents/what%27s%20new/jdj waera-2011jointsubmissionfinala.doc

Delong, J., Whitehead, J., Dhungana, P., Vaughan, M., & Mishra, S. (2021). *Accepting Educational Responsibility: Building Living Theory Cultures of Educational Inquiry in Global Contexts.* Symposium presentations at the April 2021 Conference of the American Educational Research Association on Accepting Responsibility. Available from: https://www.actionresearch.net/writings/aera21/2021aerasymposiumfull.pdf

Delong, J., Whitehead, J., Dhungana, P., Vaughan, M., & Rawal, S. (2022). *Cultivating Equitable Education Systems for the 21st Century in Global Contexts through Living Educational Theory Cultures of Educational Inquiry.* Successful proposal for a session presentation at the April 2022 Conference of the American Educational Research Association on Cultivating Equitable Education Systems for the 21st Century, in San Diego, California. Available from: https://www.actionresearch.net/writings/jack/AERA2022sessionprop.pdf

Delong, J., Whitehead, J., Dhungana, P., Vaughan, M., & Ratnum, T. (2023). *Successful Proposal for Presentation at AERA 2023 on Interrogating Consequential Education Research in Pursuit of Truth in Living Theory Educational Research.* Available from: https://www.actionresearch.net/writings/aera2023/aera2023overviewproposal220722.pdf

Delong, J., Whitehead, J., & Huxtable, M. (2019). Where do we go from here in contributing to 'the action learning and action research legacy for transforming social change?' *ALARj*, 25(1), 65–73. Workshop presentation at the 2019 ALARA Conference in Norwich University, Vermont, USA. Available from: https://www.actionresearch.net/writings/jack/jddjwmhalarj19.pdf

de Sousa Santos, B. (2014). *Epistemologies of the South: Justice against Epistemicide.* London: Routledge.

Dhungana, P. (2007). *Portrayal of Motherhood in Plath's Poetry.* Unpub. Master Dissertation, Tribhuwan University.

Dhungana, P. (2013). *The Concept of Beauty in the Twenty First Century.* Unpub. M.Phil. Dissertation, Pokhara University.

Dhungana, P. (2020). 'Living love': My living-educational-theory. *Educational Journal of Living Theories*, 13(1), 45–70. Available from: https://ejolts.net/files/356.pdf

Dhungana, P. (2021). *Accepting Educational Responsibility: Building Living Theory Cultures of Educational Inquiry in a Nepal/Global Context.* A contribution to a symposium presentation on 'Accepting Educational Responsibility: Building Living Theory Cultures of Educational Inquiry in Global Contexts' at the April 2021 Conference of the American Educational Research Association on 'Accepting Responsibility' with Jacqueline Delong, Shivani Mishra, Parbati Dhungana, Michelle Vaughan and Jack Whitehead.

Donmoyer, R., Imber, M., & Scheurich, J. J. (Eds.) (1995). *The Knowledge Base in Educational Administration: Multiple Perspectives.* New York: State University of New York.

Eisner, E. (1988). The primacy of experience and the politics of method. *Educational Researcher*, 17(5), 15–20.

Eisner, E. (1993). Forms of understanding and the future of educational research. *Educational Researcher*, 22(7), 5–11.

Eisner, E. (1997). The promise and perils of alternative forms of data representation. *Educational Researcher*, 26(6), 4–10.

Ellis, C., & Bochner, A. P. (2000). Autoethnography, personal narrative, reflexivity: Researcher as subject, pp. 733–768 in Denzin, N. & Lincoln, Y. (Eds.), *Handbook of Qualitative Research*, 2nd Edition. Thousand Oaks, CA: Sage Publications.

Erben, M. (Ed.) (1998). *Biography and Education: A Reader.* London: Routledge.

Erickson, F. (1986). Qualitative methods in research on teaching, 3rd Edition, pp. 119–161 in Wittrockk, M. (Ed.), *Handbook of Research on Teaching.* New York: MacMillan.

Farren, M, Whitehead, J., & Bognar, B. (Eds.) (2011). *Action Research in the Educational Workplace.* Palo Alto, CA: Academia.

Feyerabend, P. (1990). *Against Method.* London: Verso.

Forrest, M. (1983). *The Teacher as Researcher*, unpublished Masters Dissertation, University of Bath.

Foucault, M. (1977a) Discipline and Punish. New York; Pantheon books.

Foucault, M. (1977b). Intellectuals and power—A conversation between Michel Foucault and Giles Deleuze, in Bouchard, D. F. (Ed.), *Michel Foucault, Language, Counter-Memory, Practice.* Oxford: Basil Blackwell.

Freire, P. (1998). *Teachers as Cultural Workers: Letters to Those Who Dare Teach.* Boulder, CO: Westview.

Gadamer, H. G. (1975). *Truth and Method*, 2nd Edition. London: Sheed and Ward.

Gertz, C. (1973). *On Cultural Theory: The Interpretation of Cultures.* New York: Basic books.

Ginott, H. (1972). *Teacher and Child.* New York: Colliers Books Macmillan Publishing Company.

References

Gjøtterud, S. (2009). Love and critique in guiding student teachers. *Educational Journal of Living Theories*, 2(1), 68–95. Available from: https://ejolts.net/files/journal/2/1/Gjotterud2(1).pdf

Glenn, M. (2006). *Working with Collaborative Projects: My Living Theory of a Holistic Educational Practice.* Ph.D. Limerick University. Available from: https://www.jeanmcniff.com/glennabstract.html

Glenn, M. (2020). *A Case for a 'Slow Approach' to Action Research.* CARN2020 Virtual Conference October 24–25. CARN 2020 Online Conference Abstracts.

Griffin, C. (2011). *How Can I Improve My Practice by Living My Values of Love, Trust and Authenticity More Fully?* Master of Education Research Project, Brock University. Available from: http://www.spanglefish.com/ActionResearch-Canada/index.asp?pageid=255602

Habermas, J. (1976). *Communication and the Evolution of Society.* London: Heinemann.

Halsall, N., & Hossack, L. (Eds.) (1996). *Act, Reflect, Revise, Revitalize.* Mississauga: OPSTF.

Harper, S. R., Davis, L. P., Jenkins, T. S., & Soodjinda, D. (2020). *Accepting Educational Responsibility.* AERA 2021 Annual Meeting Theme. Available from: https://www.aera.net/Events-Meetings/Annual-Meeting/2021-Annual-Meeting-Theme

HCPC (2016). *Standards of Conduct, Performance and Ethics.* London: Health and Care Professions Council.

Hirst, P. (Ed.) (1983). *Educational Theory and its Foundation Disciplines.* London: RKP.

Huxtable, M. (2009). How do we contribute to an educational knowledge base? A response to whitehead and a challenge to BERJ. *Research Intelligence*, 107, 25–26. Available from: https://s3-eu-west-1.amazonaws.com/s3.spanglefish.com/s/1298/documents/papers/bera-ri107.pdf

Huxtable, M. (2012). *How do I Evolve Living-Educational-Theory Praxis in Living-Boundaries?* Ph.D. University of Bath. Available from: https://www.actionresearch.net/living/mariehuxtable.shtml

Huxtable, M., & Whitehead, J. (2015). *How Does Living Educational Theory Research Enable Individuals to Research into Their Higher Education to Improve It and Contribute to Educational Knowledge?* Paper presented at BERA HE SIG, Researching into Higher Education: Innovative Research Methods, 8 May 2015, Institute of Education, London.

Huxtable, M., & Whitehead, J. (2017). Enhancing Professionalism in Education through Inquiry Learning: A Living Theory Research Approach, in Boyd P. & Szplit, A. (Eds.), *Teachers and Teacher Educators Learning through Inquiry: International Perspectives.* Kielce Krakow: Wydawnictwo Attyka. Available from: https://www.actionresearch.net/writings/jack/mhjwboyd2017.pdf

Huxtable, M., & Whitehead, J. (2020). Enhancing educational influences in learning with a living theory approach to pedagogical action research in higher education. *Educational Action Research*, 29(2), 310–327. Available from: https://www.tandfonline.com/doi/full/10.1080/09650792.2020.1779771

Ilyenkov, E. (1977). *Dialectical Logic*. Moscow: Progress Publishers.

IPDA (2020). *Key Questions for 2020 IPDA Virtual Conference*. Available from: https://ipda.org.uk/ipda-international-conference/conference2020/

Jacobs, D. T. (2008). *The Authentic Dissertation; Alternative Ways of Knowing, Research, and Representation*. London: Routledge.

John, K., & Pound, R. (2011). *Creativity and Well Being*. Available from: https://www.youtube.com/watch?v=WOnXxPQjBmI

Keizer-Remmer, A. (2017). *Underneath the Surface of Cosmopolitanism: In Search of Cosmopolitanism in Higher Education*. Utrecht, The Netherlands: University of Humanistic Studies. Available from: https://www.actionresearch.net/writings/keizer/keizer.pdf

Kitchen, J., Berry, A., Bullock, S., Crowe, A., Taylor, M., Guojonsdottir, H., & Thomas, L. (2020). *2nd International Handbook of Self-Study of Teaching and Teacher Education Practices*. Rotterdam, The Netherlands: Springer.

Laidlaw, M. (1996). *How can I create my own living educational theory as I offer you an account of my educational development?* Ph.D. Thesis, University of Bath, U.K.

Linds, W. (2001). In Hocking, B., Haskell, J. & Linds, W. (Eds.), *Unfolding Bodymind: Exploring Possibility through Education*. Volume Three of the Foundations of Holistic Education Series. Brandon, VT: Psychology Press/Holistic Education Press.

Lohr, E. (2006). *Love at Work: What Is My Lived Experience of Love, and How May I Become an Instrument of Love's Purpose?* Ph.D. University of Bath. Available from: https://www.actionresearch.net/living/lohr.shtml

Lyotard, F. (1986). *The Postmodern Condition: A Report on Knowledge*. Manchester: Manchester University Press.

MacIntyre, A. (1988). *Whose Justice, Which Rationality*. London: Duckworth.

Marcuse, H. (1964). *One Dimensional Man*. London: Routledge and Kegan Paul.

Marshall, J. (1999). Living life as inquiry. *Systematic Practice and Action Research*, 12(2), 155–171.

Maxwell, N. (2021). *The World in Crisis – and What to Do About it: A Revolution for Thought and Action*. London: World Scientific.

McDonagh, C., Roche, M., Sullivan, B., & Glenn, M. (2019). *Enhancing Practice Through Classroom Research: A Teacher's Guide to Professional Development 2nd Edition*. London: Routledge.

McNiff, J., & Whitehead, J. (2009a). *Doing and Writing Action Research*. London: Sage.

McNiff, J., & Whitehead, J. (2009b). *You and Your Action Research Project*. London: Routledge.

McNiff, J., & Whitehead, J. (2011). *All You Need to Know About Action Research*. London: Sage.

Miller, A. (2009). Pragmatic radicalism: An autoethnographic perspective on pre-service teaching. *Teaching and Teacher Education*, 25(6), 909–916.

References

Mishra, S. (2021). *Accepting Educational Responsibility: Building Living Theory Cultures of Educational Inquiry in an Indian/Global Context*. Presented in the AERA 2021 Symposium on Accepting Responsibility. Available from: https://www.actionresearch.net/writings/aera21/2021aerasymposiumfull.pdf

Morgan, G. (1988). *Riding the Waves of Change*. San Francisco, CA: Jossey-Bass.

Morgan, G. (1993). *Imaginization*. Newbury Park: Sage.

Moore, K., & Wáhiakatste, D.-D. (2021). For Senator Murray Sinclair, leadership is defined by humility. *Globe and Mail*, 25 January 2021.

Mounter, M. (2008a). *The Time is Right Now! 'How can I enhance the educational influence of my pupils in their own learning, that of other pupils, myself and the school?'* 3rd MA Educational Enquiry May 2008. Available from: https://www.actionresearch.net/writings/tuesdayma/joymounteree3.pdf

Mounter, J. (2008b). *Understanding Learning and Learners Assignment, Can Children Carry Out Action Research about Learning, Creating their Own Learning Theory?* MA unit, University of Bath. Available from: https://www.actionresearch.net/writings/tuesdayma/joymounterull.pdf

Mounter, J. (2019). *MA in Values-led Leadership*. Available from: https://www.findcourses.co.uk/training/the-learning-institute/ma-values-led-leadership-1525460

Neeb, G. (2020). An action research project on improving students' written communication in mathematics. *Ontario Action Researcher*, 14(2). Available from: http://oar.nipissingu.ca/archive-Vol4No2-V424E.htm

Nyanjom, J. (2020). Calling to mentor: The search for mentor identity through the development of mentor competency. *Educational Action Research*, 28(2), 242–257.

Plato (1910). *Five Dialogues of Plato Bearing on Poetic Inspiration*. London: Everyman's Library.

Polanyi, M. (1958). *Personal Knowledge: Towards a Post-Critical Philosophy*. London: Routledge and Kegan Paul.

Popper, K. (1963). *Conjectures and Refutation*. Oxford: Oxford University Press.

Popper, K. (1975). *The Logic of Scientific Discovery*. London: Hutchinson & Co.

Potts, M. (2012). *How can I Reconceptualise International Educational Partnerships as a Form of 'Living Citizenship'?* Ph.D. Thesis, Bath Spa University, UK. Available from: https://www.actionresearch.net/living/markpotts.shtml

Potts, M. (2019). How can I live my life as a living-global-citizen? From action research to political activism. *Educational Journal of Living Theories*, 12(2), 20–35. Available from: https://ejolts.net/files/347.pdf

Potts, M., Coombs, S., & Whitehead, J. (2013). *Developing Cultural Empathy and the Living Global Citizenship Agenda: The Social Role and Impact of Technology in Supporting Global Partnerships*. A presentation at the 2013 Annual Conference of the British Educational Research Association, University of Sussex, 5th September. Available from: https://www.actionresearch.net/writings/bera13/markstevejackbera010913.pdf

Reiss, M. J., & White, J. (2013). *An Aims-Based Curriculum. The Significance of Human Flourishing for Schools.* London: Institute of Education Press.

Ryle, G. (1973). *The Concept of Mind.* Harmondsworth: Penguin.

Shakeshaft, C. (1995). A cup half full: Gender critique of the knowledge base in educational administration, in Donmoyer, R., Imber, M. & Scheurich, J. J. (Eds.), *The Knowledge Base in Educational Administration: Multiple Perspectives.* New York: State University of New York, 139–155.

Shotter, J. (2011). Embodiment, abduction, and expressive movement: A new realm of inquiry? *Theory and Psychology*, 21(4), 439–456.

Skolimowski, H. (1994). *The Participatory Mind: A New Theory of Knowledge and of the Universe.* London: Penguin.

Smith, L. T. (1999). *Decolonizing Methodologies: Research and Indigenous Peoples.* London: Zed Books.

Smith L. T. (2012). *Decolonizing Methodologies: Research and Indigenous Peoples*, 2nd Edition. London: Zed Books.

Stake, R. E. (2005). Qualitative case studies, in Denzin, N. K. & Lincoln, Y. S. (Eds.), *The Sage Handbook of Qualitative Research*, 3rd Edition. London: Sage, 443–466.

Thayer-Bacon, B. (2003). *Relational (E)pistemologies.* Oxford: Peter Lang

Thayer-Bacon, B. (2017). *Relational Ontologies – Counterpoints: Studies in Criticality.* Oxford: Peter Lang.

The Common Cause Handbook (2012). The common cause handbook: A guide to values and frames for campaigners, community organisers, civil servants, fundraisers, educators, social entrepreneurs, activists, funders, politicians, and everyone in between. *Public Interest Research Centre.* Available from: https://commoncausefoundation.org/_resources/the-common-cause-handbook/

Tierney, W., & Renn, K. (2012). *American Educational Research Association 2013 Annual Meeting Call for Submissions.* Available from: http://www.aera.net/

Tight, M. (2016). Phenomenography: The development and application of an innovative research design in higher education research. *International Journal of Social Research Methodology*, 19(3), 319–338.

Van Tuyl, G. (2009). *From Engineer to Co-Creative Catalyst: An Inclusional and Transformational Journey.* Ph.D. University of Bath. Available from: https://www.actionresearch.net/living/gvt.shtml

Vasilyuk, F. (1991). *The Psychology of Experiencing: The Resolution of Life's Critical Situations.* Hemel Hempstead: Harvester Wheatsheaf.

Vaughan, M. (2019). Learning who I am: The exploration of my guiding values through a living theory methodology. *Educational Journal of Living Theories*, 12(1), 62–80. Available from: http://ejolts.net/node/336

Vaughan, M. (2021). *Accepting Educational Responsibility: Building Living Theory Cultures of Educational Inquiry in a USA/Global Context.* Paper presented in

References

a Symposium at the 2021 AERA Conference. Available from: https://www.actionresearch.net/writings/aera21/michelle.pdf

Vaughan, M., & Delong, J. (2019). Cultures of inquiry: A transformative method of creating living-theories. *Educational Journal of Living Theories*, 12(2), 65–88. Available from: http://ejolts.net/node/349

Vickers-Manzin, J., & Johnston, J. (2013). *A Living Educational Theory of Knowledge Translation: Improving Practice, Influencing Learners, and Contributing to the Professional Knowledge Base*. Master of Education research project, Brock University. Available from: documents/brock_vickers-manzin_jen_-and-_johnston_jan_2013.pdf at http://www.spanglefish.com/ActionResearch-Canada/index.asp?pageid=227469

Whitehead, J. (1967). *The Way to Professionalism in Education?* Unpublished Special Study for the Diploma of Education Course at the Newcastle University, Department of Education. Available from: https://www.actionresearch.net/writings/jack/jackstudy1967all.pdf

Whitehead, J. (1985). An analysis of an individual's educational development - the basis for personally orientated action research, pp. 97–108 in Published in Shipman, M. (Ed.), *Educational Research: Principles, Policies and Practice*. Falmer: London. Available from: https://www.actionresearch.net/writings/jack/jw1985analindiv.pdf

Whitehead, J. (1989a). Creating a living educational theory from questions of the kind, "How do I improve my practice?" *Cambridge Journal of Education*, 19(1), 41–52. Available from: https://www.actionresearch.net/writings/livtheory.html

Whitehead, J. (1989b). How do we improve research-based professionalism in education?-A question which includes action research, educational theory and the politics of educational knowledge. 1988 presidential address to the British educational research association. *British Educational Research Journal*, 15(1), 3–17. Available from: https://www.actionresearch.net/writings/jwberapres.html

Whitehead, J. (1993). *The Growth of Educational Knowledge. Creating Your Own Living Educational Theories*. Bournemouth: Hyde Publications. Available from: https://www.actionresearch.net/writings/jwgek93.htm

Whitehead, J. (1999). *How Do I Improve My Practice? Creating a New Discipline of Educational Enquiry. Vol.2- Including Vol.1*. Ph.D. Thesis, University of Bath. Available from: https://www.actionresearch.net/living/jackwhitehead2.shtml

Whitehead, J. (2005). Living inclusional values in educational standards of practice and judgement. Keynote for the Act, Reflect, Revise III Conference, Brantford Ontario. 11th November 2005. *Ontario Action Researcher*, 8(2). Available from: http://oar.nipissingu.ca/PDFS/V821E.pdf

Whitehead, J. (2006a). *How Do I Express and Communicate Embodied Values of Ubuntu in an Explanation of their Educational Influence in My Own Learning and in the Learning of Others?* Draft paper, 12 March 2006.

Whitehead, J. (2006b). Generating living theory and understanding in action research studies. *Action Research*, 7(1), 85–99. Available from: https://www.

researchgate.net/publication/249747675_Generating_living_theory_and_understanding_in_action_research_studies

Whitehead, J. (2008). Using a living theory methodology in improving practice and generating educational knowledge in living theories. *Educational Journal of Living Theories*, 1(1), 103–126. Available from: http://ejolts.net/node/80

Whitehead, J. (2009). How do i influence the generation of living educational theories for personal and social accountability in improving practice? Using a living theory methodology in improving educational practice. Last draft before publication in Tidwell, D., Heston, M. & Fitzgerald, L. (Eds.), *Research Methods for the Self-Study of Practice*. Dordrecht: Springer. Available from: https://www.actionresearch.net/writings/jack/jwLTM080508.pdf

Whitehead, J. (2012). *To Know Is Not Enough, Or Is it?* Paper presented on the 14th April at the 2012 AERA Conference in Vancouver in the Symposium, To Know Is Not Enough: Action Research As The Core of Educational Research. Available from: https://www.actionresearch.net/writings/jack/jwaera12noffke200212.pdf

Whitehead, J. (2013). *A Living Logic for Educational Research*. A presentation at the 2013 Annual Conference of the British Educational Research Association, University of Sussex, 5th September. Available from: https://www.actionresearch.net/writings/bera13/jwbera13phil010913.pdf

Whitehead, J. (2016). Book Review of: de Sousa Santos, B. (2014). *Epistemologies of the South: Justice against Epistemicide*. London: Paradigm Publishers. *Educational Journal of Living Theories*, 9(2), 87–98. Available from: https://www.actionresearch.net/writings/jack/jwreviewdesantos2016.pdf

Whitehead, J. (2019a). The action learning, action research experiences of professionals - ALARj 25(1), 11–27. A keynote presentation to the 10th World Congress of the Action Learning Action Research Association with the theme of "The Action Learning and Action Research Legacy for Transforming Social Change: Individuals, Professionals, and Communities" Developments, Organizational Advancements, and Global Initiatives', 18 June 2018 in Norwich University, Vermont, USA. Available from: https://www.actionresearch.net/writings/jack/jackkeynoteALARA.pdf

Whitehead, J. (2019b). *Connecting Curriculum Development, Creativity and Professional Learning Through Living Theory Research*. Paper presented at the International Professional Development Association (IPDA) conference on 29–30 November 2019 at Aston University, Birmingham, UK. Available from: https://www.actionresearch.net/writings/jack/jwipda2019.pdf

Whitehead, J. (2019c). Creating a living-educational-theory from questions of the kind, 'how do I improve my practice?' 30 years on with living theory research. *Educational Journal of Living Theories*, 12(2), 1–19. Available from: https://www.actionresearch.net/writings/jack/jwejolts2019.pdf

Whitehead, J. (2020a). *The Identity, Ethics and Response-Ability of an Educator with and Beyond Professional Standards and with Values of Living-Global-Citizenship, Human Flourishing and Living Educational Theory Research*. A presentation at

References

the Virtual International Professional Development Association Conference on Imagining the post-professional: Identity, ethics and response-ability beyond professional standards. 27th–28th November 2020. Available from: http://www.actionresearch.net/writings/jack/jw2020ipdaindividual.pdf

Whitehead, J. (2020b). *How am I Creating a Living-Educational-Theory from Questions of the Kind, 'How do I Improve My Practice?' 30 Years on With Living Educational Theory Research.* A presentation at the Virtual International Professional Development Association Conference on Imagining the post-professional: Identity, ethics and response-ability beyond professional standards. 27th–28th November 2020. Available from: http://www.actionresearch.net/writings/jack/jw2020forsymposium.pdf

Whitehead, J. (2020c). Imagine tomorrow: Practitioner learning for the future in living educational theory research. *Action Learning, Action Research Journal,* 26(2), 17–43.

Whitehead, J. (2020d). Contributing to moving action research to activism with living theory research. *Canadian Journal of Action Research,* 20(3), 55–73. Available from: https://journals.nipissingu.ca/index.php/cjar/article/view/467

Whitehead, J., Delong, J., & Huxtable, M. (2017). *Participation and Democratization of Knowledge: Living Theory Research for Reconciliation from ARNA 2015-ARNA 2017.* A presentation at the 2017 Conference of the Action Research Network of the Americas 12–16 June 2017 in Cartagena, Colombia. Available from: https://www.actionresearch.net/writings/jack/jwjddmharna070617.pdf

Whitehead, J., Delong, J., Huxtable, M., Campbell, E., Griffin, C., & Mounter, M. (2020). Self-study in elementary and secondary teaching: A living theory approach, in Kitchen, J., Berry, A., Bullock, S., Crowe, A., Taylor, M., Guojonsdottir, H. & Thomas, L. (Eds.), *2nd International Handbook of Self-Study of Teaching and Teacher Education Practices.* Rotterdam, The Netherlands: Springer. Final draft before publication. Available from: https://www.actionresearch.net/writings/jack/STEPchpt4june2020.pdf (Accessed 9 March 2021).

Whitehead, J., & Huxtable, M. (2006a). *How Are We Co-creating Living Standards of Judgement in Action-Researching Our Professional Practices?* Multi-media text presented at the World Congress of ALARPM and PAR 21–24 August 2006 in Groningen. Available from: https://www.actionresearch.net/writings/jack/jwmh06ALARPMmulti.pdf

Whitehead, J., & Huxtable, M. (2006b). *How Are We Co-Creating Living Standards of Judgement in Action-Researching Our Professional Practices?* Printed text in the Conference Proceedings of the World Congress of ALARPM and PAR 21–24 August 2006 in Groningen. Available from: https://www.actionresearch.net/writings/jack/jwmhalarpmtext06.pdf

Whitehead, J., & Huxtable, M. (2010). *How Are We Sustaining Educational Relationships to Improve Educational Practices with Teachers and Pupils in the Generation of Educational Knowledge?* Paper presented at the British Educational Research Association Annual Conference, University of Warwick, 1–4 September 2010. Available from: https://www.actionresearch.net/writings/jack/jwmh2010.pdf

Whitehead, J., & Huxtable, M. (2015). *Notes for a Workshop on Living Theory Research: Innovative Research Methods in Researching One's Own Higher Education.* University of Cumbria, Carlisle, 3rd June 2015. Available from: https://www.actionresearch.net/writings/jack/jwmhcumbria310515.pdf

Whitehead, J., & Huxtable, M. (2016). Creating a profession of educators with the living-theories of master and doctor educators. *Gifted Education International*, 32(1), 6–25. Available from: https://www.actionresearch.net/writings/gei2015/geicontents2016.pdf

Whitty, G. (2005). *Education(al) Research and Education Policy Making: Is Conflict Inevitable?* Presidential Address to the British Educational Research Association, University of Glamorgan, 17 September 2005. Available from: https://www.bera.ac.uk/wp-content/uploads/2014/02/gwberapresidential-address_0001.pdf?noredirect=1

Wolvaardt, E. (2013). *Over the Conceptual Horizon of Public Health: A Living Theory of Teaching Undergraduate Medical Students.* Ph.D. University of Pretoria. Available from: https://www.actionresearch.net/writings/wolvaardtphd/Wolvaardtphd2013.pdf

Wolcott, H. F. (1992). Posturing in qualitative inquiry, pp. 3–52 in LeCompte, M. D., Millroy, W. L. & Preissle, J. (Eds.), *The Handbook of Qualitative Research in Education.* San Diego, CA: Academic Press.

Yamamoto, K. (1988). To see life grow: The meaning of mentorship. *Theory into Practice*, 27(3), 183–189. Available from: http://www.jstor.org/stable/1477189

Zuber-Skerritt, O. (Ed.) (2017). *Conferences as Sites of Learning and Development: Using Participatory Action Learning and Action Research Approaches.* Abingdon: Routledge.

Index

Action Research history 32, 53–54
Action Research Network of the Americas (ARNA) 176
Africa 128, 141, 155, 157, 162, 184, 198
American Educational Research Association (AERA) 3, 49, 124, 126, 134, 158, 167, 200
Aristotle. 46, 131
Avon LEA 93

Bath Spa University 204
Becoming Critical 32
Biesta, G. 163, 197
Bluewater Action Research Network (BARN) 69
Bochner, A. 61, 201
Bognar, B. 179, 201
Bohm, D. 181, 197
British Educational Research Association (BERA) 48–49, 124, 134, 136, 197, 204, 206
Bruce Ferguson, P. 56
Buber, M. 21, 197

Cambridge Journal of Education 206
Campbell, E. 9, 11, 13–14, 22, 25–26, 33, 64, 66–67, 71, 77, 115, 123, 126, 159, 167, 174, 183, 195, 197–198, 200
Canada 14, 67, 143–144, 155, 167, 184, 198–202
Carr, W. 32, 53–54, 198
China 14, 74, 156
Collaborative Action Research Network 124, 134, 165
Coombs, S. 161–164, 198

Corey, S. 32, 53, 198
Creswell, J.W. 32, 61, 71, 198
critical friend 10–11
Croatia 116, 165, 176, 200
Culture of inquiry vi, 11–13, 30, 34–35, 76, 80, 85, 89, 117, 181, 186

Dadds, M. 6–7, 13, 60–62, 192, 198
data collection and analysis 18–26
democracy 9, 34, 50, 68, 106, 164, 168, 179, 194
description and explanation 49–50
Dhungana, P. 14
dialectical 54, 85, 100, 105, 130, 131–132, 203
dialectical logic 130–132, 203

educational influences 1–16, 23–24, 27, 32–34, 42, 45, 59–66, 71–74, 77–79, 81, 84–85, 89, 91, 118, 122–123, 127–128, 130–133, 135, 156, 164–168, 179, 181, 187, 191–192, 202
Educational Journal of Living Theories (EJOLTS) 66, 72, 75, 134, 163, 164, 191
Educational Practice and its Theory 31
educational research 2, 3, 5, 6, 21, 40, 45, 47, 51, 70, 73, 74, 77, 82, 87, 97, 100, 101, 104, 112, 125, 127, 128, 129, 130, 132, 133, 136, 137, 139, 141, 148
Educational Theory 1, 12, 18
Eisner, E. 74–75, 201
Elliott, J. 7

211

Index

Ellis, C. 61, 201
empathetic resonance 7, 64, 127, 174, 176, 180–182, 199
energy-flowing values 7, 22, 62–64, 67, 85, 127, 129, 192–194, 196
ethics 18

Farren, M. 179, 201
Forrest, M. vii, 72, 80, 83, 90–98, 201
Foucault, M. 51, 73, 201

Gadamer, H. 88, 201
Glenn, M. 69, 71, 86–87, 182–183, 202
Google 32, 53
Griffin, C. 12, 63–64, 77, 126, 167, 198, 200

Habermas, J. 32–34, 54, 62, 81–83, 118, 127–202
Hart, S. 6–7, 13, 60–62, 192, 198
Hirst, P. 48, 51, 202
human flourishing 2, 7, 50, 55, 66, 71, 73, 85, 89, 112–113, 154, 156, 160–163, 166, 169, 171–173, 188, 193–194, 196
Huxtable, M. 18, 75, 77, 123–124, 127–128, 165–167, 181, 187

Ilyenkov, E. 131, 203
India 155, 167–168, 173, 177, 194, 204
International Conference of Teacher Research 66
Ireland 86, 191

Jensen, M. 9
Jones, C. 112, 133, 135, 137–139
journals 20, 24

Kemmis, S. 32, 53–54, 198
Kok, P. 99–110

Laidlaw, M. 4, 14, 42, 74, 203
Larter, A. 8–9
life-affirming energy 7, 13, 22, 62, 64, 66, 127–130, 158–159, 174, 176, 181, 191, 193, 196
living contradictions 9, 31
living-educational-theory i–ix, 1, 5, 7, 32–33, 41–42, 55, 81, 150
Living Educational Theory Planner 16–20
Living Educational Theory research ix, 1, 5, 29–30, 33, 41–42, 60

Living Theory research ix, 4–5, 15, 23, 31, 41–42, 61, 66, 84, 85, 89, 136, 161, 164, 166, 188, 202, 207, 208
Living Theory researchers 154
Lohr, E. 125, 203
Lomax, P. 119

Malaysia 155, 190
Mandela 141, 157, 163, 198
Marcuse, H. 130, 203
McDonagh, C. 86–87, 203
McNiff, J. 32–33, 54, 61, 67, 71, 80, 119, 202, 203
methodological inventiveness 13, 22, 60, 68, 192
methods and methodologies 31–33
Mumbai 169

Network Educational Action Research Ireland (NEARI) 86–87, 191
New Orleans 197, 200
Newcastle University 206
Noffke, S. 207

Ontario 40–41, 80, 119, 144, 155, 199, 204–205
ontological values 42, 50, 56, 70, 123–124, 127–128, 131

Peters, R. 204
Phaedra 195
phenomenology 31, 61, 71
Pinnegar, S 63, 161
Plato 195, 204
Polanyi, M. 135, 173, 204
Popper, K. 80–81, 124, 127, 130–131, 204
Potts, M. 57, 113, 155, 161–163, 168, 183, 198, 204

relational value 127
Research Intelligence 202
Roche, M. 86–87, 203
Ryle, G. 46–47, 205

Schön, Donald 140
Singapore 107, 110
Smith, L.T. 18
Socrates 66, 195
de Sousa Santos, B. 74, 76, 166, 184–185, 200
South Africa 141, 157, 162, 198
Stake, R. E. 62, 205
Sullivan, B. 86–87, 203

Tight, M. 54, 61, 205

Ubuntu 157, 168, 206
University of Bath 80, 120, 129, 141

validation group 33–34
values 8–10, 78, 164, 169, 173, 194
values of human flourishing 50, 55, 66, 71, 73, 85, 89, 140, 156, 160–163, 166, 172
Vasilyuk, F. 128–129, 205

Vaughan, M. 4, 13, 35, 76, 85, 88–89, 155, 173–174, 176, 181–182, 192–193, 195
Visual data 21–22, 63–66

Way To Professionalism In Education 206
Whitty, G. 48–49, 209
Winter, R. vii, 65, 84, 99–101, 105, 109
World Congress on Action Learning, Action Research and Process Management 165, 207–208

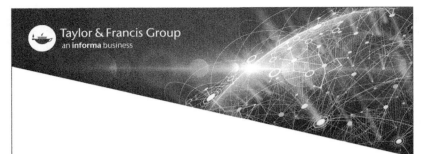